D1739069

Cities of the Prairie Revisited

Cities of the Prairie Revisited

The Closing of the Metropolitan Frontier

Daniel J. Elazar
with Rozann Rothman, Stephen L. Schechter,
Maren Allan Stein, and Joseph Zikmund II

University of Nebraska Press
Lincoln and London

The paper in this book meets the guidelines for permanence and durability of the Committee on Production Guidelines for Book Longevity of the Council on Library Resources.

Library of Congress Cataloging-in-Publication Data
Main entry under title:

Cities of the prairie revisited.

Sequel to: Cities of the prairie.
Bibliography: p.
Includes index.
1. Municipal government—Middle West—Case studies.
2. Cities and towns—Middle West—Case studies.
3. Metropolitan government—Middle West—Case studies.
4. Metropolitan areas—Middle West—Case studies.
I. Elazar, Daniel Judah. II. Elazar, Daniel Judah.
Cities of the prairie. III. Title.
JS434.C58 1986 307.7'64'0977 85-24245
ISBN 0-8032-1853-2 (alk. paper)

To the memory of Shirley Raskin Abelson,
who spent her life serving the people of the prairie

Contents

Maps

Figures

Tables

Acknowledgments

Faculty participants in the resurvey of the cities of the prairie included: Daniel J. Elazar, Bar Ilan and Temple Universities, project director; Stephen L. Schechter, Russell Sage College, project coordinator; Thomas A. Drolesky, Illinois State University at Normal; John Kincaid, North Texas State University (first involved as a research assistant); Rozann Rothman, University of Illinois at Urbana; Heywood Saunders, University of Illinois at Normal; Benjamin R. Schuster, Temple University (first involved as a research assistant); Maren Allan Stein, Russell Sage College; and Joseph Zikmund II, Menlo College.

Research assistants on the project included: Gail L. Charette, Christine Newman, Linda Reichl, Alexis Samryk, and Joseph R. Marbach.

Staff support was provided by the Center for the Study of Federalism at Temple University, Mary Duffy, head secretary.

The research for this project was supported by the Center for the Study of Federalism of the Temple University College of Arts and Sciences and by grants from the Earhart Foundation, Ann Arbor, Michigan, and CSF Associates.

Special acknowledgment is due all those citizens of the cities of the prairie who assisted us in our research, as interviewees or in other capacities.

Introduction

The 1980 census confirms what had been at least marginally evident since 1960, that among the new centers of urban growth in the United States are medium-sized communities of 40,000 to 250,000 people (table 1). What the table does not fully reveal is that over 40 percent of all the inhabitants of metropolitan America, one-third of the nation's population, live in urban civil communities in that size range, and another 15 percent of the total live in cities approaching it. As cities, these medium-sized communities constitute the largest single class in the United States and have done so for better than half a century.

The trend in American settlement patterns since World War II is clear from the United States Census breakdown. In 1950 large cities of over 500,000 population constituted the largest single group: 17.6 percent of the total population of the United States. Small cities of 10,000 to 50,000 were second with 13.4 percent, and medium-sized cities were third with 12.3 percent. By 1960 the large cities' share had dropped to 15.9 percent, which was almost matched by the small cities' 15.5 percent. The medium-sized cities had also gained, reaching 13.3 percent. Between 1960 and 1970 the large cities dropped slightly to 15.6 percent and were surpassed by the small cities, which reached 16.4 percent. They were almost matched by the medium-sized cities at 14.7 percent. By 1980 the medium-sized cities constituted 16.2 percent of the total population, with large cities declining to only 12.5 percent.

In fact, these figures underestimate the medium-sized category as defined here and in the original Cities of the Prairie study, which uses a population breaking point of 40,000 at the lower limit and 200,000 at the upper. The larger cities in the census's medium-sized category tend to share the lower or even negative growth rates of the cities in the two categories above, while those between 40,000 and 50,000 tend to be growing. A recalculation using those categories rather than those of the United States Census Bureau would probably place the medium-sized group in the number one position among the five categories of cities.

This pattern carries over into the metropolitan areas. Those under 500,000, dominated by medium-sized cities, have been growing faster than

Table 1. Distribution of United States Population by Size of Place, 1950–80

			Urban Places 1,000,000 +		500,001–1,000,000		250,001–500,000		100,001–250,000		50,001–100,000		10,001–50,000		10,000 or Less		
Year	% Urban	No. of Urban Places	No.	% of Pop.	No.	% of Pop.	No.	% of Pop.	No.	% of Pop.	No.	% of Pop.	No.	% of Pop.	No.	% of Pop.	% Rural
1950	64.0	4,743	5	11.5	13	6.1	23	5.5	65	6.3	126	5.9	1,030	13.7	3,479	10.1	36.0
1960	69.9	6,041	5	9.8	16	6.2	30	6.0	81	6.5	201	7.7	1,566	18.1	4,142	10.1	30.1
1970	73.5	7,062	6	9.2	20	6.4	30	5.1	100	7.0	240	8.2	1,905	19.3	4,761	16.4	26.5
1980	73.7	8,765	6	7.7	16	4.8	34	5.4	117	7.5	290	8.7	2,440	22.5	5,862	17.1	26.3

Source: U.S. Bureau of the Census, *Statistical Abstract of the United States,* 1950 and 1980.

those above 500,000, at least since the mid-1960s.[1] Medium-sized cities are growing both within larger metropolitan regions and as centers of small metropolitan areas in their own right. Their growth reflects certain fundamental changes in the social patterns of the already urbanized and developed countries of the world, including new economic conditions, new approaches to the organization of local government services, and changing value choices by citizens. Moreover, their impact on the national and world scene is growing as the large cities decline and the more manageable civic life of smaller places generates a cosmopolitan leadership in a wide variety of fields, consisting of those who are beginning to reach beyond their local environment. A small sign of the times was the election of Richard J. Carver, Peoria's mayor, to the presidency of the United States Conference of Mayors in the mid-1970s. Yet in the concern for studying the very large metropolis, as the focus of urbanization in past decades, or the very small town, seen as a manageable place to examine the intricacies of urban life, the medium-sized civil community has been substantially neglected as a focus of study. This neglect is all the more a problem in light of the statistical findings on optimal city size, which suggest that cities in this size range achieve optimum performance on most measures.

One exception is the Cities of the Prairie project, a comparative study of medium-sized civil communities in ten metropolitan areas in the upper Mississippi–Missouri valley, initiated in 1959. In that project thirteen civil communities, in ten metropolitan areas, were studied intensively:

1. Champaign–Urbana, Illinois
2. Decatur, Illinois
3. Duluth, Minnesota
4. Joliet, Illinois
5. Belleville, Illinois, in the Madison–St. Clair counties area
6. Peoria, Illinois
7. Pueblo, Colorado
8. Rock Island and Moline, Illinois, and Davenport, Iowa, three of the "Quad Cities"
9. Rockford, Illinois
10. Springfield, Illinois

Six civil communities in the same metropolitan areas were studied less intensively:

1. Superior, Wisconsin, in the Duluth–Superior standard metropolitan statistical area (SMSA)
2. Alton and East St. Louis, Illinois in the Madison–St. Clair counties area
3. East Peoria and Pekin, Illinois, in the Peoria SMSA
4. East Moline, Illinois, part of the Quad Cities

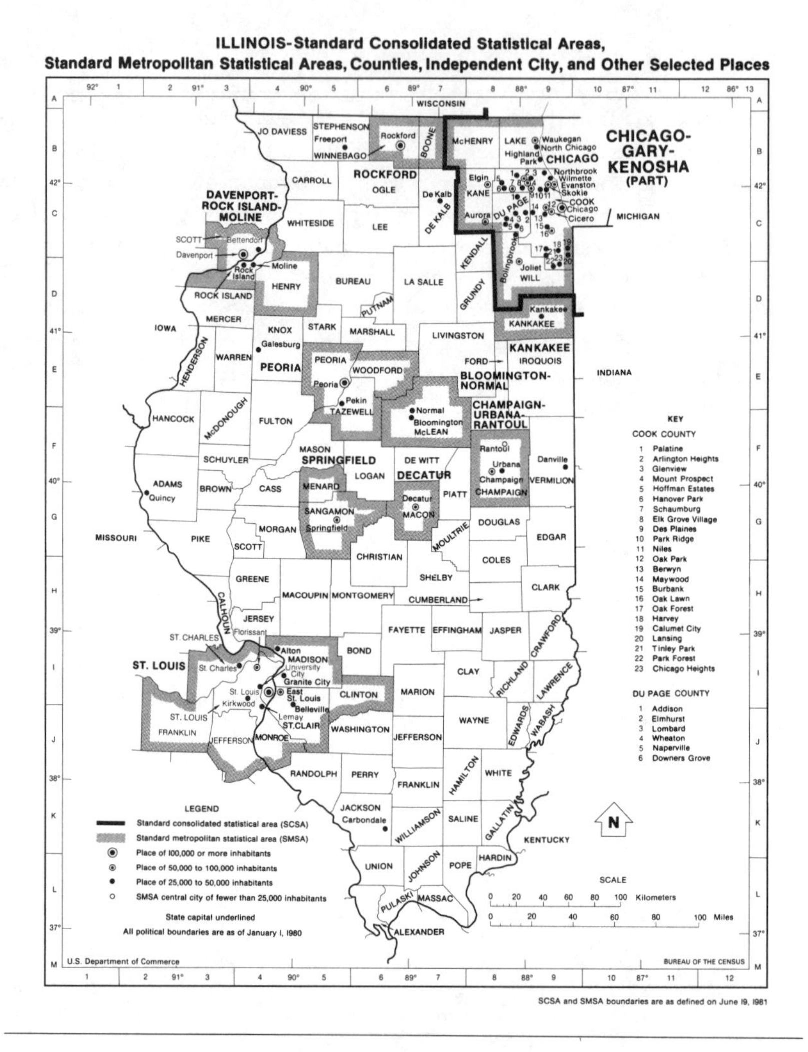

Map 1. Metropolitan areas in Illinois, 1977.

The initial work, undertaken between 1959 and 1963, was conducted under the auspices of the Institute of Government and Public Affairs of the University of Illinois. Since 1967 the project has continued under the auspices of the Center for the Study of Federalism of Temple University. One of the first comparative studies of urban politics in the United States, its findings were published in two books, *Cities of the Prairie: The Metropolitan Frontier and*

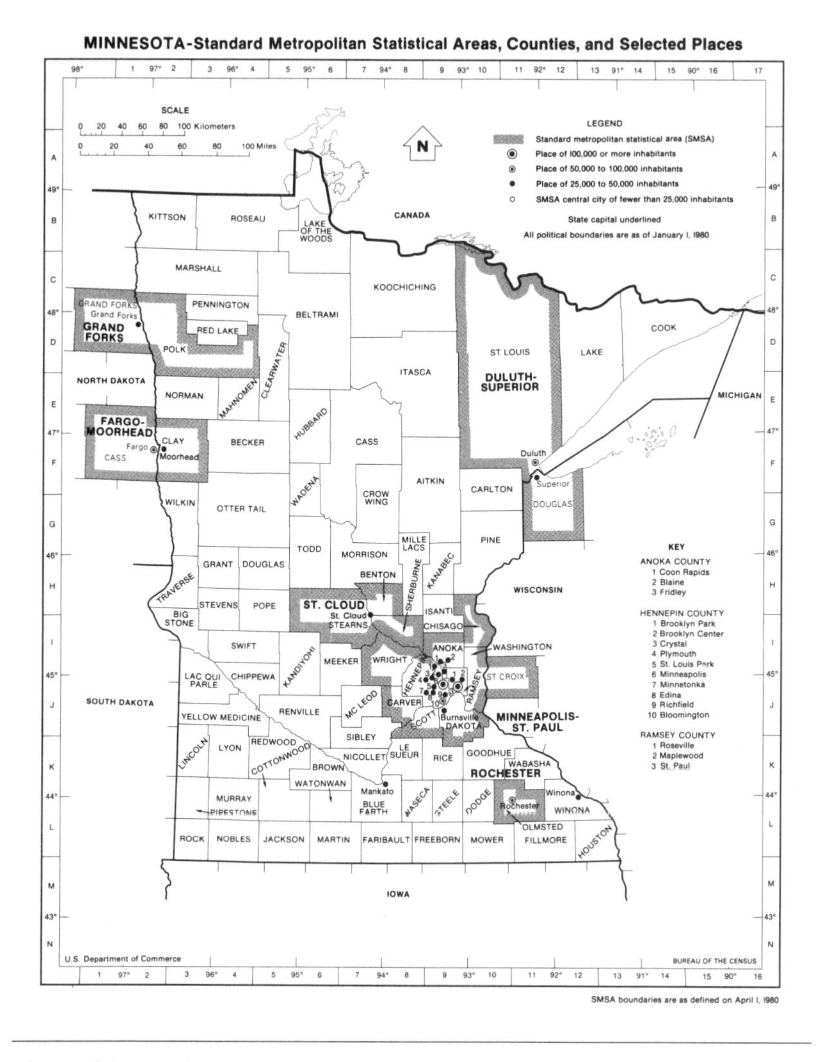

Map 2. Metropolitan areas in Minnesota, 1977.

American Politics and *The Politics of Belleville: A Profile of the Civil Community*, as well as in a number of separately published articles. The latter have been collected and revised for inclusion in *Building Cities in America*. Significantly, several of the central theses developed in that study and presented in *Cities of the Prairie*—particularly those delineating the patterns of American political culture and the character of local-state-federal relations—are now widely

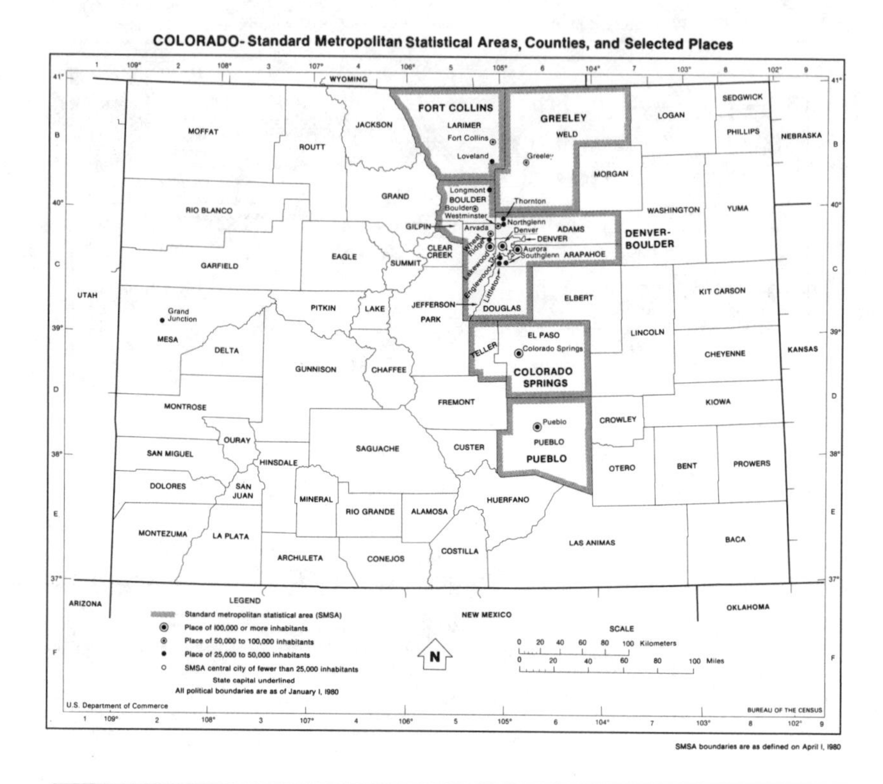

Map 3. Metropolitan areas in Colorado, 1977.

accepted as standard elements in current political science theory and have been the basis for extensive research within that and other disciplines.

When I began the initial work, I committed myself to a long-term study of the same cities and metropolitan areas. The idea was to restudy them periodically over at least a generation. I did so because of great dissatisfaction with the snapshot character of most urban research and the lack of longitudinal coverage. In 1970, with the assistance of graduate students, staff, and faculty associates of the Center for the Study of Federalism, I resumed studies in selected civil communities from among the original group, specifically Champaign–Urbana, Moline, Rockford, and Springfield, Illinois; Davenport, Iowa; Duluth, Minnesota; and Pueblo, Colorado. Subsequently we returned to Decatur, East St. Louis, Joliet, and Peoria, Illinois, as well.

In addition to replicating the earlier work, these new studies added new dimensions of specificity—probing the influence of foundings and reconstitutions, the relation between economic and political power, the associational frameworks of civic life, and the expansion of the role of government locally as a developmental phenomenon. In all cases the central focus was the effect on local government and politics of the greatly increased federal intervention of the 1960s and early 1970s. This represented a natural follow-up to the original study, which focused on the changes of the first half of the postwar generation (1946–61).

In the interim, the number of medium-sized civil communities in the states from which the original group was chosen has at least doubled, a sign of the accuracy of the forecast that emerged from the first study. Colorado and Minnesota have each added four more medium-sized metropolitan civil communities, and Illinois has added five. Among the fastest-growing cities in the 25,000 to 50,000 class in the United States between 1960 and 1970, for example, were Brooklyn Park (147.2 percent and fifteenth in the nation), Coon Rapids (104.3 percent and thirty-second), and Fridley (92.7 percent and thirty-ninth), Minnesota; Arvada (159.1 percent and sixteenth), Littleton (93.6 percent and thirty-eighth), and Fort Collins (73.2 percent and fifty-first), Colorado; Northbrook (134.6 percent and twentieth), Palatine (126.4 percent and twenty-second), North Chicago (106.1 percent and twenty-eighth), Normal (97.6 percent and thirty-fifth), Mount Prospect (85.1 percent and forty-third), and DeKalb (78.4 percent and forty-sixth), Illinois; and Menominee Falls (73.4 percent and forty-ninth), Wisconsin.

On the other side of the ledger, Alton, Illinois, lost 7.8 percent of its population in that period, one of the fifty cities in that category with the steepest decline and the only one in the Cities of the Prairie study to be included in that category. Virtually all of the rapid-growth cities were in major metropolitan regions, the exceptions being Normal, Illinois, part of the Bloomington–Normal metropolitan area, one of the new medium-sized metropolitan areas in that state, and DeKalb, Illinois, and Fort Collins, Colorado, both on their way to becoming small metropolitan centers in their own right.[2]

During the same period, most of the civil communities of the original study had their own demographic ups and downs. While all but one had modest population gains between 1960 and 1980, half of the central cities lost population. Except in the case of Superior, which had been losing population since its 1910 peak at the end of its land frontier, those losses represented a reversal of the previous trend and reflected the general pattern of older central cities, especially in the Northeast. Indeed, the central cities that did grow were those two west of the Mississippi or on the periphery of the greater Northeast.

The Changing Focus of Local Political Studies

This study replicates the original research design, examining major political developments during the fifteen-year period from 1962 to 1977, thereby completing the examination of those civil communities over a full generation and creating the basis for a more systematic and substantial longitudinal comparison than has ever been undertaken in the study of urban politics.

Interest in the systematic study of community power and local politics has its origins in the Progressive Era, in the work of journalistic probers of urban bossism in America. Those journalists, including such figures as Lincoln Steffens and Ida Tarbell, approached their inquiries on a comparative basis, but as journalists without a scientific orientation.[3] After the First World War, sociologists and political scientists began to enter the field in a more systematic manner. The sociological inquiries of Robert S. Lynd and Helen M. Lynd are landmarks in the effort.[4] They were paralleled in political science by the work of Charles E. Merriam and his associates at the University of Chicago, particularly Harold F. Gosnell.[5] After World War II this line of inquiry was advanced by the work of C. Wright Mills, Floyd Hunter, Robert Dahl, and Edward Banfield, all of whom have provided the present basis for assessments of community power and politics.[6] Their work has been supplemented by what is by now a substantial list of studies by their colleagues and students.

One feature common to all these studies is an almost exclusive focus on the urban political community as an entity detached from its larger political environment. This indeed was, in some respects, a necessary first step in establishing the structure and patterns of local politics as existing in their own right. At the same time, it represented a grave deficiency in the ultimate character of the works.

While this basic work in community politics was being undertaken within this limited framework, Morton Grodzins and his colleagues at the University of Chicago (including Banfield, who is far more prone to include external factors than other authors) initiated explorations of local government, metropolitan and nonmetropolitan, within the context of the American federal system.[7] The Cities of the Prairie project was an outgrowth of the Grodzins school and represented, from the first, an effort to study American urban politics within the larger context of the American political system and its sociocultural environment.

Thus a central premise of this study is that it is neither possible nor desirable to study local political systems apart from their larger geohistorical, cultural, economic, and political settings. Communities are located not only in space, but also in time (history) and culture. Not only is it possible, for example, to "map" the geohistorical and cultural location of a particular community, but it is necessary to do so to understand how it functions socially and politically and how it relates to the larger civil society of which it is a part. Refining the Grodzins model, the first project focused explicitly on urban politics within the larger context.

The project was based on the thesis that the American political system in its local as well as its larger dimension has been shaped by four decisive forces: the frontier and its continuing stimulation of technological innovation and social change; migration and the transplantation of cultures; sectionalism and the development of distinctive geohistorical settings for American politics; and federalism that has provided the operating principles and framework for political and social response to these factors. The civil communities of the study were examined within the context of these four themes and in light of the particular temporal rhythm of American politics, in an effort to indicate how they have interacted with them. The results have led to what we believe are the foundations for an integrated multidimensional theory of metropolitan politics within the American federal system that can be extended, with appropriate modifications, to an examination of urban politics in other political systems as well.

The Resurvey

The first survey covered the first half of the postwar generation (1946–61). Since that time there have been a number of significant developments in the communities, not the least of which involves the massive infusion of federal funds during the height of the "Great Society" programs in the mid-1960s. Taking a long view of history, the rapid institution building and the widening scope of government activity during that period marked the peak of the postwar generation, and the culmination of a form of politics most powerfully enunciated by the New Deal.

The most immediate objective of the resurvey was to examine the significant issues and events of the second fifteen-year period and the changes that had occurred since the end of the first period. In our investigation we were particularly interested in local responses to those national trends and issues of the 1960s and early 1970s that bore directly on the themes of our study. The original themes and specific issues examined in the resurvey include:

1. *Civil Community and Federalism,* the position of the civil community within the state and national political systems, and the influence of the "Great Society" and "New Federalism."

2. *Metropolitanism,* the position of the medium-sized civil community

within its metropolitan region, and the effects of recent state and federal efforts to stimulate "substate regional planning" and "intergovernmental co-operation" within metropolitan areas.

3. *Democracy and Republicanism,* the representation of different factions and groups within the civil community, and the local effects of the black and ethnic revolution vocalized during the previous decades as expressed in political and institutional changes and reflected in challenges to the legitimacy of local power systems and institutions.

4. *Constitutionalism,* the position of government and government reform in the local civil community, and the effects of post-1961 legislation regarding redistricting, reapportionment, home rule, planning, electoral reform, campaign practices, and the like.

5. *Frontier and Sectionalism,* the diffusion of technological and managerial developments, and the changing geohistorical location of the civil community in response to the metropolitan-technological frontier as it reached its peak.

6. *Political Culture,* the effect of the foregoing changes on the local public's expectations from government, politics, and political leaders.[8]

Following the original research design, the investigation involved: (1) selective interviewing of political and community activists in depth; (2) systematic observation; (3) extensive review of the local press; (4) collection of socioeconomic and voting data; and (5) utilization of other relevant studies as well as public documents and special reports. Because the investigation involved a resurvey, special steps were taken to utilize and extend earlier findings in a number of ways: (1) reinterviewing key respondents interviewed in the early 1960s to review the findings and probe for both attitudinal and behavioral changes in the ensuing fifteen years; (2) updating earlier findings by following up on issues that were initiated before the first survey but resolved after, and by collecting newly released information on the first survey period; (3) comparing qualitative changes in the types of community activists interviewed and in the ease and manner of the interview process; as well as (4) the primary research task of identifying major shifts in the location of the civil communities and analyzing both survey and resurvey data for salient patterns and medium-range trends of the postwar generation.[9]

Amplification of Earlier Findings

The skills and field research efforts of a larger and more varied research staff enabled us to amplify as well as update earlier findings. The mutually reinforcing effects of these two tasks have been successfully tested by various members of the research team through topical and historical studies.

As a result of the first survey, I was able to obtain the surface and immediate subsurface information needed to construct a basic political map for each of the civil communities under investigation. Following the general comparative analysis of these maps, we were able to return to the case study approach to investigate those most typical and atypical communities more intensively.

Two published case studies resulted from the first effort: *The Politics of Belleville* and "Constitutional Change in a Long-Depressed Civil Community: A Case Study of Duluth, Minnesota." The former study was designed to serve as a more detailed illustration of the general model developed in the earlier analytical volume, *Cities of the Prairie,* and to contribute to a more general understanding of the inner workings of one of many relatively autonomous medium-sized communities that function rather successfully within greater metropolitan regions. As I noted in the introduction to that study: "An understanding of the Bellevilles of the United States, how and why they are and remain independent civil communities within great metropolitan regions, and what makes them tick, is crucial to understanding the nature of American urbanization, and perhaps more important, to understanding how an urbanized and metropolitanized America can possibly retain human scale in its social and political life."[10]

The second case study, of Duluth, analyzed local politics in a relatively unsuccessful and long-depressed civil community outside the mainstream of the American economy and urban development. Though the city was atypical as a "boom and bust" metropolis with a marginal economy, Duluth's politics of adversity were found to share important similarities with the politics of relative prosperity found in Belleville and other cities studied. Within this context, "Duluth may be considered a paradigm of the civil community caught in the backwash of the American economy and a testing ground in which to examine notions of the nature of community political systems developed in more prosperous civil communities."[11]

Though broadly historical in approach, these case studies were particularly concerned with the most recent time segment of each civil community's history. Drawing on these and other studies, Stephen L. Schechter built a historical and development dimension into the resurvey design itself through studies in Pueblo, Colorado, and Springfield, Illinois. Through exploratory research, he was able to identify certain critical periods of development for more intensive investigation (of foundation, incorporation, industrial expansion, depression, recovery, and reform) and to develop surrogate measures for mapping the civil communities' political characteristics during these periods and their transition from one period to another.

In another comparative case study, this one on a topical theme, Benjamin Schuster wrote his dissertation on the relationships between economic and political elites in three civil communities (Rockford, Davenport, and Duluth).[12] Rozann Rothman completed a book-length case study of Champaign–Urbana, with special emphasis on the local implications of the home rule and reapportionment provisions of the new Illinois state constitution.[13] Shorter case studies were completed by Maren Stein on Decatur and Joseph Zikmund on Joliet.

Expanding the Scope of the Study

Although the research design was first tested in American cities of the upper Mississippi–Missouri valley, from the first the intention was to produce a research design and models that would be more widely applicable. Since the first survey, the research design has been tested in other cities both within and outside the original area of investigation. Within the boundaries of the first study, we mapped the migration, settlement, and eventual meeting of different cultural streams in selected civil communities of the greater West. While those civil communities shared the common characteristics of that sphere, because of their particular geohistorical location, most also reflected the characteristics of adjacent spheres, as follows: (1) civil communities of the industrial north (Joliet); (2) civil communities of the central prairie (Champaign–Urbana, Decatur, Peoria, Springfield); (3) civil communities of the border south (Madison and St. Clair counties); (4) civil communities of the upper midwest (Duluth); (5) civil communities of the West (Pueblo, Quad Cities). This made the broader generalizations of the original study both possible and reasonable.[14]

In the expansion, Stephen Schechter and John Kincaid retraced the three great westward streams to their American sources in the New England, Middle Atlantic, and southern states. Representative civil communities were selected on the basis of their "goodness of fit" within their respective regions and their comparability with each other and with the civil communities in the original study. Retaining the essential case study character of the original work, the choices emphasized sectional location and "socioeconomic" (in the broadest sense of the term) positions within the respective social systems.

John Kincaid did a comprehensive in-depth study of Jersey City, New Jersey, as the epitome of the Middle Atlantic industrial city, from its entrepreneurial beginnings in the eighteenth century through its period as a haven for immigrant workers from Europe and the machine politics of that time, down to its present status as a port of entry for the most recent waves of Asian and Latin American immigrants and its continuing struggle with machine politics. His work delineates and analyzes the pathology of phenomena that appeared in much more moderate form in certain of the Illinois cities of the prairie, whose geohistorical location clearly had a moderating effect on such tendencies. In doing so, it adds a whole new dimension to our understanding of machine politics and "boss rule."[15]

Stephen Schechter adopted a different approach, undertaking a broadly comparative effort in ten cities classified as: (1) the satellite cities of southern New York (White Plains and Mount Vernon); (2) the river cities of central New York (Albany and Schenectady); (3) the piedmont cities of central North Carolina (Raleigh and Durham); (4) the prairie cities of central Illinois (Springfield and Decatur); (5) the oasis cities of southeastern Colorado (Pueblo and Colorado Springs). His work focuses on foundings and refoundings; the stages of development of the civil communities and the continuities and discontinuities in their responses; patterns of urbanization and metropolitanization; the nature of political conflict and competition; the character of political leadership; local government organization and the politics of government change; and public policy formulation and administration.[16]

Finally, I did parallel exploratory surveys in Colorado Springs, Colorado, and Rochester, Minnesota, which became medium-sized civil communities in this period, and in the far western civil community of Pasadena, California.

This book presents the results of our return to the cities of the prairie. It does not go beyond those civil communities to incorporate the results of the studies of my colleagues, most of whom will publish their own books in due course. The book itself is divided into two parts. The first is an analytic overview of the cities' responses to major themes of the original study, and the second consists of case studies of particular civil communities and topics that further elucidate the analysis.

By replicating the research project longitudinally, we hope that we have contributed significantly to the scientific investigation of local politics. In our opinion, the resurvey itself represents a significant methodological advance over the single snapshot character of most urban studies. The half-generation seems to be an appropriate unit of time for such restudies, allowing comparative analysis over a full generation of thirty to forty years; hence, at the end of this decade we hope to be back with another installment in the continuing study of the cities of the prairie.

Part 1. Overview

1. The Civil Community in the Federal System

The high social and geographic mobility characteristic of American life has prevented the formation of communities as traditionally defined (e.g., the gemeinschaft of Toennies) based on stable populations or situated within a single set of political boundaries.[1] At the same time, functioning, self-perpetuating local communities clearly do exist and may be even more powerful politically than were the more comprehensive communities of premodern times. As a result, new definitions and delineations of community in political terms are required to explain this phenomenon.

In seeking to better define and understand the local political system, the original study identified the civil community as its focal point. A civil community is a consociation of individuals and groups within a particular locality that acquires a separate identity and the power to undertake common actions for political or civil purposes. In the United States, it is a species of locality containing many government institutions not necessarily coterminous with city boundaries or metropolitan limits, but served by a single comprehensive local political system. In brief, the civil community is the organized sum of the political institutions that function in a given locality to provide it with the bundle of government services and activities that can be manipulated locally to serve local needs in the light of local values.

Common politically significant components of the civil community include formally established local governments; the local agencies of state and federal governments; nongovernment public bodies; political parties or their equivalent; interest groups; and the locality's body of written constitutional material and unwritten traditions that define the rules of the local political "game." Taken together, these elements are interlinked through a communications network that provides the basis for the civil community's local political system.[2]

In their structural characteristics the civil communities of the cities of the prairie cover the gamut of such phenomena in the United States. The simplest are the single-center civil communities, consisting of one central city, no satellite cities, and perhaps some suburbs or suburban areas. Decatur, Peoria, Pueblo, Rockford, and Springfield are civil communities of this kind (see maps 1.1, 1.2, 1.3, 1.4, 1.5).

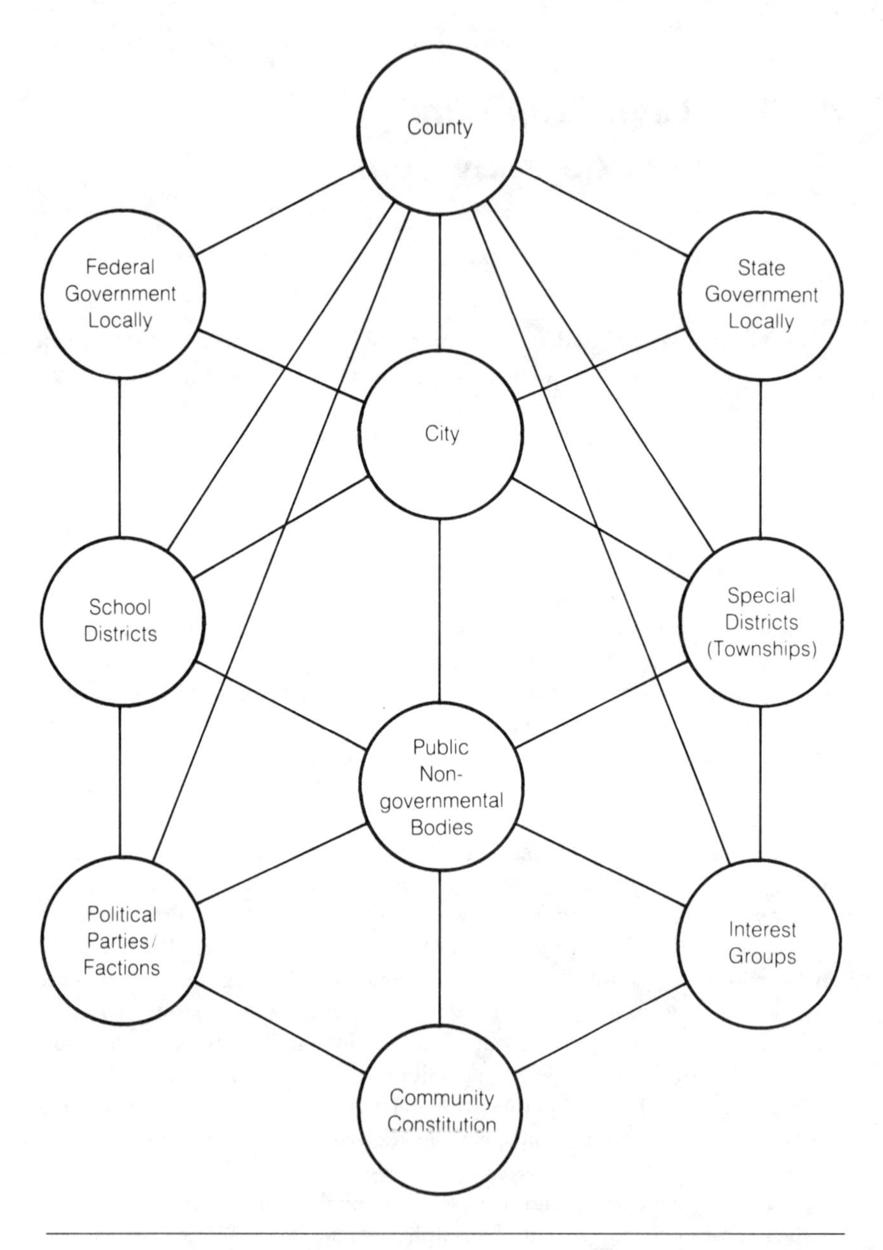

Fig. 1.1. The civil community and its components. From Daniel J. Elazar, *The Politics of Belleville: A Profile of the Civil Community* (Philadelphia: Temple University Press, 1971).

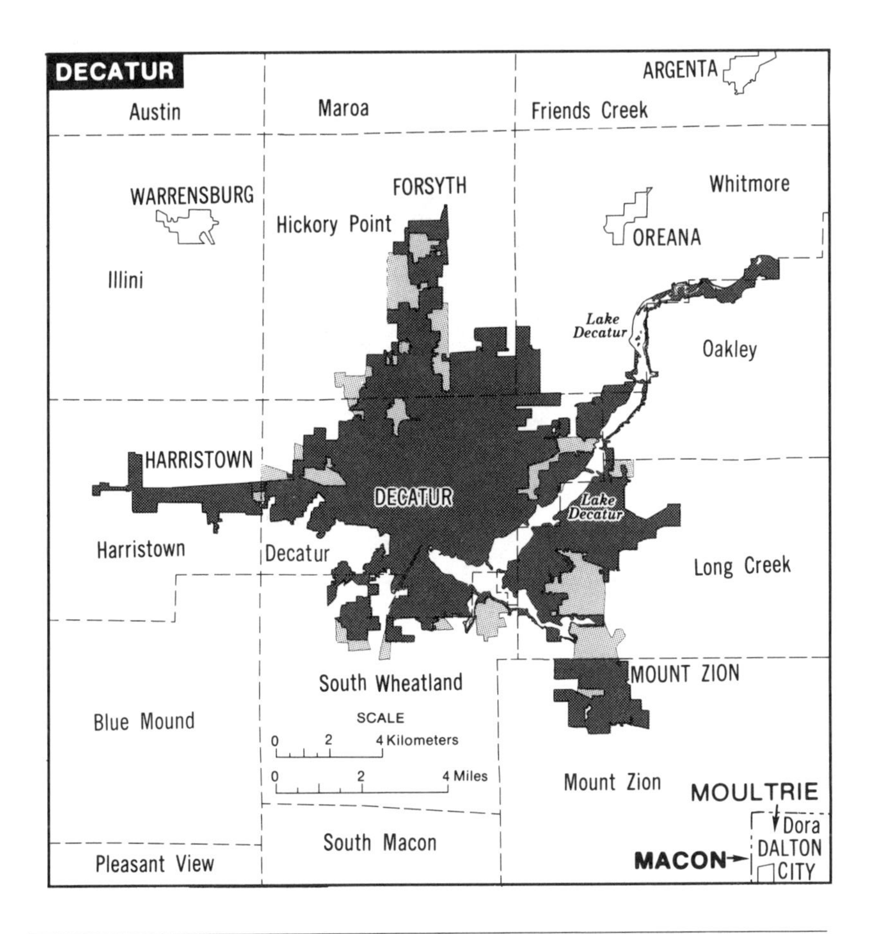

Map 1.1. The Decatur civil community.

Somewhat more complex are twin cities, of which Champaign–Urbana (map 1.6) and Duluth–Superior (map 1.7) are the only examples in this study. A more complex model is that of the integrated metropolitan civil community network, where more than two adjacent cities share an integrated socioeconomic pattern and a rudimentary communitywide politics. The Quad Cities area (map 1.8), with its three central cities and two satellite cities plus suburbs and exurbs, is a classic example of this genre.

On the other hand, there is the multiple-centered metropolitan area that includes several, if not many, civil communities adjoining one another

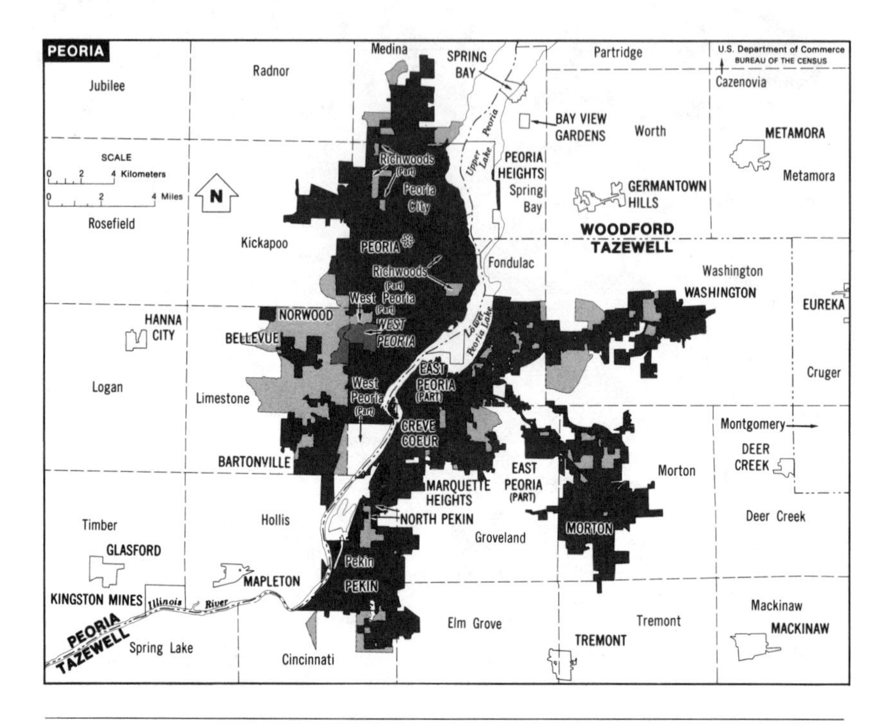

Map 1.2. The Peoria civil community and urbanized areas.

but with minimal integration among them. Madison and St. Clair counties (map 1.9), with six central cities and three to five satellite cities plus suburbs, most of which work hard at putting distance between themselves, constitute a classic example of this type. Joliet (map 1.10), within the northeastern Illinois metropolitan region, which includes Chicago, is a different example of the same phenomenon.

The civil community concept is paralleled by the economists' conception of the urban economy as a three-sector system consisting of the business sector, the household sector, and the urban public sector, each distinct but interacting with the other (fig. 1.2). Urban outcomes in the private business sector that affect the civil community include levels of economic activity, income, employment, wages, and investment in the urban area. The household sector includes the size, composition, and spatial distribution of the population, the composition of the housing stock, and the number of people per housing unit in the geographic area. The urban public sector includes all local governments, which we define as the first component of the civil community. For the urban public sector, the major outcomes include the

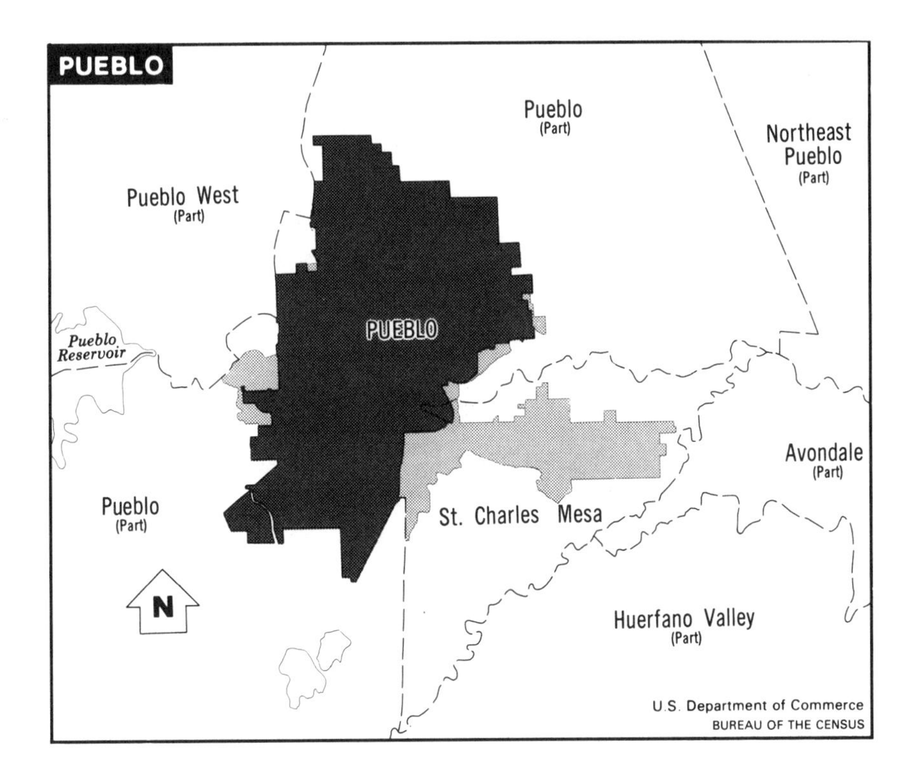

Map 1.3. The Pueblo civil community.

level of public services and the magnitude and composition of the public expenditure by the residents (table 1.1).[3]

Economists utilize this model in the way political scientists study policy determinants and outcomes through the civil community model. The linkage of the two models offers a basis for drawing a comprehensive picture of any civil community. For example, in the original Cities of the Prairie study, the important public contribution of the residential sector in providing physical amenities to the civil community was related to the American style of city, with its emphasis on freestanding housing. The cost of maintaining trees and lawns throughout the urbanized area was borne principally by that sector and would have been prohibitive for the public sector to assume.[4] This is only one way this economic model can be of use in systematically investigating the public contribution of the residential and business sectors, just as it is important to understand the influence of the public sector on the other two.

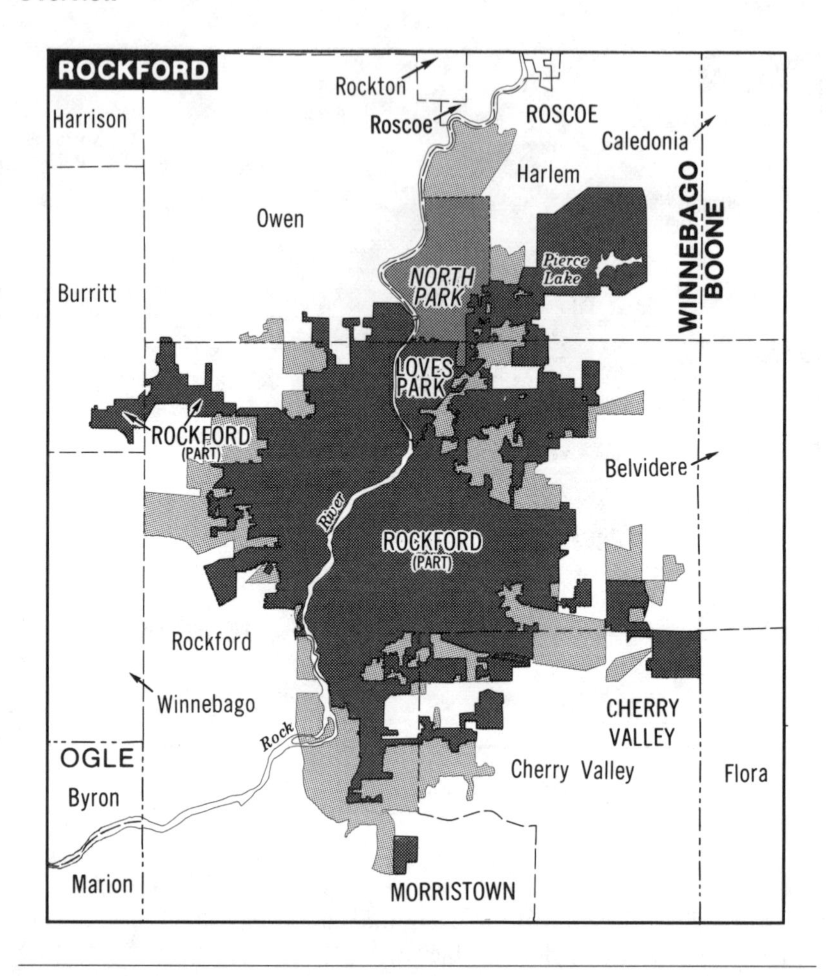

Map 1.4. The Rockford civil community.

Outside Influences on the Civil Community

American civil communities possess reasonably complex and actively functioning political systems of their own. Nevertheless, it would be a distortion to view the communities or their political systems as detached from any other. The casual civics student knows that local governments are creatures of the state and that the states are linked in a union under a federal government whose influence is widespread and whose hand is felt in many ways in the local community. It is equally misleading to view local political systems as

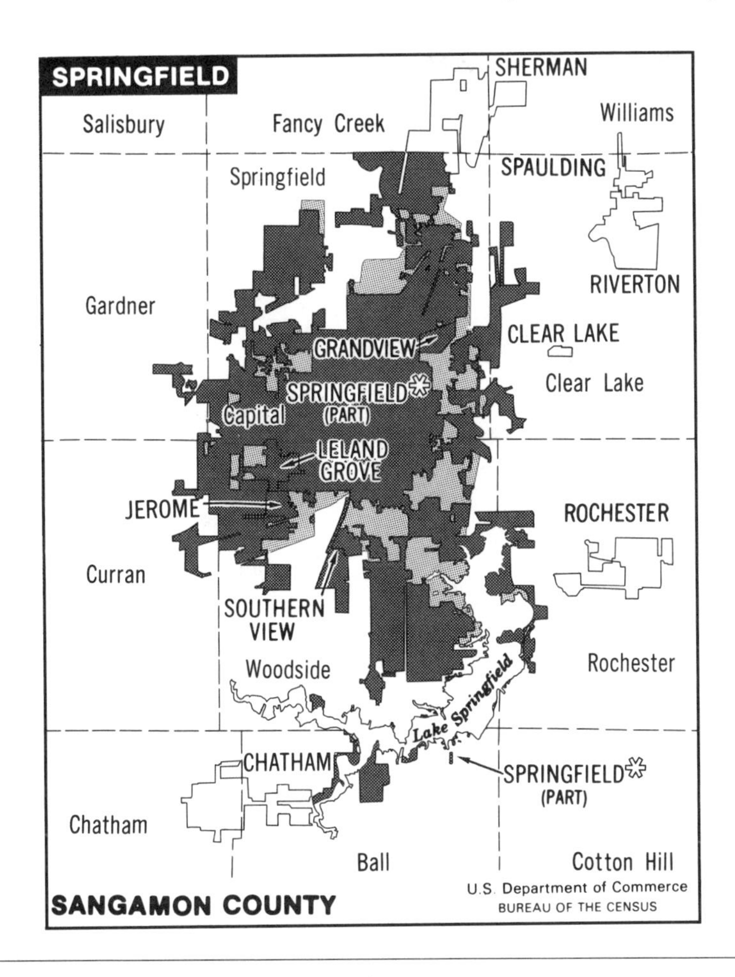

Map 1.5. The Springfield civil community.

subordinate or limited to a particular sphere by the state and federal governments.

Constitutionally dependent upon their states for their very existence, local communities are protected by the same political diffusion of power that protects the states vis-à-vis the federal government. Most of them have been able to use their political power to secure a greater measure of autonomy than is formally theirs under constitutional law. This has given them a measure of control over all government activities within their limits, regardless of the level of government responsible for them.

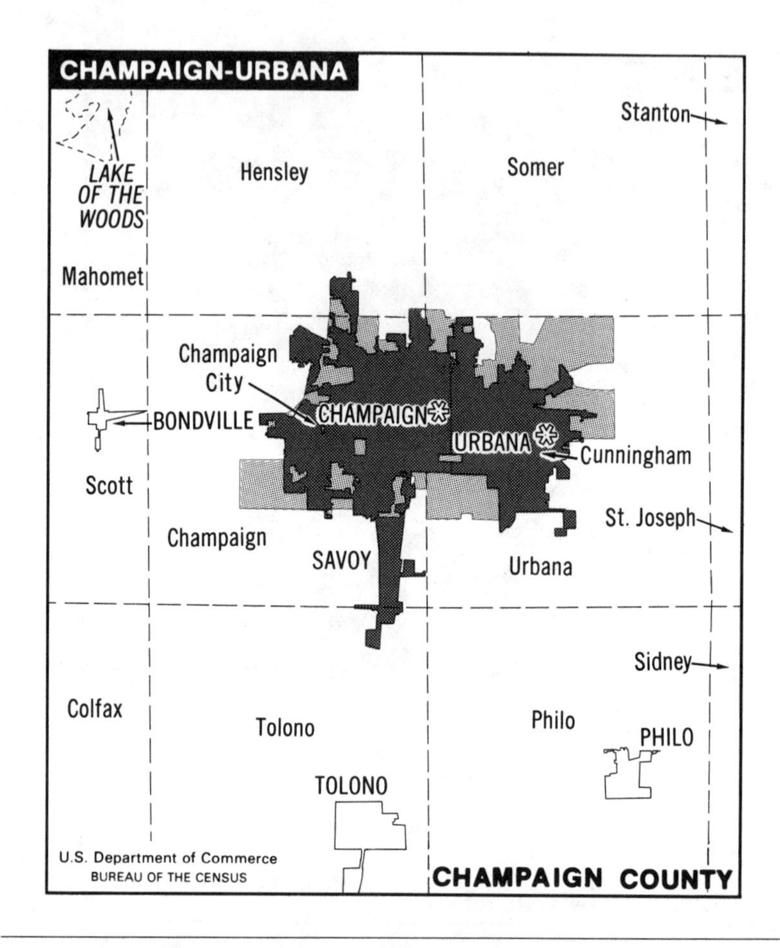

Map 1.6. The Champaign and Urbana civil communities.

Similarly, local communities intermesh with the state and federal governments in many ways and for many purposes. City officials seek expert advice on building a jail; park commissioners seek financial aid in developing a local recreational facility; local businessmen seek funds for airport improvement and for transfer of a military installation to their city; public and private parties seek the right to issue bonds for industrial development and seek grants of fire-fighting equipment under the civil defense program. All require outside assistance, and assistance for all but the last two items can be acquired from either level of government, depending upon which is most convenient. Because the federal principle of noncentralization extends

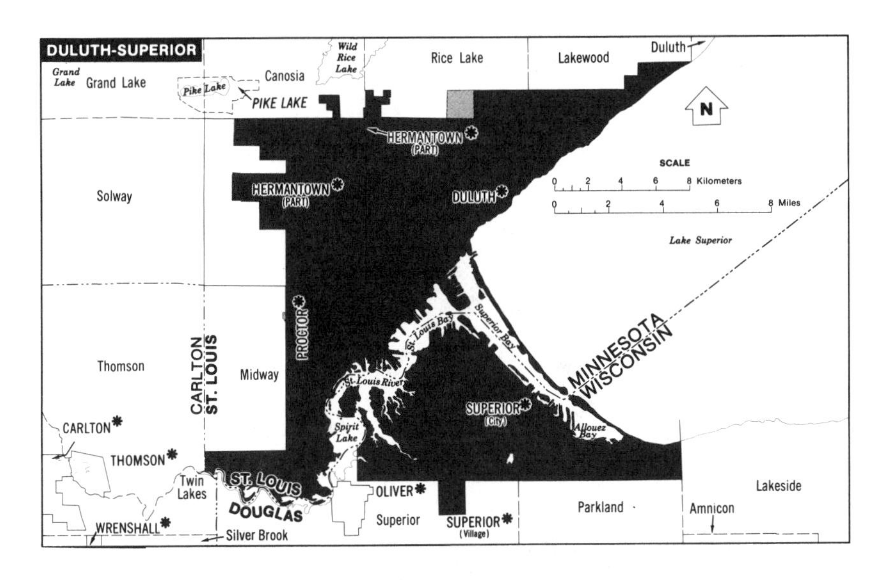

Map 1.7. The Duluth and Superior civil communities.

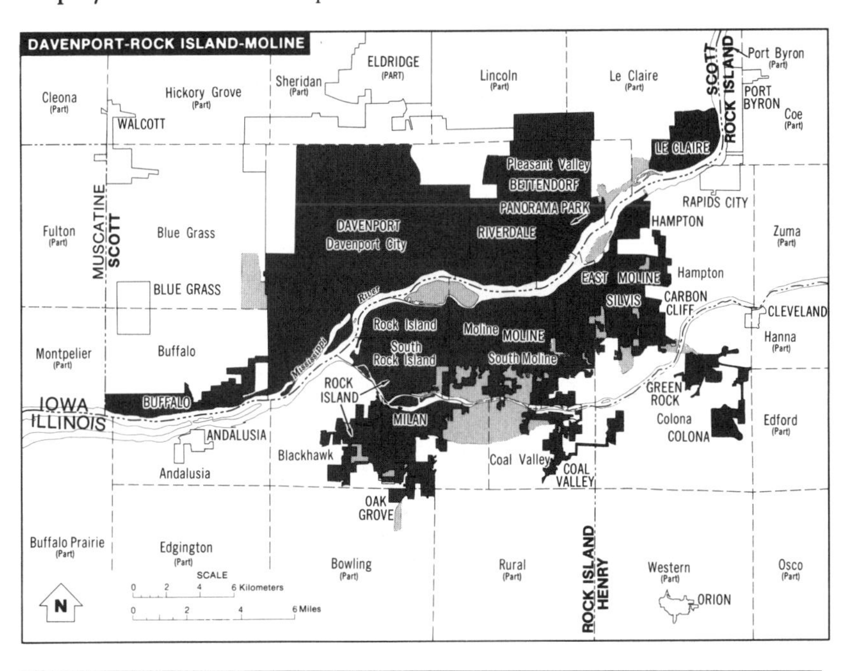

Map 1.8. The Quad Cities urbanized area.

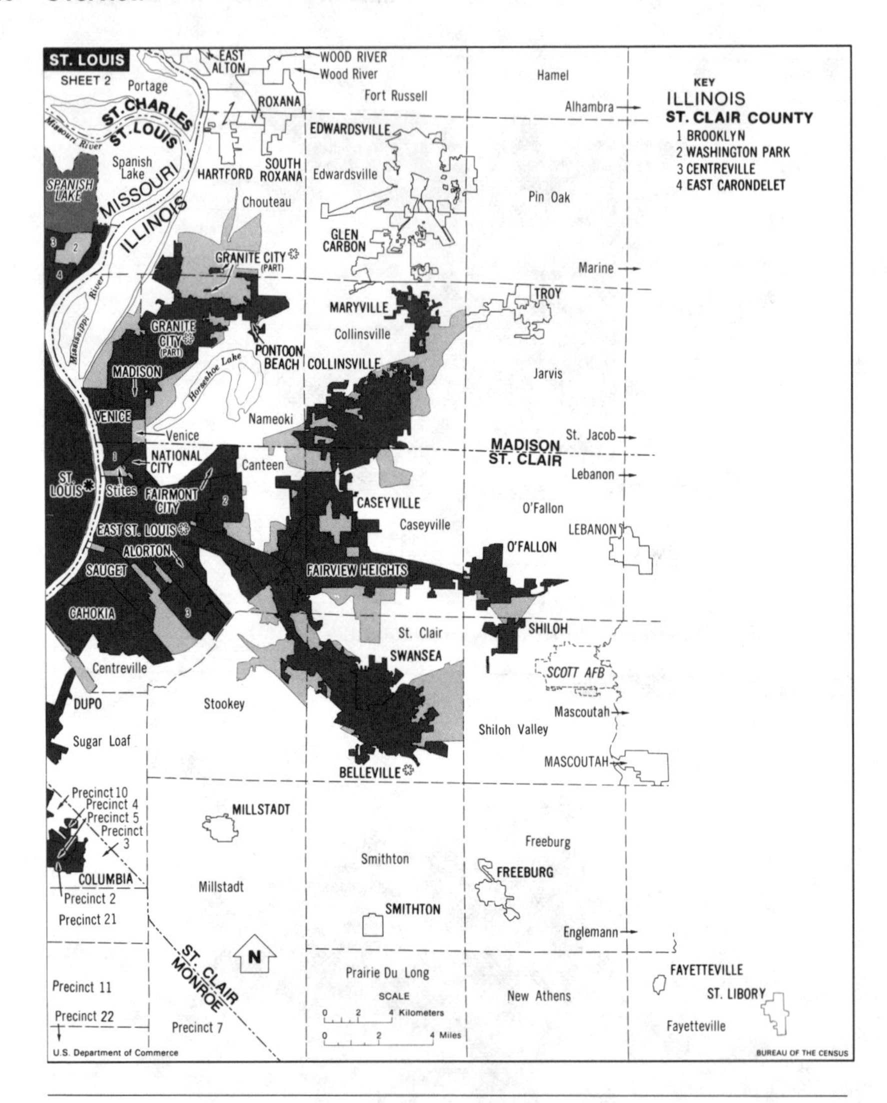

Map 1.9. The Madison-St. Clair counties urbanized area.

to the local plane, even outside contributions—financial, technical, or political—can be assimilated and managed locally for local ends.

Since the founding of the republic, operations in the American federal system have been predominantly cooperative, involving the sharing of functions by all planes of government in partnership, thus avoiding both a separation of function by plane or system and centralization of power in

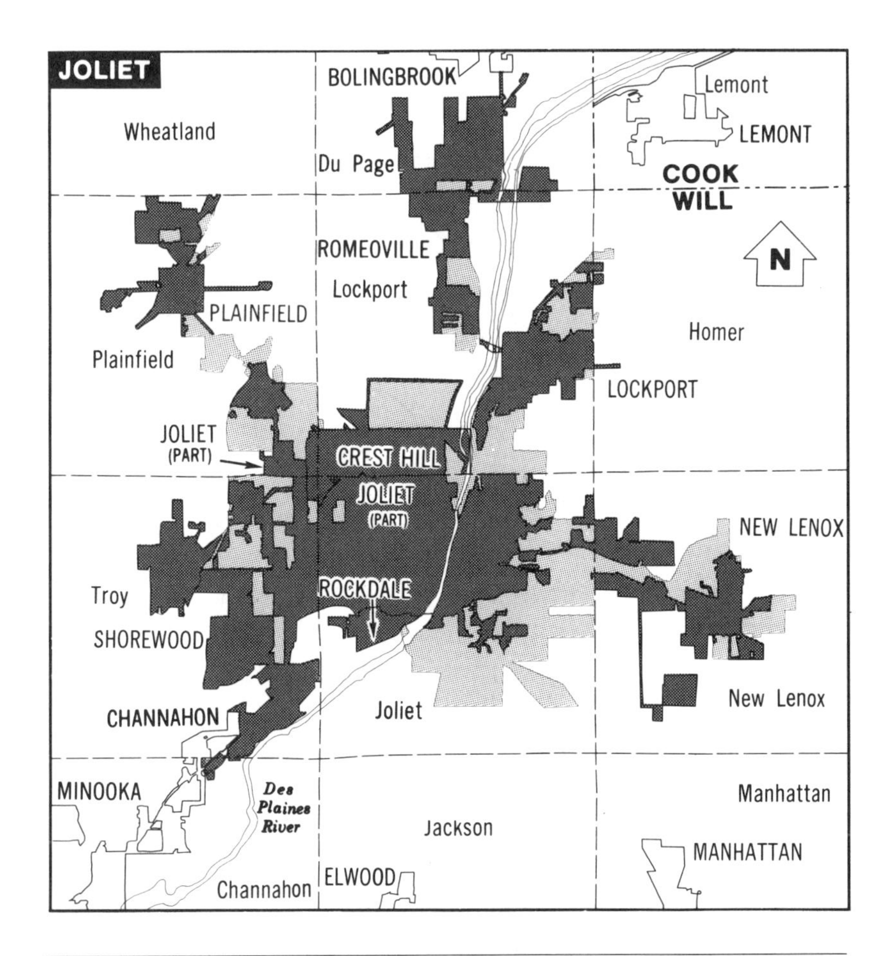

Map 1.10. The Joliet civil community.

the national government.[5] The civil communities are part of larger and more complex political systems that impinge upon them to the point where neat separation of activities is existentially impossible and theoretically inaccurate.

Contractual noncentralization—the structured dispersion of power among many centers whose legitimate authority is constitutionally guaranteed—is the key to the widespread and entrenched diffusion of power that remains the principal characteristic of the American federal system. Noncentralization is not the same as decentralization, though the latter term is frequently—and erroneously—used to describe the American system. De-

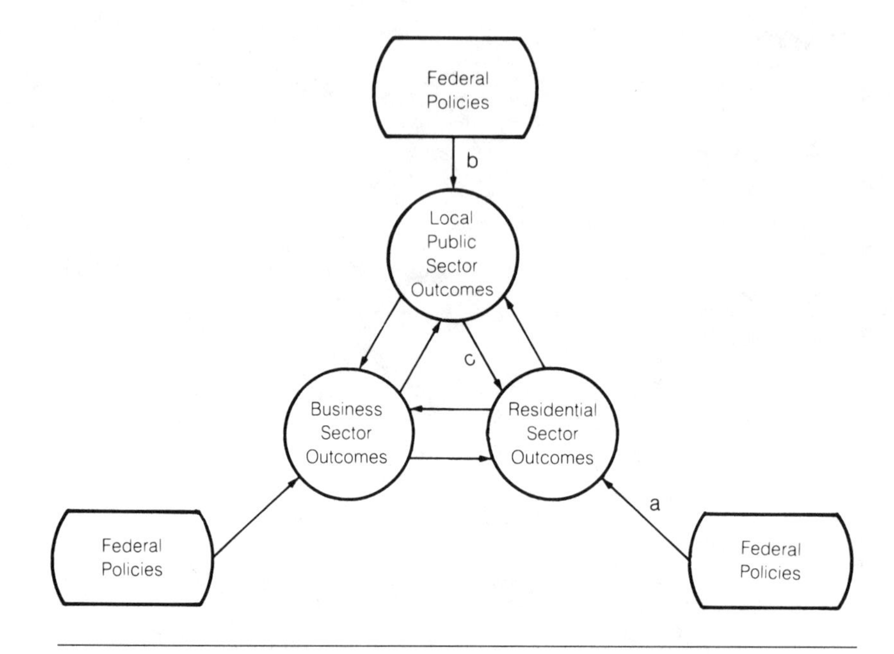

Fig. 1.2. The three-sector approach to urban impact analysis. From Herrington Bryce, ed., *Small Cities in Transition: The Dynamics of Growth and Decline* (Cambridge, Mass.: Ballinger, 1977), p. 218.

centralization implies the existence of a central authority, a central government. The government that can *de*centralize can *re*centralize if it so desires. Hence in decentralized systems the diffusion of power is actually a matter of grace, not right, and as history reveals, in the long run it is usually treated as such. In a noncentralized political system, power is so diffused that it cannot legitimately be centralized or concentrated without breaking the structure and spirit of the constitution.

In contemporary social science language, centralization and decentralization are extremes of the same continuum, while noncentralization represents another continuum altogether. In systems on the former continuum, it is rather simple to measure the flow of power one way or another. In noncentralized systems, however, such measurement is considerably more difficult. In the American case, as this study demonstrates, simple evidence of national government involvement in a particular field does not tell us enough about the relative strength of the various power centers in policymaking, administration, or what have you. The primary diffusion of power makes

Table 1.1. Major Determinants of Outcomes in the Three Sectors of the Urban Economy

Sector	Decision-Making Units	Major Outcomes	Main Determinants of Outcomes
Private business sector	Firms	Output Investment Employment Wages Magnitude Composition Spatial distribution	Demand for output Consumer demand Population characteristics Income from economic activity Transfer payments Personal taxes Business demand (for intermediate goods) Public demand Federal purchases State/local purchases Factor supply Supply of labor Access Transportation of goods Transportation of persons Supply of raw materials Supply of energy Supply of land Supply of capital funds Public services and taxes Amenities Subsidies and restrictions Technology
Residential sector	Households	Population and housing stock Magnitude Composition Spatial distribution	Demand for housing Income (including transfer payments) Socioeconomic characteristics Neighborhood characteristics Access/transportation Amenities: physical and social

Table 1.1. Continued.

Sector	Decision-Making Units	Major Outcomes	Main Determinants of Outcomes
			Public services and taxes
			Housing subsidies and tax benefits
			Availability and cost of mortgage credit
			Supply of housing
			Factor supply
			Housing construction
			Housing operation
			Public infrastructures
			Supplier subsidies and tax benefits
			Availability and cost of credit
			Production and marketing restrictions
Local public sector	Local governments	Public services	Revenue sources
		Level	Local revenue base
		Mix	Residential/personal
		Distribution	Business
		Taxes	Tax spillovers
		Level	Outside aid
		Composition	Federal and state grants
			Revenue subsidies (tax expenditures)
			Expenditure demands
			"Need" factors (population characteristics)
			Service costs
			Service spillovers
			Scope of local service responsibility
			Mandated expenditures

Source: Herrington J. Bryce, ed., *Small Cities in Transition: The Dynamics of Growth and Decline* (Cambridge, Mass.: Ballinger, 1977), pp. 220–21.

"involvement" take on many different meanings. As those involved in the governmental process well know, even apparently unilateral programs may be substantially shaped by the other governments through the political process. As those who study local government also know, he who pays the piper may or may not call the tune, and not necessarily in proportion to the amount of money provided.

The local presence of federal and state governments is only partially illustrated in table 1.2. In fact, there has never been a time when it was possible to put neat labels on separate federal, state, and local programs. Federal and state grants of land, money, and services have long stimulated local activity in fields where local governments have hesitated to act on their own resources alone. Direct federal and state activities in the civil community, ranging from river and harbor improvements to youth work with potential juvenile delinquents, have *supplemented* local government efforts. Federal and state "government locally"—the post office, the state employment office—have become integral parts of the bundle of government activities included in the political system of every civil community.

Finally, there is the special character of state-local relations. The state is constitutionally the source of authority for all its created local governments. In addition, the immediate determination of the legal rights and powers of local government is vested in the state government as written into state law and as interpreted by the state courts. Furthermore, each state has the exclusive right and obligation to regulate the way its elections are conducted. This also includes the regulation of political parties, candidates, and the form of ballot. The states maintain a special, continuing, and omnipresent relationship with their civil communities in the realm of public regulation—of transportation, of public utilities, of matters involving public health and morals. The state also is a direct actor in and supporter of local government in an increasing number of fields.

In the second half of the postwar generation, the roles of the federal and state governments increased dramatically, as is reflected in greater funding of local programs and in an increased presence in the civil community. From 1962 to 1975, federal aid to state and local governments nationwide increased by 494.9 percent to approximately $47 billion per year, growing at an annual average rate of 14.6 percent. Over the same period, state aid to localities increased by 434.5 percent, from approximately $11.6 billion to $62 billion, an average annual growth rate of 15.8 percent. Of that, aid to municipalities grew from $2.5 billion in 1962 to $19.6 billion in 1975, an increase of 684 percent, increasing at an average annual rate of 17.1 percent.[6] Whereas in 1962 cities as a class were the least dependent units of general-purpose

Table 1.2. Major Federal and State Institutions in the Cities of the Prairie

Civil Community	Immediate Cause of Founding	Early Federal Institutions	Early State Institutions	Federal Institutions in 1970	Contemporary State Institutions in 1970
Champaign	Illinois Central RR[a] division point		University of Illinois[a]	Chanute Air Force Base	University of Illinois[a]
Urbana	Designated county seat by state		University of Illinois[a]	Chanute Air Force Base	University of Illinois[a]
Decatur	Designated county seat by state				
Joliet	Center of construction for Illinois and Michigan Canal		Illinois and Michigan Canal[a] State penitentiary	Illinois Waterway Locks	State penitentiary
Alton	Riverboat landing		State penitentiary (1829–61)	Alton Lock and Dam	Alton State Hospital[a]
Belleville	Designated county seat by territory			Scott Air Force Base	Southern Illinois University[a]
East St. Louis	Ferry crossing and terminus of national railroads				Southern Illinois University[a] Cahokie Mounds State Park
Peoria	Federal military post (Fort Peoria)	Fort Peoria			Peoria State Hospital
Davenport–Bettendorf	Federal military post (Fort Armstrong)	Rock Island Arsenal		Rock Island Arsenal	
E. Moline–Silvis	Location of factories for National Corps	Rock Island Arsenal		Rock Island Arsenal	East Moline State Hospital

Moline	Industrial site	Rock Island Arsenal		Rock Island Arsenal	
Rock Island	Federal military post (Fort Armstrong)	Rock Island Arsenal		Rock Island Arsenal	Black Hawk State Park[a]
Rockford	Industrial site and stagecoach crossing	Camp Grant (1917–18, 1940–46)		District Office U.S. Corps of Engineers	University of Illinois Medical School and Regional Academic Center[a]
Springfield	Designated county seat by state	United States Land Office	State capital State fair	Federal regional offices	Sangamon State University[a] State capital State fair
Duluth	Designated terminus for Northern Pacific RR[a]	United States Land Office Federal Harbor Control		Federal Harbor Control USAF Air Defense Force	University of Minnesota (Duluth)[a]
Superior	Lake port and designated county seat by state	Federal Harbor Control		Federal Harbor Control	State college[a]
Pueblo	Gold rush	United States Land Office	State fair	Pueblo Ordnance Depot U.S. Department of Transportation Test Center U.S. Document Center	Colorado State Hospital Colorado State Fair Colorado State Museum University of Southern Colorado[a]

Source: Daniel J. Elazar, *Cities of the Prairie: The Metropolitan Frontier and American Politics* (New York: Basic Books, 1970), pp. 384–85, as updated.
[a]Received or receives extensive federal aid.

local government within the state-local system, by 1975 they were more than twice as dependent as the states on outside funds, had exceeded the dependency level of townships, and were rapidly approaching the dependency level of counties. Over the thirteen-year period the dependency of cities grew more than three times as fast as that of the states. However true this was across the country, it was much less true in the cities of the prairie. Their use of state and federal aid also grew, but to a far lesser extent, in part because they ignored opportunities to acquire outside aid that did not come automatically, and in part because in some cases they actually resisted outside money. Table 1.3 shows the extent of federal and state aid to cities of the prairie, by county or multicounty SMSA for 1971–72, the high point of Great Society expenditures.

This phenomenon was common among cities of their size; the smaller the city, the less per capita expenditure, the less per capita aid, and the less dependency as shown in table 1.4. Throughout the period, medium-sized cities tended to be below the national average in dependency and in growth of dependency. In part this was also a function of geohistorical location. Illinois and Colorado ranked fortieth and forty-first among the fifty states and the District of Columbia in municipal dependency on state and federal aid, and Iowa and Minnesota ranked sixteenth and twenty-third respectively. Only Wisconsin ranked high, in fifth place. If we take federal aid alone, then Wisconsin ranked fiftieth, Minnesota forty-third, Illinois forty-eighth,

Table 1.3. Cities of the Prairie: Sources of Local Government Revenue, 1971–72 (millions of dollars)

Standard Metropolitan Statistical Area	Total Revenue*	State Funds	Federal Funds
Champaign–Urbana	63.8	20.9	3.5
Davenport–Rock Island, Moline	172.2	51.7	5.4
Decatur	54.5	18.9	0.8
Duluth–Superior	201.6	82.7	4.3
Joliet (Will County)	105.4	31.1	1.8
Madison–St. Clair counties	239.4	89.2	16.9
Peoria	137.1	40.0	1.9
Pueblo	61.9	23.3	2.1
Rockford	116.6	39.9	4.4
Springfield	82.4	23.3	1.2

Source: U.S. Bureau of the Census, *Local Government in Metropolitan Areas,* 1971–72.
*Excluding interlocal.

and Colorado forty-fourth. Only Iowa was the exception, ranking thirteenth. Wisconsin's high overall ranking reflected the fact that it was fourth in state aid. Minnesota was fifteenth, Iowa twenty-first, Illinois twenty-sixth, and Colorado thirty-sixth. Indeed, Colorado was one of the states whose municipalities received more aid from the federal government than from their states up to that year.[7]

The five states also ranked low in the growth of municipal dependency on state and federal aid between 1962 and 1975, with Colorado forty-ninth, Wisconsin forty-first, Illinois thirty-seventh, Iowa thirty-third, and only Minnesota ranking above the median at seventeenth. With regard to federal aid alone, Minnesota was eighth and Wisconsin thirteenth, but beyond that Illinois was twenty-ninth, Iowa thirtieth, and Colorado forty-fifth. Colorado was equally low with regard to state aid, ranking forty-eighth; Illinois was thirty-sixth, Iowa thirty-third, Wisconsin twenty-seventh, and Minnesota fifteenth.[8] Hence not only did local decisions count in this regard, but the general pattern in their respective states strongly influenced the fact that the cities of the prairie passed through the Great Society years with less change than the national average.

The consequence of this policy pattern was that General Revenue Sharing had more of an impact on medium-sized and smaller cities than any other form of federal aid, since it came automatically and did not involve state or local decisions other than whether to accept the checks. General Revenue Sharing represented 11.2 percent of total aid package in 1975 for all the municipalities in the United States, but 14.5 percent for those in the 100,000 to 199,999 range and 16.2 percent for those in the 50,000 to 99,999 range. Similarly, General Revenue Sharing was higher as a percentage of federal aid and in relation to federal aid and own-source revenue in those years.

The specific data from the cities of the prairie reflect this, as the contrasting examples of East St. Louis and Rockford indicate. East St. Louis was the poorest of all the cities and most dependent on outside aid. In 1975, $13 million of the city's $20 million total budget came from the federal government. Total federal outlays in the civil community, including welfare, job training, and highway and public works programs, had reached $52 million in 1970 and rose to $95 million in 1976.

Approximately 80 percent of the East St. Louis school district budget came from state and federal sources, and East St. Louis had the only junior college district in Illinois that was entirely state supported. In 1976 East St. Louis School District 189 received 61 percent of its budget from the State of Illinois, 17 percent from the federal government, and only 19 percent from local sources. Its per-pupil assessed valuation placed the city 427th among the 442 school districts in the state.[9]

Table 1.4. Per Capita Expenditure, per Capita Aid, and Dependency,

City Size	Per Capita Expenditures, 1962	Per Capita Expenditures, 1975	Annual Average Rate of Growth in per Capita Expenditures, 1962–75	Per Capita Aid, 1962	Per Capita Aid, 1975
All municipalities	$113.56	$358.65	9.20%	$22.66	$144.76
1,000,000 +	219.11	844.44	10.89	49.50	437.83
500,000–999,999	166.49	531.95	9.30	39.53	216.68
300,000–499,999	124.06	413.96	9.65	25.11	156.07
200,000–299,999	126.87	395.31	9.05	22.59	153.57
100,000–199,999	122.73	340.66	8.13	23.24	118.60
50,000–99,999	111.25	295.62	7.75	19.11	90.76
Less than 50,000	63.16	193.55	8.98	10.44	62.84

Source: ACIR Staff computations based on data from U.S. Bureau of the Census, *Compendium of City Government Finances*

The erosion of the city's local tax base meant that in 1975 only 30 percent of the city's operating funds came from property taxes. Between 1965 and 1974, the assessed valuation of real property dropped 25 percent and retail sales fell 34 percent. As a result, the city's property tax rates are the highest in St. Clair County.

Even with the outside revenue, the city could meet its expenditure needs. With the exception of four years, after 1951 East St. Louis has used a process known as "judgment funding" whereby creditors, with the approval of the city, obtained court judgments against it, enabling the city to sell revenue bonds to satisfy those judgments. This method obviated the necessity for referenda to increase taxes, since state law allowed property tax rates to be raised automatically to meet the requirements of indebtedness. It also meant that about one-half of all property tax revenues were set aside to pay the principal and interest on judgment funding bonds. Between 1973 and 1975, federal revenue sharing dollars enabled the city to avoid this procedure, but the growth of expenditures rapidly absorbed even that additional income, bringing the city back to this process by the end of the generation. The major role played by public employment, public welfare, and public housing in the city (see below) also adversely affected local revenue prospects.

Rockford, on the other hand, was the most independent of the cities, by design. Not only did its relative prosperity reduce its need, but the city by City Population Size Class, 1962, 1975, and Growth, 1962–75

Annual Average Rate of Growth in per Capita Aid, 1962–75	Aid ÷ Own Source Revenue, 1962	Aid ÷ Own Source Revenue, 1975	Annual Average Rate of Growth in Dependency 1962–75	Number of Cities, 1962	Number of Cities, 1975
15.27%	25.85%	65.1%	7.32%	–	–
18.22	28.50	90.50	9.25	5	6
13.94	32.23	71.50	6.25	17	20
15.07	27.08	60.76	6.37	21	20
15.83	23.53	64.22	6.35	19	17
13.35	24.43	54.56	7.98	68	95
12.68	22.21	46.55	5.80	180	229
14.75	21.23	47.07	6.24	17,690	18,130

in 1962, and U.S. Bureau of the Census, *Compendium of City Government Finances in 1975,* various tables.

fathers were generally cool to requesting or receiving outside aid. In fiscal year 1976, Rockford's total revenue was $29,400,000, of which $15,300,000 came from purely local sources, $6,850,000 from the city's share of the state sales tax, $3,600,000 from state revenue sharing, and $2,500,000 from federal revenue sharing funds.[10]

At the same time, all the cities of the prairie ranked very low in the Nathan-Adams municipal hardship index. There were a few medium-sized cities that appeared in the higher ranks of that index, principally depressed industrial cities of the Northeast with large minority populations. Only one, Grand Rapids, was even in the same geohistorical section. Almost no medium-sized cities appeared in the medium range of the index.[11]

The changes that were reflected in changed funding levels were also reflected in the growth of government offices. Table 1.5 compares federal, state, and local government offices in the Rockford civil community in 1960 and 1980. The number of federal offices in the civil community increased by some 50 percent in twenty years. It is important to note in this context that the number of federal civilian offices almost tripled, while the number of federal military offices declined by half. The number of state offices quadrupled, closing in on the number of federal offices in the civil community. This reflects the intensification of a prior trend for the state to establish a direct presence in the civil community and not work only through the county

Table 1.5. Federal, State, and Local Government Offices in the Rockford Civil Community, 1960 and 1980

	1960	1980
Federal agencies	24	38
Civilian	13	32
Military	11	6
State agencies	9	36
Local government offices	66	95
City	28	40
County	27	39
Township	5	6
Special districts	9	9
School districts	3	1

government. At the same time, the county, once conceived as the local arm of the state as well as a form of local government, is increasingly emphasizing the latter aspect of its dual character. Tables 1.6 and 1.7 list the offices for the two years.

Local government offices still far outnumber those of outside governments, having increased proportionately over the two decades. The situation is even further complicated by the high level of "horizontal" division of local government within the civil community. So-called "fragmentation" of government within the local arena is widely discussed and frequently denounced.[12] The extensive division of authority locally appears to be another corollary of the basic American proposition of limiting government through separation of powers and functions. It is derived in part from the great diversity of interests that must compete for the limited attention and resources of governments, each of which seeks as fully independent a governmental framework as possible to serve its purposes.[13]

The Civil Community's Response

Within this national system of systems the civil community serves in five major capacities: as *acquirer* of outside aid for local needs; as *adapter* of government actions and services to local values and conditions; as *experimenter* with new functions and services (or readaptation of traditional ones); as *initiator* of government programs of particular relevance locally; and as the means by which the local aggregation of people can secure an effective voice

Table 1.6. Federal, State, and Local Government Offices in the Rockford Civil Community, 1960

Federal agencies with local offices (24)

- CIVILIAN (13)
  - *Department of Agriculture*
  - Soil Conservation Service
  - Winnebago County A.S.C.[a]
  - *Department of Commerce*
  - Civil Aeronautics Administration
  - Federal Mediation and Conciliation Service
  - Weather Bureau
  - *Department of Defense*
  - Selective Service Boards[a]
  - Veterans Administration
  - *Federal Housing Administration*
  - *Department of Health, Education, and Welfare*
  - Social Security Administration
  - *Department of Justice*
  - Federal Bureau of Investigation
  - *Department of Labor*
  - Bureau of Apprenticeship
  - *Post Office Department*
  - *Treasury Department*
  - Internal Revenue Service
- MILITARY (11)
  - *Department of the Air Force*
  - Air Reserve Center
  - Chicago Air Procurement District (Production Representative)
  - Industrial Property Office
  - Air Force Recruiting Office
  - *Department of the Army*
  - Army Recruiting Station
  - Army Reserve Area Command
  - *Department of the Navy*
  - Inspector of Naval Material
  - Organized Naval Reserve
  - Navy Recruiting Substation
  - Marine Corps Recruiting Station
  - Marine Corps Reserve Company

State agencies with local offices (9)

- *Military and Naval Department*
- Illinois National Guard
- *Illinois Public Aid Commission*
- *Department of Public Welfare*
- Division of Vocational Rehabilitation
- *Secretary of State*
- Driver's License Department
- *Department of Public Works and Buildings*
- Division of Highways Maintenance Garage
- *Department of Mines and Minerals*
- Oil Inspection Laboratory
- *Youth Commission*
- *Veterans Commission*

Local government offices (66)

- City
  - Rockford (20)
  - Loves Park (8)
- Winnebago County (27)
- Rockford Township (5)
- Special districts (9)
- School districts (3)

Source: Daniel J. Elazar, *Cities of the Prairie: The Metropolitan Frontier and American Politics* (New York: Basic Books, 1970), p. 381.

[a]Formally a state office as well but listed as a federal one in the telephone directory.

Table 1.7. Federal, State, and Local Government Offices in the Rockford Civil Community, 1980

Federal agencies with local offices (38)

CIVILIAN (32)

Department of Agriculture
Soil Conservation Service
Winnebago County Assistance Office
Bankruptcy Court
Department of Commerce
National Weather Service
Department of Defense
Defense Logistics Agency
Defense Supply Agency
Defense Contract Administration Services
District Court
Equal Employment Opportunity Commission
Federal Aviation Administration
Federal Bureau of Investigation
Federal Housing Administration
Federal Mediation and Conciliation Service
Food and Drug Administration
Department of Health, Education, and Welfare
Social Security Administration
Supplemental Security Income
Medicare Social Security Administration
Internal Revenue Service
Department of Justice
Immigration and Naturalization Service
Department of Labor
Bureau of Apprenticeship and Training
Wage and Hour Division
Nuclear Regulatory Commission—Region III
Office of Personnel Management
Federal Job Information Center
Post Office

State agencies with local offices (36)

Appellate Court
Bureau of Scientific Services
Department of Children and Family Services
Commerce and Community Affairs
Cooperative Extension Service (University of Illinois)
Department of Corrections
Adult Division
Division of Crippled Children
Division of Highways Materials Labs
Division of Criminal Investigation
Driver's License Department
Environmental Protection Agency
Guardianship and Advocacy Commission
Illinois Young Adult Conservation Corps
Department of Labor
Job Service—Illinois State Employment Service
Employment Service
Temporary Employment
Veterans Employment Representative
Unemployment Insurance
Department of Mental Health and Developmental Disabilities
Bureau of Special Investigations
National Guard
Nature Preserves Commission
Department of Public Aid
Regional Office Building
Correction—Juvenile Division
Illinois Commission of Delinquency Prevention
Crippled Children Services
Administrative Services
Public Aid—Support Enforcement
Rehabilitation Services
Department of Revenue
Lottery
Secretary of State

Table 1.7. Continued

Probation, Parole, and Pretrial Service	Investigation Department
Department of Transportation	*State Police*
Federal Aviation Administration	*Department of Veterans Affairs*
Department of the Treasury	*WIN Program*
Internal Revenue Service	*Winnebago County Department of Public Aid*
U.S. Customs Service	*Northern Illinois Law Enforcement Commission*
U.S. Secret Service	Local government offices (85)
U.S. Marshal's Office	City (40)
U.S. Representative	Rockford (28)
Veterans Administration	Loves Park (12)
MILITARY (6)	Winnebago County (39)
Department of the Air Force	Rockford Township (3)
Air Force Recruiting Office	Special districts (9)
Recruiting Station	School districts (1)
Department of the Army	
Reserve Center	
Recruiting Station	
Marine Corps	
Recruiting Station	
Department of the Navy	
Navy Recruiting Station	

in state and national government decisions affecting them. Thus it is neither possible nor desirable to study the civil community as separate from the larger civil society of which it is a part.

The original Cities of the Prairie study documented the functioning of the civil community in these capacities in each of the cases studied. What was true then was revealed to be equally true in the course of the resurvey. The continued functioning of the civil community as acquirer and adapter was even enhanced as a result of the federal government initiatives of the mid-1960s and beyond. At the same time, the resurvey gave us an opportunity to document how the civil community held its own during a period of great federal government intervention.

The following pages deal more with the latter aspect than with the former, which was well documented in the first study at a time when the weight of presumption might have been in the other direction. The weight of presumption with regard to the period from 1964 to 1977 is heavily cast toward the expectation that, given the range and extent of new federal involvement, the civil community would lose its ability to function as an autonomous unit within the larger system. As it turns out, this was not so in the cities of the prairie; the civil communities studied held their own very nicely, adapting to federal initiatives while retaining their own character. Rockford and Springfield represent polar opposites in their characters, while Champaign–Urbana reflects the new university-centered world of the metropolitan frontier. Together they demonstrate how this was so despite massive federal and state activity locally.

Thus a decade and a half after the original study, Rockford remained Rockford, a civil community whose citizens were highly satisfied with their way of life and their community. It continued to be moralistic in its self-definition and committed to a highly qualitative vision of the good life, a bit of the Upper Midwest in Illinois.

In a demonstration of the way a civil community functions best, the City of Rockford, Rockford Township, and Winnebago County worked together to provide maximum utilization of federal revenue sharing funds for local purposes. Public safety and law enforcement functions were the major beneficiaries of the first several rounds of revenue sharing of all three governments, with Rockford Township actually transferring nearly a million dollars to the county over the first four years of the revenue sharing program. Some $2.5 million of township funds went to health and social services, primarily for special clinics to deal with alcohol and drug abuse, mental health, and the like. Modest sums of money were used as special grants for education and other purposes; for example, in 1977 Rockford's public library received more than $200,000 to tide it over a financial crisis.

The range of public governmental and nongovernmental bodies that benefited from federal revenue sharing itself demonstrated the civil community concept in action. Recipients of federal aid in the Rockford civil community included the Rockford police department (via the City of Rockford), the Winnebago County sheriff's office (via Winnebago County and the City of Rockford), the city-county health department (via the city, county, and township), the Rockford public library (via the city), and such public nongovernmental institutions as the county health and welfare council, Big Brothers, Goodwill Industries, the Rockford Arts Council, the paramedics, the women's crisis center, the YWCA, alcohol and drug control centers, and the retarded children's center.[14] From the state, Rockford gained a medical school, a regional higher education center, and funding for a community college, giving it public institutions of higher education for the first time. As a result, college enrollments in Rockford rose by 418 percent between 1960 and 1970—from 751 to 3,388.

If Rockford remains the outsider in Illinois and a stronger civil community as a result, Springfield remains the quintessential Illinois city, combining both the seamy and the idealistic sides of politics in that curious conglomerate that is Illinois and has been ever since the state was settled. Springfield achieves this synthesis without the turbulence that marks Chicago; it maintains calm waters as always. The shadow of Abraham Lincoln lies over the city in the 1970s as it did in the 1950s, when the centennial of Lincoln's rise to political prominence was the feature of any number of local celebrations. Under that shadow, the state's lobbyists and legislators play, and the venerable institutions of local government continue along the same road they have traveled for well over a century.

In the first half of the postwar generation, Springfield emerged from its condition as a small state capital and laid the groundwork for its transformation into a medium-sized city, in character as well as in population. The expansion of state government and the reform of local government in the 1950s were the keys to this change, but it came to fruition in the 1960s and early 1970s as state government took off in size as well as scope and the civil community began to accommodate its new population. The city itself grew by over 10 percent between 1960 and 1970, and the population growth of the civil community as a whole was even greater because many of the newcomers settled directly on the city fringes.

A new base of public industries was added to the city's economy. Springfield, long the largest city in the country without a four-year college, was endowed by the legislature with Sangamon State University, which immediately developed a major public affairs division related to state government. A medical school was established, also by the legislature, and a community college formally funded by local government also benefited from state aid.

Growth in state government brought with it an expansion of federal government locally as federal agencies opened state and regional headquarters in Springfield. It also brought an increase in the number of offices of special interest groups committed to lobbying state government. This expanded the transient population, that is to say, people not permanently wedded to the Springfield area; but it also brought in many people who became a long-term part of the local scene. Government's position as the largest industry was reinforced. All told, approximately one-third of the civil community's 79,000 nonagricultural workers are employed by state, local, or federal government, and hardly more than 10 percent are in manufacturing. In 1970 nearly 30 percent of the city's labor force was employed as "clerical or kindred workers," more than in any other city in the state. The new migrants were generally better-educated administrators, managers, and academics. The percentage of professional and technical workers was exceeded only in Champaign and Urbana, because of their role as university towns.

Indeed, the only major private industry to grow in the Springfield area was the insurance industry, which reinforced the same tendencies in the labor force.

This represents a substantial shift from the situation before World War II, when local manufacturing, particularly coal mining, was a major source of employment and state government was still a modest economic force in the civil community. When the last mine closed in 1952, an era came to an end. In the interim, Springfield's efforts to attract heavy industry, such as they are (and there is considerable question whether major efforts are made), have not had much success. Finally, in the 1970s, the city government and local business groups began to take action. The city issued industrial revenue bonds, and business groups helped to develop industrial parks. More often than not, they worked separately rather than together. Their efforts have brought modest success, but no more than that. The efforts have included attracting foreign investors, with the same mixed results. The Allis Chalmers heavy equipment assembly plant, the largest local manufacturing industry, was sold to Fiat during the second half of the postwar generation, and a local electronics firm was bought out by a Belgian conglomerate and then moved to the Sun Belt. City growth of the public sector kept this from being a problem until the very end of the generation, when government growth slowed to a halt and the wave of industrial layoffs and plant closings reached Springfield as well.

As a commercial center Springfield benefited in the postwar generation from the new interstate connections that gave the civil community good access to the national highway network in all directions. In addition, as a state capital with a reputation for good restaurants and a relaxed atmosphere, Springfield attracted many state conventions. Tourists came to see the seat of Illinois government and, most important, the home and tomb of Abraham Lincoln. Restoration of Lincoln's home and the street on which he lived in the 1850s added to the area's attraction for tourists, and New Salem, the restored village near Springfield, remained a major part of the Lincoln "package."[15] Thus Springfield remained itself—a "self" directly shaped by outside forces.

The most pronounced characteristic of the Champaign-Urbana civil community is that over half of the county's wage and salaried workers are employed by institutions of the state and federal governments. The University of Illinois is the largest single employer in the county, and Chanute Air Force Base in Rantoul is the second. Even so, the civil community remains part and parcel of the prairie, with agriculture its largest source of income (approximately 35 percent) and education second with 30 percent. Local industry is based almost entirely on agriculture, and services are geared to the university or the agricultural sector so that the entire local economy is connected to one or the other.

The cities' responses to state and national politics in the second half of the postwar generation brought few surprises. By and large, Democratic strongholds remained Democratic, and Republican bastions became even more Republican. Except for Minnesota, where the Democratic-Farmer-Labor party grew in strength, making it a maverick within its sphere, the secular trend in the states and cities was toward Republicanism in presidential elections and an increasingly apartisan response in gubernatorial contests, with attractive candidates or dissatisfaction with incumbents taking precedence over party loyalties. Tables 1.8 to 1.10 summarize the pattern for each of the five states as a whole and the individual counties of the cities of the prairie.

The Quality of Life in the Cities of the Prairie

By and large, the quality of life in the cities of the prairie remained high throughout the second half of the postwar generation. Unemployment was minimal (although that was to change in the later years of the 1970s and to become a critical problem early in the 1980s), the crime rate was stable or even slightly down, medical services expanded to keep pace with new developments in the field, and the standard form of housing remained owner-occupied, freestanding homes. Perhaps the greatest citizen discontent was registered with regard to the quality of elementary and secondary education, with a general feeling growing that school standards were declining. Otherwise, high percentages of the population were satisfied or very satisfied with the quality of life and public services. This, indeed, remained one of the most significant dimensions of living in medium-sized cities. It was apparent to the study team throughout the fieldwork for both Cities of the Prairie studies. For the second, we have additional evidence in the form of two surveys undertaken by the Center for the Study of Middle-Size Cities at Sangamon State University in Springfield, Illinois, covering nine of the Illinois cities of the prairie (plus Bloomington and Normal), conducted in 1976 and 1978. The results of those surveys are unequivocal and conveniently sum up the high level of citizens' satisfaction with their civil communities at the end of the postwar generation.[16] Significantly, there was a general feeling that government had little influence on the quality of life, though local government was given credit for the most positive effect, with state government second. The federal government took the most blame for worsening the quality of life, local government taking the least. Only in East St. Louis (18.2 percent) and Decatur (11.4 percent) did more than 10 percent of

Table 1.8. State Partisan Political Preferences, 1964–80 (based on presidential and gubernatorial elections)

	Illinois		Iowa		Wisconsin		Minnesota		Colorado	
Year	Governor	President	Governor	President	Governor	President	Governor	President	Governor	President
1964	D	D	D	D	R	D	–	D	–	D
1966	–	–	D	–	R	–	R	–	R	–
1968	R	R	R	R	R	R	–	D	–	R
1970	–	–	R	–	D	–	D	–	R	–
1972	D	R	R	R	–	R	–	R	–	R
1974	–	–	R	–	D	–	D (DFL)[b]	–	D	–
1976	R[a]	D	–	R	–	D	–	D	–	R
1978	R	–	R	–	R	–	R (IR)[c]	–	D	–
1980	–	R	–	R	–	R	–	D	–	R

Sources: Richard M. Scammon and Alice V. McGillivray, comps. and eds., *America Votes 14* (Washington, D.C.: Congressional Quarterly, 1978); Congressional Quarterly, *Politics in America,* 1979; Michael Barone and Grant Ujifusa, *The Almanac of American Politics, 1982* (Washington, D.C.: Barone and Company, 1982).

[a]Special two-year term to shift the state's gubernatorial election to nonpresidential years.

[b]Democratic-Farmer-Labor.

[c]Industrial-Republican.

Table 1.9. Cities of the Prairie: Partisan Political Preferences, 1968–80

	Illinois Statewide		Champaign County (Champaign-Urbana)		Macon County-Decatur		Madison County (Alton, etc.)		Peoria County (Peoria)	
Year	Governor	President	Governor	President	Governor	President	Governor	President	Governor	President
1968	R	R	R	R	D	D	R	D	D	R
1972	D	R	R	R	R	R	R	R	R	R
1976	R	R	R	R	R	R	R	R	R	R
1978[a]	R	—	R	—	D	—	D	—	R	—
1980	—	R	—	R	—	R	—	R	—	R

	Rock Island County (Rock Island, Moline, East Moline)		Sangamon County (Springfield)		St. Clair County (East St. Louis, Belleville—23)		Will County (Joliet—17)		Winnebago County (Rockford—16)	
Year	Governor	President	Governor	President	Governor	President	Governor	President	Governor	President
1968	R	D	R	R	D	D	R	R	R	R
1972	R	R	R	R	D	R	R	R	D	R
1976	R	R	R	R	R	D	R	R	R	R
1978[a]	R	—	R	—	D	—	R	—	R	—
1980	—	R	—	R	—	D	—	R	—	R

Sources: Congressional Quarterly, *Politics in America,* 1979; *World Almanac,* 1981.
[a]In 1978 there was a special two-year term to shift state's gubernatorial elections to nonpresidential years.

Table 1.10. Cities of the Prairie: Partisan Political Preferences, 1972–80

	Scott County, Iowa (Davenport–1)		Douglas County, Wisconsin (Superior–7)		St. Louis County, Minnesota (Duluth–8)		Pueblo County, Colorado (Pueblo–3)	
Year	Governor	President	Governor	President	Governor	President	Governor	President
1972	R	R	–	R	–	D	–	R
1974	R	–	D	–	D	–	D	–
1976	–	R	–	D	–	D	–	R
1978	R	–	R	–	R	–	D	–
1980	–	R	–	D	–	D	–	D

Sources: Richard M. Scammon and Alice V. McGillivray, comps. and eds., *America Votes 14*, 1980; Congressional Quarterly, *Politics in America*, 1979; *World Almanac*, 1981.

the local population see local government as making the quality of life worse, and in most cities over 50 percent thought that it had not changed the quality of life. In Peoria and Springfield, 49.5 percent and 45.4 percent, respectively, thought that local government had improved matters.

The citizens' evaluation of local government is slightly more positive than their evaluation of state government and considerably more positive than their evaluation of the federal government. While none of these civil communities gave state government as low a rating as East St. Louis gave its local government, in five of them more than 10 percent did believe that the state worsened the quality of life, and the overall percentage of those who saw state government as improving the quality of life was a few percentage points lower than for local government. Characteristically, Rockford, which is constantly locked in political conflict with state government in its efforts to protect its own political culture, gave state government the lowest rating for having improved conditions.

In eight of the nine Illinois cities of the prairie, over 15 percent of the citizens surveyed viewed the federal government as having worsened the quality of life. Only in East St. Louis was the figure as low as 10.6 percent. In six of the nine, over 20 percent of the residents surveyed held a negative view of the federal government, and this rose to a high of 29.1 percent in Peoria. What is apparent in the survey is that there are stronger opinions in both directions about the federal government than about either state or local government, with a tendency to the negative side.

Overall, the residents of the Illinois cities of the prairie see the quality of life in their cities as about the same as before or better. Only in East St. Louis do a majority see it as worse than it was in the early 1970s. In no other city did the negative figure approach 20 percent. Residents of Peoria and Moline see the greatest improvement, with over 42 percent in both cities suggesting that the quality of life is better than it was.

With regard to safety on the streets, only in East St. Louis was there a general feeling that the streets were not safe (63.5 percent). Rock Island and Moline were perceived to have the safest streets, with nearly half of Moline's residents viewing the streets as very safe.

Neighborhood satisfaction was also very high except in East St. Louis, and even there some 67 percent were either somewhat satisfied or very satisfied with their neighborhoods. Again, the people of Moline were the most satisfied, although in six of the nine cities surveyed over 60 percent were very satisfied with their neighborhoods.

Over 70 percent of Moline's residents were very satisfied with their city as a place to live, leading the list of generally satisfied responses. East St. Louis trailed all the others with 41 percent somewhat or very dissatisfied. In five of the nine cities, over half of the residents were very satisfied with their city as a place to live, and in no place other than East St. Louis were as many as 20 percent dissatisfied.

The prevailing form of residence in the Illinois cities was a freestanding house, with over three-quarters of the population of every one of the cities except Champaign and Urbana living in such houses. These two failed to reach that percentage only because of their high student population living in apartments and dormitories. Even in East St. Louis, 76.4 percent of the residents lived in freestanding homes. Although the people in that city rated their housing conditions more poorly than did residents of any of the other cities, only 6.5 percent viewed those conditions as fairly bad or very bad, with 90.6 percent viewing them as fairly good or very good. Again, Moline led in satisfaction, with 72.6 percent viewing their housing conditions as very good and none viewing them as very bad. Five percent was the highest dissatisfaction level in any of the cities other than East St. Louis.

The public schools produced the greatest dissatisfaction in the Illinois cities of the prairie, with over 20 percent of the population of Springfield and East St. Louis viewing them as poor or very poor. The schools were viewed as very good by 20 percent or more of the residents of Peoria, Champaign, Urbana, and Moline, with the latter registering 45.7 percent. Most people viewed their schools as fair to good, a relatively poor rating compared with the other local services.

With regard to medical care, over 70 percent of the residents of Springfield, Decatur, and Peoria were very satisfied, as were over 60 percent in Rock Island, Rockford, and Moline. In no community, not even East St. Louis, were as many as 20 percent of the people dissatisfied with the quality of medical care.

The general assessment was that the standard public services (sanitation, fire protection, public transportation, parks and recreation) were good or very good. Again East St. Louis was the exception, with just under 40 percent believing those services were fair and 27.5 percent viewing them as poor or very poor. On the other hand, 85 percent of Urbana residents saw those services as good or very good, as did over 75 percent of the residents of Moline, Rock Island, and Champaign. Approximately two-thirds of the residents of the remaining cities also saw their public services as good or very good.

While voting participation was down in cities of the prairie, as elsewhere, there seems to be a very high level of interpersonal contact between the citizens and public officials. In the Sangamon State University survey, approximately one-third of all the citizens in the Illinois cities reported contact with city departments or officials in the course of the year, ranging from a high of close to 47 percent in Springfield and Urbana to a low of 30.5 percent in East St. Louis. These contact figures compare favorably with those of the voting turnout in local elections, suggesting that territorial democracy still has great meaning because of the way it encourages access to public officials as well as participation in choosing them.

This assumption is reinforced by the citizens' satisfaction level which the same survey reported with regard to how people were treated by public officials. Only in Decatur and East St. Louis were more than 15 percent dissatisfied with the way their problems were handled, and even in Decatur over 32 percent were very satisfied, a singular figure toward the low end of the response record for the nine cities. Moline residents were most satisfied, with 67.5 percent estimated very satisfied and only 20 percent dissatisfied. The overall satisfaction rate was over 60 percent in Peoria and Urbana as well. If anything, the residents' rating of the efficiency with which their problems were handled was as high as or higher than it was earlier.

There was an equally widespread feeling on the part of the citizens that they were treated fairly by their officials. Of the people in East St. Louis, 21.2 percent thought that public officials did not treat them at all fairly, but in no other community did as many as 10 percent feel dissatisfied with their treatment. The people of Decatur felt most satisfied, with 48.9 percent seeing public officials as treating them very fairly. Springfield and Peoria also registered over 40 percent. Basically, the residents of cities of the prairie saw public officials as treating them somewhat fairly.

The same citizens did not express clear-cut opinions about the overall responsiveness of local government officials, dividing almost equally between those who thought they responded most to a majority of the citizenry or to a few influentials or did what they themselves thought was best. Of the residents of East St. Louis, 54.8 percent saw that last category as dominant in their community, not surprising considering the realities of political life in that city, in which public officials have consistently run the city for their own profit. The residents of Peoria were most likely to see local officials as responsive to the majority of the citizenry, but only 37.2 percent viewed them in that way.

Needless to say, taxation was generally considered too high in light of the facilities and services needed, with the people of East St. Louis being most strongly of that opinion (78.4 percent) and over 50 percent of those in Rockford, Champaign, and Rock Island sharing that view. Over 50 percent of the residents of Decatur, Peoria, Urbana, and Moline thought taxes were about right. Only in Springfield and Rock Island did as many as 5 percent view taxes as too low.

In the last analysis, the interplay of local, state, sectional, and national forces encouraged local self-expression as least as much as it inhibited it, and probably far more. In the following chapters those forces are traced, utilizing the same themes as the original study.

2. Closing the Metropolitan Frontier

The Continuing American Frontier[1]

For Americans, the word frontier conjures up, first and foremost, images of the rural-land frontier of yesteryear—of explorers and mountain men, of cowboys and Indians, of brave pioneers pushing westward in the face of natural obstacles. Subsequently, they expanded their picture of the frontier to include the inventors, the railroad builders, and the captains of industry who created the urban-industrial frontier. Recently television has begun to celebrate the entrepreneurial ventures of the automobile and oil industries, portraying the captains of those industries and their families in the same larger-than-life frame once used for the heroes of the first frontier.

As is so often the case, the media responsible for determining and catering to popular taste tell us a great deal about ourselves. The United States was founded with the opening of its rural-land frontier, a frontier that persisted for three hundred years until World War I, more or less, and that brought with it the first settlement of this continent, spreading across the land farms, ranches, and towns catering to the extractive industries.

Early in the nineteenth century, the rural-land frontier generated the urban frontier that was based upon industrial development, just as the rural frontier was based upon the availability of free land. The creation of new wealth through industrialization transformed cities from mere regional service centers to producers of wealth. That frontier persisted for more than one hundred years as a major force in American society as a whole and, as we shall soon have reason to note, perhaps another sixty years as a major force in various parts of the country. The population movements and attendant growth on the urban-industrial frontier created the second settlement of the United States in freestanding cities built around the new industrial base from coast to coast.

Between the world wars, the urban-industrial frontier gave birth in turn to a third frontier stage, one based upon the new technologies of electronic communication, the internal combustion engine, the airplane, synthetics, and petrochemicals. These new technologies transformed every aspect of life and turned urbanization into metropolitanization. This third frontier stage generated a third settlement of the United States, this time in metropolitan regions from coast to coast, involving a mass migration of tens of millions of Americans in search of opportunity on the suburban frontier.

The continuing American frontier has all the characteristics of a chain reaction. In a land of great opportunity, each frontier once opened has bred its successor and has in turn been replaced by it. Each frontier has created a new America with new opportunities, new patterns of settlement, new occupations, new challenges, and new problems. As a result, the central political problem of growth is not simply how to handle the physical changes brought by each frontier, real as they are. It is how to accommodate newness, population turnover, and transience as a way of life. This is the American frontier situation. It is a recurring one in American history and needs to be understood if Americans are to find ways to solve their problems, or at least meet them adequately, and at the same time to preserve those characteristics that have enabled America to continue to develop far longer than has been true for other countries and societies.

The foregoing is meant to suggest that the frontier is not merely a dramatic imagery but a very real process, indeed the basic sociotechnical process that informs the American experience. As a process, it is dynamic and essentially progressive, though fraught with problems of its own, like every other dimension of human life.

Government and the Course of the Metropolitan Frontier

The American people entered the twentieth century in the generation that began with Woodrow Wilson's "New Freedom" and America's entry into World War I. That generation extended through World War II to the point in the late 1940s when the United States became committed to increasingly activist government and a permanent role in world affairs. We are all aware of the radical transformations wrought in this century of earlier values, ways of life, and the very organization of American society.

World War I brought the last gasp of the rural-land frontier in the continental United States—the settlement of the Great Plains from North Dakota to west Texas by farmers or putative farmers seeking to capitalize on the war-generated wheat bonanza. That effort burst with the collapse of world food markets in the aftermath of the war, creating an agricultural depression that preceded the Great Depression by a decade. At approximately the same time, early in the 1920s, the first phase of the oil frontier, the last of the great extractive booms of the land frontier, came to a close, with the great corporations replacing individual wildcatters in the exploration as well as production of oil and gas. During the 1920s, the movement of the urban-industrial frontier also ground to a halt, bringing the American people into the first hiatus in the frontier process since the British government closed (temporarily) the land frontier in the mid-eighteenth century.

Although the World War I years, or more accurately the Wilson administration, brought the first of the twentieth-century style of federal programs, virtually all those programs were directed toward problems created by the rural-land frontier. They were designed to aid agriculture and rural Americans, who continued to form a majority of the total population until 1920. (In fact, in light of the United States Census definition of an urban place as one with 2,500 people or more, rural and small town Americans constituted a majority of the population until after World War II.) About the only major program that addressed itself to the problems of the urban-industrial frontier was the vocational education program, whose major purpose was to equip young people from rural areas and small towns with the basic skills to seek their fortunes on the urban frontier. The federal-aid highway program may have been intended as a response to frontier conditions, to "get the country out of the mud" and thereby make possible the spread of the automobile; but as interpreted and funded by Congress, it too became essentially a rurally oriented program with secondary benefits from connecting urban areas with each other.

The crash of 1929 and the depression that followed brought a first governmental response to the problems created by the urban frontier in the form of the New Deal. However, it too devoted much of its effort to the previous generation's problems, namely the farmers' revolt. A pattern was set that reemerged in the 1960s. The Congresses of the 1930s had a strong agricultural bloc that was able to secure federal legislation appropriate to the conditions of the 1890s, when the farming pattern produced by the rural-land frontier was in its heyday. In much the same way, the Congresses of the 1960s had a strong urban bloc that was able to secure the enactment of federal legislation more appropriate to the 1920s, when the city produced by the urban-industrial frontier was in its heyday.

The Great Depression of the 1930s was the last and greatest of the business cycles produced by the urban-industrial frontier—cycles that had been characterized by boom and bust since the 1830s. Because the urban frontier had ended for the country as a whole, this depression could not rely upon earlier mechanisms, namely the frontier process itself, to reverse the downward trend. As we now know, the New Deal, despite its very great benefits, did not end the depression. It took World War II and the prosperity it generated to do that. For the moment it seemed that the United States was following the classic pattern of the Old World, whereby prosperity would depend upon wars rather than upon frontiers.

The postwar period dispelled that possibility. With the return of the World War II veterans and the concomitant release of America's productive energies came the opening of the metropolitan-technological frontier in earnest. Already in the previous generation there were signs that such a frontier was developing. The automobile was creating the first of the new style suburban areas outside the central cities; radio was transforming communications; the airplane was beginning to be a useful commercial tool; and the oil industry was beginning its transformation into the petrochemical industry. But these were still initial manifestations. Significantly, none of them were seriously arrested by the depression; but it was only after World War II that they succeeded in coming together to transform American society.

What followed was one of the major movements in American history, the opening and settlement of the metropolitan-technological frontier. We are still too close to that movement to fully appreciate it; however, we can put ourselves in the position of historians of fifty or one hundred years hence looking back at the generation from 1946 through 1976, particularly the first half of that generation until roughly the Vietnam War in the mid-1960s. Many tens of millions of Americans moved from rural to metropolitan areas or followed the "old tenement trail" (in Samuel Lubell's felicitous words) from decayed cores of older industrial cities into new suburban lands.[2] New towns were built at the edge of the metropolitan frontier by the hundreds, if not the thousands. Over 100 million Americans moved and housed themselves, most along a moving line of suburban settlement that could be traced year after year at the edges of each metropolitan region. The American people transformed their way of life—first their housing and their jobs and then their values and aspirations. Affluence reached unprecedented heights, and with it came a whole new set of possibilities and problems. Myriad new opportunities were created, and millions of people took advantage of them, each in his or her own way.

It can fairly be said that, with the possible exception of a similar experience in the late nineteenth century, when the last migrations of the rural frontier coincided with the mass migrations from Europe to the United States associated with the urban frontier, no such mass movement of population, with the attendant rehousing, reemployment, and redesigning of life-styles, has ever taken place so peacefully in the whole history of mankind. This is important to recall as we look at the problems generated by this movement and the entire phenomenon of the metropolitan frontier. In trying to reckon with those problems, we should not overlook the essential success of this voluntary movement of free people in which the role of government was to help the process along rather than interfere with it.

The generation just concluded was the heyday of the metropolitan frontier. Indeed, after 1965 the thrust of the frontier tapered off so that by the early 1970s, though the processes unleashed by that frontier continued, they did so in almost routine fashion, with much of the frontier excitement gone from them.

The Latter Days of the Metropolitan Frontier

A major theme of this study has been the adjustment of the several civil communities to different frontier stages, from their founding on the rural-land frontier through the urban-industrial frontier and on to the metropolitan-technological frontier that engulfed them after the Second World War. The first study demonstrated that the geohistorical location of each civil community was directly shaped by its relation to the dominant frontier stage at any given time. The initial study was completed at the height of the influence of the metropolitan-technological frontier. In the restudy we have followed the course of that frontier during the rest of the postwar generation.

Universities continued to serve as gateways to the new frontier. After major efforts, Pueblo, Rockford, and Springfield, which had lacked local higher education facilities, gained universities for themselves. Pueblo's city fathers considered the establishment of Southern Colorado State College in 1963 (now the University of Southern Colorado) one of their prime accomplishments, although by the generation's end it had proved something of a disappointment. Springfield was equally successful in securing the establishment of Sangamon State University, which because of its location rapidly became a major force in the state as a continuing education center for state employees and a base for policy-related academic activities and other state affairs.

In Rockford, although Rockford College continued in its ultraconservative path, by 1964 it was no longer the sole provider of higher education in the civil community. That year Rock Valley College, a two-year community college, opened its doors and soon reached an enrollment of some 6,000 students. Six years later the University of Illinois opened a college of medicine in Rockford, and in 1974 the Rockford Regional Academic Center was established to coordinate college programs for all of northern Illinois west of Chicago.

The continued growth of Champaign–Urbana is a manifestation of the importance of the university on the metropolitan frontier. Table 2.4 presents the situation in figures since 1950, when students were first counted as local residents by the United States Census. After eliminating the overlap between university employees who are also graduate students and estimating average family size, it is not unreasonable to assume that two-thirds of the population of the two cities was university related in 1970, without considering the share of the private business sector whose income was university based. While the University of Illinois as an institution assiduously stays out of local politics except insofar as it must protect its direct interests, the university population has become an important factor on the local political scene. As described in *Cities of the Prairie,* the first serious attempts of university based political activists to achieve local political power came in the mid-1950s as an outgrowth of the Stevenson presidential campaigns. They laid the groundwork for a virtual takeover of the Urbana Democratic party in the late 1960s.

In general, in-migration has ceased to be a significant factor in all the cities of the prairie except Pueblo and Champaign–Urbana. In the latter two there is a large population turnover because of the university. In the former the sunbelt migration remains significant. Duluth and Superior have consistently been losing population. According to the Sangamon State University survey, in none of the other Illinois cities of the prairie did as many as 6.5 percent of those surveyed indicate that they had not lived in their cities five years earlier. The 1970 and 1980 censuses confirm this (table 2.5).

In some respects the metropolitan frontier had its greatest impact in the latter half of the generation. This was particularly so in terms of the social and political change brought about through the elimination of the last vestiges of the "two cities" and the integration of the excluded ethnocultural streams into the local polity and economy and increasingly into local society as well. The completion of the integration of the "two cities" will be discussed in some detail in chapter 3. It could also be seen in the relocation of local commerce in shopping centers at the periphery of each civil community, at the expense of the central business district. Most of all, it was felt in the transformation of "life-styles" that took place in the late 1960s and after. This transformation occurred as a backlash to frontier-induced patterns of the 1950s. Those children of the metropolitan frontier who were unhappy with the restraints imposed on them in the 1950s or unsettled by the frontier conditions it generated formed the vanguard for the country as a whole to intensify certain aspects of the frontier that had only begun to gain expression, and then very hesitantly, during the first half of the generation.[3]

The decline of the central business district was a common frontier-related change in the cities of the prairie. The case of Urbana demonstrates how little effect attempts at intervention had on the process. In the mid-1960s that city made a major effort to save its central business district with the assistance of Carson Pirie Scott and Company, one of the major Chicago department stores then reaching out to build branches downstate. Carson's management was committed to the notion of saving the central business district and located its stores in the central business districts of the various cities of the prairie, trying to bring the essence of the suburban shopping center into the heart of the town by developing a department store with a number of satellite specialty shops around it and providing off-street parking to encourage shoppers. Urbana's was one of the most important of these efforts.[4] In the last analysis, however, they did not succeed in stopping the shift of retail commerce to the periphery of the metropolitan areas where the cutting edge of the frontier was situated. Even their attempt to bring frontier technology into older areas was not sufficient to overcome the complex of factors that continued to make the suburban shopping center attractive while the metropolitan frontier was at its peak.

Central business districts lost out to regional shopping centers on the geographic peripheries of the civil community, and every one of the cities that depended upon an economic base developed during the urban-industrial frontier was thrust into a period of painful readjustment. Joliet did not have the benefit of outside assistance for increasing trade.[5] Peoria, a larger city with a far more substantial business district, was the site of another such Carson Pirie Scott experiment, which also failed to halt the shift to the suburbs. There the situation was even worse than in Urbana, for the distance between center and periphery was greater and thus there was less incentive for people living away from the city center to fight the traffic or take the time to drive in to shop.[6] Cities like Rockford, Moline, and Rock Island, which did not have the advantage of such focused outside efforts to strengthen their central business districts, suffered even more from the changeover, losing virtually all the viability of their central cores.[7]

Rockford's central business district has suffered an even more drastic decline than some of its sister cities of the prairies. By the mid-1970s a necklace of suburban shopping centers and malls had replaced the central business district as the main locus of retail trade. The major department stores and virtually all of the specialty shops had abandoned the central business district, despite efforts in the 1960s to remedy the situation by building a downtown mall.

Lacking any other choice, the city fathers have sought to restore a central focus to the civil community by replacing privately sponsored activities with public ones, in the form of a new convention center, a remodeled county courthouse, a new city-county public safety building, state and federal office buildings, and an arts and science center converted from the old post office. An old department store was converted into a center for senior citizens. High-rise housing for senior citizens was also built downtown, and two semi-professional theater groups have moved into vacated downtown buildings with the city fathers' encouragement. With the exception of the government services and senior citizens' programs, the major attractions in this renewed central area are by their nature sporadic, and it is doubtful whether public activities can generate life at the level it was when people came downtown to shop. However, there does not seem to be any alternative.[8]

The problem in Rockford was compounded by the historical pattern of the city's development. There are two other older shopping districts within the city limits—East Seventh Street and East State Street. Both have suffered the same problems of obsolescence and have tried the same techniques of shopping malls and building renovations, with the same limited results.

Rockford is a classic product of the synthesis of the rural-land and urban-industrial frontiers, an industrial city almost from its birth, when the water power district established in 1850 provided the private sector with incentives for local industrial development. As was discussed in the original Cities of the Prairie study, Rockford made an easy transition from the urban-industrial frontier to the metropolitan-technological frontier. It is not clear whether it will make so easy a transition to the next frontier stages. Its automotive and farm implement industries are not good candidates for the transition, but its machine tool industries may be.

What Rockford has is an excellent population stock as well as a reputation for being a "good place to live" and the right ingredients for a good business climate, namely a tax structure reasonably favorable to business development, good transportation facilities, and moderate housing costs. Nevertheless, at the generation's end structural unemployment was rising in the community. With all these assets, its citizens may be able to overcome a declining industrial base.

In Duluth and Pueblo the metropolitan frontier had a rather unusual impact on the central business district. Duluth's topography, declining population, and lack of a substantial metropolitan hinterland gave the central business district opportunities to remain viable not present in the other cities. Since Duluth was hardly touched by any manifestations of the local metropolitan frontier, those opportunities could be somewhat realized by a combination of local and outside initiatives.

What developed as Duluth's response to the new regionwide recreational travel pattern of the metropolitan frontier was an expanded civic center, anchored in a new hotel, built by the Radisson hotel chain as a result of local initiative to cater to travelers and conventions in a city whose major outside income was increasingly drawn from tourism. It was built alongside the government center erected in the previous generation. The shopping segments of the central business district responded somewhat sluggishly to the new opportunities, but it was not upon them that development rested. Indeed, once the civic center was in place, the same forces acquired the old railroad depot and transformed it into an art museum, an attraction for tourists as much as for locals, and certainly a civic enterprise of regional scope, rather than a private enterprise of a commercial nature, to enhance the attractiveness of the city and its center.[9]

Pueblo made more of an effort to improve the commercial facilities of its central business district, which had been extraordinarily poor before the opening of the metropolitan frontier and hence more in need of development than of redevelopment. In doing so it, like Duluth, focused its energies downtown on civic projects rather than commercial ones, most particularly an arts center that included the city's first concert hall and art museum. Here Pueblo, in its by now familiar manner, turned to the federal government for aid, in this case to the Economic Development Administration, which declared the city a depressed area and therefore eligible for such aid. Otherwise Pueblo let the frontier take its course and did not so much fight the trends as attempt to amalgamate them into a common communitywide package. As a result, its best hotel accommodations were situated on the city's periphery rather than in its center, whose facilities and attractiveness to travelers continued to decline.[10]

The responses of both Duluth and Pueblo to the metropolitan frontier were influenced by the original Cities of the Prairie study, a fact that became known to the study team only in the course of the resurvey. In both cases aspects of the conceptual framework that emerged from the original study and were presented in "Constitutional Change in a Long-Depressed Civil Community: A Case Study of Duluth, Minnesota," and in *Cities of the Prairie* itself struck home with key policymakers in the two communities, took root, and became the basis for their respective strategies.

In Duluth, Ben Boo became mayor in 1964, and shortly thereafter he obtained a copy of the case study of his city, which made the point that since Duluth was unable to capitalize directly on the current frontier stage, it was able to succeed only to the extent that it could mobilize outside (federal, state, and private) investment and even initiatives for local development. Mayor Boo proceeded to build his development strategy according to that thesis. He saw to it that every one of his senior officials and department heads had a copy of the article for guidance and for understanding the Duluth civil community generally.[11]

The mayor's strategy succeeded. Through a massive effort, he mobilized a great deal of state, federal, and outside private assistance. The University of Minnesota expanded its Duluth branch into a full-fledged campus. The interstate highway connection to the Twin Cities and a high bridge of Superior (which enabled traffic to move freely between the two cities without disruption by port activities) were completed. The civic center hotel and convention hall complex discussed above was built. The state of Minnesota expanded the port of Duluth, and the federal government enlarged the United States air base just outside town.

Although Mayor Boo did not turn the city around as he had hoped, he dramatically arrested its decline for at least a decade. Moreover, he created a moderately positive atmosphere locally. Shortly after he left office, Duluth began to decline again, and it continues to do so.

In Pueblo the key figure in the adoption of the *Cities of the Prairie* strategy was Alvin Bloomquist, executive director of the regional planning commission and one of the two initiators of Pueblo's revival. Bloomquist (also originally from Minnesota) was particularly moved by the civil community concept as it appeared in some preliminary articles before *Cities of the Prairie* was published, and he adopted as his goal the development of a strong civil community along the lines outlined in those pieces. He proceeded to develop a strategy of institution building and leadership mobilization designed to achieve that goal.[12]

The superb, comprehensive structure that emerged, with its broad civic base, is a concrete demonstration of the power of the civil community concept as a community-building device. Significantly, it was the concepts that emerged from the Cities of the Prairie study that were of most use to the policymakers involved. While those concepts needed concrete illustration to provoke subsequent concrete application, the policymakers who adopted them were more interested in acquiring a conceptual basis for a strategy than advice on tactics—in the latter field they no doubt excelled by virtue of their own intelligence and experience. It was in the conceptual area that political science could make its contribution. This unanticipated result of our efforts reinforces the thesis presented in the discussion of research methodology in *Cities of the Prairie,* namely that social science is itself a frontier phenomenon, a means of exploring an increasingly complex environment to open it up for "cultivation" rather than a humanistic branch of physics seeking to be predictive.[13]

The cities of the prairie were less affected by life-style changes than other parts of the country. There too, however, the kind of permissiveness and hedonism associated with the metropolitan frontier in the 1960s became far stronger influences on social behavior as the civil communities tried to accommodate them. Perhaps the sharpest contrast to be found was between Champaign-Urbana, which as the locus of a major university attracted strong expressions of those trends, and its neighbor Decatur, a mere half-hour's drive away, where homeostasis seems to be built into the very fabric of the civil community.

By the same token, the differences from one civil community to another found expression in the different ways local leaders sought to accommodate the changes. In Pueblo, for example, following its pattern of civic involvement, the city fathers promoted discussions of the proper and improper use of marijuana and other drugs and of whether users should be prosecuted by city law enforcement agencies. Very early on, they adopted a relatively relaxed view that would have been quite out of place in most other cities of the prairie.

Peoria, like Champaign and Urbana, remained politically conservative through the second half of the postwar generation, seeking to make its adjustments to the nationwide changes with the minimum of local alteration. On the other hand, the city also remained something of an open town with regard to the "old style" vices—liquor, gambling, and prostitution.

Shifts in Geohistorical Location

A central premise of the Cities of the Prairie study is that the capacity of a particular civil community to function effectively within this broader political context is determined not only by socioeconomic factors but also—and more importantly—by its geohistorical and political cultural foundations. During the second half of the postwar generation, the geohistorical location of the cities of the prairie shifted substantially in its temporal dimension, albeit less so than the country as a whole, and modestly in its spatial dimension. Temporarily, the cities were catapulted into the new American life-style, as was the whole country, but in their usual fashion they were able to conserve many more of the old ways. They were helped in this by being far from the arenas where the cultural change was occurring.

The civil communities most affected were Champaign and Urbana because the University of Illinois was in their midst. Illinois was not as troubled as the east- and west-coast universities or even the University of Chicago, 140 miles to the north. Still, as a major American institution of higher learning, it had its share of student disturbances, including riotous demonstrations against the Vietnam War that led to the sharpest confrontation between town and gown in the history of the region. Less visible but equally potent were changes in social behavior, whether the introduction of a drug culture among certain segments of the student body or the newly permissive attitude toward premarital sexual relations that led the university to abandon its prior commitment to serve "in loco parentis" and instead to allow the students to determine their own life-styles, many of which shocked the townspeople in both cities.

These new developments could have led to a near-permanent state of confrontation in the streets. Then, at the height of this period, the United

States Supreme Court handed down a decision forbidding local governments to deny students the right to establish local residency for voting purposes. This decision, coupled with the reduction of the voting age to eighteen, enfranchised nearly 30,000 new voters in the two cities, more than the total number of permanent residents entitled to vote. This new voting bloc soon secured unprecedented freedom to maintain its own life-style and introduced an even more active student presence into local politics, particularly into the politics of Urbana, within whose city limits most of the students (dormitory and nondormitory) resided.[14]

This particular temporally induced effect was more muted in the other cities. On the other hand, that aspect of temporal change that was manifested in the decline of central cities affected most of the civil communities, as table 2.1 indicates. Central-city population declined in twelve of them, and in the other it did not only because of a successful annexation policy (see table 2.2). Even East St. Louis, with few incentives and virtually surrounded by incorporated areas, was able to annex some adjacent land. Duluth, with so much vacant land within its city limits for years and with a rapidly declining population, added five square miles to its previous sixty-two, and adjacent Hermantown Township incorporated as Hermantown, though its population was essentially static (6,737 in 1970 and 6,759 in 1980). Nine of the cities increased their area by a third to two-thirds between 1960 and 1975 and three by more than two-thirds.

Adjacent to Champaign, Savoy emerged as a growing suburban municipality. Its population in 1960 was 339; by 1970 it had become 592, and by 1980 it was 2,126.

Peoria remains one of the more cosmopolitan cities of the prairie, perhaps because its economic base rests upon Illinois River commerce and industries that are heavily involved in international trade. Of all the civil communities it, along with the Quad Cities, has shifted least in geohistorical location. Observers of the Peoria scene, from the first research done there in the 1930s through Betty Friedan, a Peoria native who went home in 1980 to celebrate some milestone in the feminist movement, have continued to comment on how solid a city it is—not spectacular in any single respect, not even on the "quality of life" measures, but comfortable in a way that seems to defy quantification.

At the same time, the city proper would have lost its intrametropolitan locational struggle had it not succeeded in its annexation policy. Between 1950 and 1960, the central city lost 7.8 percent of its population, dropping from 111,856 to 103,162, less than its population in 1930. The city's 23.1 percent growth between 1960 and 1970 is entirely a result of its enlarging its boundaries. Annexations, including the Western Hills and Charter Oaks areas,

Table 2.1. Growth of the Ten Metropolitan Areas, 1960–80

Standard Metropolitan Statistical Area	1960	1970	1980
Champaign–Urbana	132,436	163,281	168,392
Champaign	49,583	56,837	58,133
Urbana	27,294	33,976	35,978
Outside central cities	33,443	46,906	54,120
Decatur	118,257	125,010	131,375
Decatur	78,004	90,397	94,081
Outside central city	40,253	34,613	37,294
Duluth–Superior	276,596	265,350	266,650
Duluth	106,884	100,578	92,811
Superior	33,563	32,237	29,571
Outside central cities	136,149	132,535	144,268
Joliet	116,585	155,500	167,475
Joliet	66,780	80,378	77,956
Outside central city	127,781	75,122	89,519
Madison–St. Clair	487,198	536,502	515,222
Alton	43,047	39,700	34,171
Belleville	37,264	41,699	41,580
East St. Louis	37,264	69,996	55,200
Granite City	40,073	40,440	36,815
Outside central cities	276,295	NA[a]	NA
Peoria	313,412	341,979	365,864
Peoria	103,162	126,963	124,160
Pekin	28,146	29,465	30,684
Outside central city	210,250	215,016	241,704
Pueblo	118,707	118,238	125,972
Pueblo	91,181	97,774	101,686
Outside central city	27,526	20,464	24,286
Quad Cities	319,375	362,638	383,958
Davenport	88,981	98,469	103,264
Moline	42,705	46,237	45,709
Rock Island	51,863	50,166	47,036
Outside central cities	135,826	167,766	187,949
Rockford	230,091	272,063	279,514
Rockford	126,706	147,370	139,712
Outside central city	103,385	124,693	139,802
Springfield	155,787	171,020	187,789
Springfield	83,271	91,753	99,637
Outside central city	72,516	79,267	88,152

Source: U.S. Bureau of the Census, *State Statistical Abstracts, Number of Inhabitants,* 1980.
[a]NA = not available.

Table 2.2. City Land Area and Population Density, 1950–75

	1950		1960		1975	
City	Area	Density	Area	Density	Area	Density
Alton	6.4	5,086	9.8	4,393	12.9	2,777
Belleville	6.4	5,113	8.5	4,384	11.5	3,805
Champaign	4.7	8,418	6.4	7,747	9.6	6,083
Davenport	18.1	4,119	46.7	1,905	59.1	1,691
Decatur	9.3	7,126	19.7	3,960	33.4	2,683
Duluth	62.3	1,678	62.6	1,707	67.3	1,396
East St. Louis	13.4	6,141	13.8	5,921	13.9	4,168
Joliet	7.7	6,701	14.2	4,703	22.1	3,367
Moline	7.1	5,267	9.2	4,642	12.8	3,482
Peoria	12.9	8,671	15.2	6,787	38.2	3,298
Pueblo	10.6	6,008	17.1	5,332	33.1	3,182
Rockford	14.0	6,638	26.0	4,873	36.1	4,029
Rock Island	10.5	4,639	10.9	4,758	14.3	3,429
Springfield	10.4	7,849	21.4	3,891	35.3	2,476
Superior	36.6	965	36.6	917	37.8	795
Urbana	NA[a]	NA	5.0	5,459	5.7	6,038

Sources: 1950 and 1960 figures: Daniel J. Elazar, *Cities of the Prairie: The Metropolitan Frontier in American Politics* (New York: Basic Books, 1970), p. 115; 1975 figures: U.S. Bureau of the Census, *County and City Data Book, 1977.*
Note: Area is given in square miles; density is given as population per square mile.
[a]NA means not available from Census because city had a population under 25,000.

brought a statistical growth in Peoria's population. Although the size of Peoria more than doubled between 1960 and 1975, from 15.2 to 38.2 square miles, as a central city it barely held its own within the total metropolitan area, with slightly more than one-third of the total metropolitan population. The city's growth is to the north and west, following the line of upper-middle-class suburbanization within Peoria County. Its annexation policy captures the best of the suburban developments; in part because most of the lower-income suburban development takes place across the Illinois River in Tazewell and Woodford counties, beyond the reach of the city's powers of annexation.[15]

By the end of the generation, however, Peoria was beginning to show signs of economic trouble. The Keystone Steel Company, one of its oldest employers, was having financial problems. Hiram Walker Distillers was making plans to close what had been at one time the largest bourbon distil-

Table 2.3. East St. Louis Population by Race

Race	1900	1910	1920	1930	1940	1950	1960	1970	1975	1976	1980
Total	29,655	58,457	66,767	74,347	75,609	82,295	81,712	69,996	57,929[b]	55,770[b]	55,200
White[a]	24,856	52,575	59,330	62,811	58,811	54,740	45,374	21,628	—[c]	—	2,449
Black	1,799	5,882	7,437	11,536	16,798	27,555	36,338	48,368	—	—	52,751

[a]"Other" races, where available, are recorded with the white population.
[b]Estimate supplied by Data Users Service, Bureau of the Census.
[c]Dash indicates data not available.

Table 2.4. Growth of the University of Illinois and Champaign-Urbana, 1950–70

Year	University Employees	University Enrollment	Population of Champaign-Urbana
1950	6,072	19,521	62,497
1960	7,076	21,955	76,877
1970	11,516	34,018	89,322

lery in the world. There was even unease at Caterpillar Tractor Company, the mainstay of Peoria's economy since the early 1900s, which was to find itself in serious trouble early in the 1980s. In sum, Peoria was beginning to be caught in the transition between frontiers, a phenomenon that was to plague other cities of the prairie in the new generation.

The annexation of Richwoods Township made a substantial difference in electoral behavior in Peoria by strengthening the cosmopolitan forces within the city limits. The change was illustrated in the two referenda regarding a bond issue to build a new public library in the late 1960s. Public libraries rarely become major community issues or acquire widespread community backing. The Peoria public library was established in 1856 after a period when various groups maintained their own subscription libraries, the last of which merged into the public library in 1880. In 1911 Carnegie funds supported the establishment of branch libraries, and by 1960 the combined circulation of the branches was more than twice that of the central library in downtown Peoria. In part this was because the central library building was no longer adequate.

In the summer of 1969 the city council approved the construction of a new library building as part of its long-range plan. Turning down an opportunity to acquire $400,000 in federal funds because of the conditions attached, the city council decided to raise $2.8 million through the sale of municipal bonds instead. As required by law, the matter was submitted to referendum and failed by sixteen votes despite a major campaign on the part of the cosmopolitan leadership in the community. Such a close result meant that a second effort would be made, and it was a year later—after the annexation of the Richwoods Township area. The result was a dramatic reversal as the newly annexed cosmopolitan voters supported the bond issue by a large margin.

Rockford remained a manufacturing community throughout the postwar generation. In 1975, 49.2 percent of all jobs in Winnebago County were derived from manufacturing, nearly double the national average, with the country lagging far behind in retail and wholesale trade. This dependency

Table 2.5. Migration and the Cities of the Prairie, 1970 and 1980

City	Percentage of Residents Still in Same House	
	1970[a]	1980[b]
Champaign	59.6	58.8
Urbana	67.5	61.4
Decatur	62.8	63.3
Joliet	73.1	67.4
Alton	76.4	73.0
Belleville	74.2	70.8
East St. Louis	71.7	76.2
Peoria	64.5	63.7
Davenport	63.5	61.8
Moline	70.6	66.4
Rock Island	70.7	67.9
Rockford	63.6	65.6
Springfield	67.4	61.6
Duluth	71.8	69.3
Superior	70.5	69.4
Pueblo	69.4	63.6

Source: U.S. Bureau of the Census.
[a]Residents lived in same house before 1965.
[b]Residents lived in same house before 1975.

upon manufacturing led to a fluctuating unemployment rate that was either higher or lower than the state average. Median family income hovered around the state average, with slightly fewer Rockford residents below the poverty line.

Labor-management relations in Rockford remained tense throughout the postwar generation, with the local owners of the major industries retaining their Yankee stubbornness in opposition to unionization and the workers displaying a militancy that came from being a cut above the average blue-collar labor force. The United Auto Workers remained the largest union but declined in militancy after Emmett Poyer, its powerful leader of the 1950s, was found to be engaged in corrupt practices (in direct violation of the local political culture) and was forced to leave town in disgrace. The Typographical Workers' Union remained the most "thinking" of the unions in the grand tradition of nineteenth-century print media workers. It was involved in two major strikes, in 1952 and 1970; the first led to the transformation of the Rockford newspapers for the better, and the second destroyed the dailies as a public force.

In general Rockford has been a union town, which has brought benefits to the workers and the local body politic. At the same time, unionization has had unanticipated deleterious consequences, driving out some marginal industries that could find better labor conditions elsewhere and discouraging others.

At the same time, Rockford has always boasted a rich cultural life for an American city its size. An effort to strengthen the city's cultural institutions and rationalize their funding was made in the latter half of the postwar generation with the establishment of the Rockford Arts Council in 1967.

Another way Rockford differs from the rest of the country is in its relatively low crime rate, which falls well below the national average. Not only that, but the Rockford Police Department has an exceptional record of solved cases, and the city's crime rate even dropped in the mid-1970s. As a result the Rockford police department spends much of its time in non-crime-related activities and deliberately cultivates its role as a public service organization.

A generally progressive force, the police pioneered an emergency ambulance service, since transferred to the fire department, a detoxification center for those arrested for drunkenness, and a drug treatment center for addicts. In 1974 the department established a chaplain's division, including a full-time police chaplain and volunteer assistant chaplain. A citizen participation crime prevention program was established with federal funds in 1975.

Rockford's population growth after World War II depended heavily on annexation, to encompass the natural growth and in-migration that raised the metropolitan area's population. The city maintained an active annexation program through the 1960s, which enabled it to grow from 93,000 to over 140,000 between 1950 and 1970. As part of that growth the black population increased substantially, and there was a small but significant influx of Hispanic families.

Perhaps the greatest losers in this effort continued to be Duluth and Superior, whose economic base continued to erode as their geohistorical location became even more disadvantageous. With the continuing shift to the Sun Belt, Duluth and Superior became even further removed from the mainstream of American society, worsening their geohistorical location. Whatever growth potential was not cut off by the shift to the Sun Belt was absorbed by the Twin Cities metropolitan region. Duluth continued to lack any significant replacement for the long closed urban-industrial and rural-land frontiers and for the industries that emerged or were introduced in response to them. The closest thing to such a replacement was the prepared-food "empire" of Duluth resident Jeno Palucchi. Characteristic of the metropolitan-technological frontier in every respect, the industry broadened Duluth's economy by developing nationwide markets, and Palucchi himself energetically pursued civic improvement. He was one of the sparkplugs in the city's redevelopment of the periphery of its downtown, demonstrating once again the close tie between frontier-based activities and the existence of the frontier spirit among those involved in them.[16]

If Duluth became increasingly obsolete, what was to be said of Superior? Its population continued to plummet, and the city even lost its port activities as the iron mines played out. Like Duluth but more so, the temporal changes that made its spatial location even more peripheral in the context of American development spelled further defeat.[17]

The latter stages of the metropolitan frontier also rendered East St. Louis increasingly obsolete. Built on labor-intensive industries, as these declined the city had no basis for recouping its fortunes in other directions. At the height of the urban frontier, the East St. Louis stockyards were, with those of Chicago and Kansas City, part of the triumvirate that dominated meat packing in the United States. Today stockyards have all shifted westward and become smaller operations. The railroads also reached their peak in the heyday of the urban frontier, and from 1920 to 1970 rail employment and income declined by 75 percent. Between 1960 and 1975 alone, there was a decline of two thousand jobs with the railroads, stimulated not only by the general decline in rail transportation but by the specific inefficiencies of the East St. Louis yards. Between 1950 and 1970 manufacturing employment dropped by 50 percent.

Thus East St. Louis's decline is a result of the changing technological and transportation patterns of the metropolitan frontier, which rendered its raison d'être obsolete. In this respect it suffered even more than the St. Louis metropolitan region as a whole, one of the areas in the country hardest hit by these changes. Almost from the first, East St. Louis provided homes for the unskilled workers who manned the stockyards, railroad yards, waterfront, and whatever transportation facilities straddled the city. Although its geographic location means that six major highways cross it today, the highways divide the city and enable people and goods to merely pass through rather than serving it in any beneficial way. In this respect it has returned to the days of its founding in 1795 when a ferry was established to cross the Mississippi from the Illinois shore to St. Louis, except then there were no people to be supported other than the ferry operators and their families, whereas today tens of thousands must find a livelihood.

The decline in jobs led in turn to the decline of the commercial base of the city. By now East St. Louis is virtually devoid of commercial establishments. At the end of the generation in 1975 the A&P warehouse, Sears, Roebuck, Swift, and W. T. Grant closed down their operations in the city. None of the national supermarket chains are represented locally, so people must shop out of town. The city's three movie theaters all closed during the postwar generation, though one reopened to show pornographic films. Between 1950 and 1976 food sales declined by 60 percent, though the population declined by only 25 percent. As a crowning blow, in 1977 the only large shopping center built since the 1950s was foreclosed for defaulting on its mortgage, with almost all of its commercial space vacant. Even the East St. Louis daily newspaper ceased publication in spring 1979. Unlike Duluth and even Superior, which, though declining, have a strong enough population mix and regional function to retrench rather than simply collapse, East St. Louis has become the ultimate in obsolescence.

Even in its heyday the railroads and stockyards that provided employment for most East St. Louis residents were situated, for the most part, outside the city limits. The city never had a proper tax base to support its population, nor did those industries have any incentive to control or contribute to local civic progress. Rather, they were absentee owned and exploited in the extreme. As they too have become obsolete, they have been abandoned without qualms by their absentee owners, leaving their workers to fend for themselves. In that respect East St. Louis represents the worst aspects of modern industrial society as it can be found in the United States.

It is not surprising that over the years East St. Louis has become nearly all black. Even in the heyday of the urban frontier during the last generation of the nineteenth century, when Irish, Slavic, and European white immigrants represented the majority of the labor force, before blacks began to move to East St. Louis in great numbers, the percentage of nonwhites was high, reaching about 15 percent of the population by 1917. Political control, however, was in the hands of the whites until the very end of the postwar generation.

Throughout, East St. Louis has lacked a sufficient middle class to balance the various ethnic and racial groups and to provide civic leadership or a tax base that could support civic improvement. The managers of the absentee-owned industries worked with the politicians to effectively limit corporate taxation. The enterprises protected themselves by establishing company towns around the city's periphery that served as tax havens, and the county politicians were in collusion with the companies to keep county tax assessments low.

Not surprisingly, the politics of East St. Louis represented the worst manifestations of the individualistic political culture. Using politics for personal gain was made easier because most of the immigrating groups were from traditional or traditionalistic political cultures and thus were relatively docile in their attitudes toward their leaders.

East St. Louis became the service center for vice in the metropolitan region, including prostitution, gambling, and off-hours drinking. Despite nominal cleanup efforts from time to time, this situation prevails today. Organized crime came into the city from Chicago in the 1940s and plays a major role in these activities.

After Illinois passed legislation enabling its cities to adopt the commission form of government, East St. Louis did so in 1919, which only enhanced the possibility of consolidating power in the hands of the politicians for corrupt purposes by eliminating all checks and balances. The commissioners, as executives, administrators, and legislators, simply divided the spoils among themselves. East St. Louis kept this system of government until 1975.

The combination of all these factors plus the declining industrial base since World War II has made East St. Louis a city of out-migration. Between 1950 and 1976 its total population declined by more than 30 percent. Not only that, but whites have been moving out since World War I, to be replaced by blacks. By 1940, 22 percent of the population was black; by 1960 it was 45 percent and is probably close to 90 percent today. The area has lost tens of thousands of jobs since 1960, so the city's unemployment rate is consistently among the highest in the country. At the end of the postwar generation nearly half the population was receiving some form of welfare assistance.

Not only has technological change rendered East St. Louis obsolete as an industrial center, but it is surrounded by other medium-sized and small cities within the southwestern Illinois metropolitan region that have absorbed its fleeing middle-class population. The city has been left to cope alone with the poor migrants into the region, overwhelmingly black and Hispanic, who have given East St. Louis a new function as their gateway to the metropolitan frontier. Because of its size, all of East St. Louis was equally affected by these two migrational trends, and the impact of its decline has been felt throughout the city.

In 1977 the largest single employer in East St. Louis was the public school district, with approximately 2,000 employees. This was the same school district that went from scandal to scandal, suggesting that many—if not all—of these employees were patronage appointments. Another 1,400 people were employed by the various federal/city programs designed to bring some measure of rehabilitation to East St. Louis. The St. Clair County Office of Public Aid employed 266, and local industry employed some 6,500 others.[18]

Since government was the most stabilizing force in the local economy, with patronage a major element in its stabilizing role, it is no wonder that the people of East St. Louis have been willing to trade off good government for jobs, especially since most of these were jobs as operatives and service workers. This is reflected in the median income of the city, which was just under two-thirds that of the state of Illinois and not much more than two-thirds that of St. Clair County as a whole.

As the tables in this book indicate, East St. Louis stands at the bottom of every positive measure of the quality of life among the cities of the prairie and at the top of every negative one. Still, though citizens are less pleased with their community than are those of any of the other cities, if the poll is representative there is far more satisfaction with the quality of life in East St. Louis than the outside observer might think. This is because there are dimensions of life in that city that go against the conventional picture of an urban slum, most of which reflect the differences between slums in large cities and those in medium-sized urban places.

Take the matter of income. Nearly two-thirds of the respondents in the Sangamon State University survey of 1978 were worried that their incomes would not meet their obligations. With so many households headed by black women, it is not surprising that the city's median income in dollars has declined relative to other areas. Even so, the survey showed that just under 79 percent of those polled indicated that their financial situation had stayed the same or had improved during the previous few years.

In 1975 the city's housing stock was estimated to be 81 percent deteriorated or substandard, with a median value considerably below the average for the county. In 1960, 24 percent of the city's housing units lacked hot and cold water, and 47 percent of those units were inhabited by nonwhites. For the most part, the improvement in housing conditions came about because out-migration allowed those in the worst buildings to move to slightly better ones, and the worst buildings were eliminated.

The school system is subject to constant criticism; its facilities are poor, and its teachers perceive themselves to be underpaid and have responded accordingly. Its financial situation is such that it cannot market new school bonds. There is a very high school dropout rate and a low achievement level. At the same time, the percentage of students graduating from high school and the median number of school years completed has increased over the generations.

Although crime is a severe local problem, according to the figures available East St. Louis is not the worst city in the state. On the other hand, the civil community has reasonable health care available, with two hospitals within the city limits and a third nearby. The health statistics reflect this general availability of medical care, and indeed one of the three hospitals is probably unnecessary, given the pattern of usage. Medical care seems to be equally accessible to whites and blacks, even if slightly below the standards of higher-income communities.

If anything, the image of East St. Louis is even worse than its reality. Again, this has long been the case; even in the 1930s a negative image of the city had spread nationwide. In an early Humphrey Bogart film, Bogart played a young man from East St. Louis seeking to break into the mob. Confronted by the big boss, he was told, "The matter with you, kid, is that you haven't been around." He responded, "East St. Louis is around enough," and he got the job. Local, regional, and national media frequently focus on East St. Louis as one of the worst examples of urban decay and political corruption. But still the people who live there have a higher opinion of their city than the image it projects, as the Sangamon State survey indicated.

Because of its geohistorical location, the residents of East St. Louis tend to be locals rather than cosmopolitans, with little sense of the city as a whole, which may be one reason they are more satisfied with their lot than the statistics show they have a right to be. In several surveys of the late 1960s, a very high level of neighborhood satisfaction was reported, just as it was in the 1978 Sangamon State survey, with very few people indicating that they wished to leave the city and many suggesting that their neighborhoods were quiet, pleasant, and populated by good neighbors. Violence was perceived as being mostly confined to people who know one another and are involved in personal disputes, rather than being random.[19]

Even though the 1978 survey showed that 59 percent of those surveyed felt the quality of life in East St. Louis was worse than it had been five years earlier, as Altes and Mendelson suggest in their article this is probably more "a reflection of national malaise than local despair, since two-thirds of the same residents said, taking all things together, they were happy."[20]

In sum, for the residents of East St. Louis, the city is like a small town. Eighty-four percent of the black population maintain church membership, and nearly all attend church activities. Blacks are also highly involved in other associational activities. Moreover, they anticipate a better future for their children. Even housing is considered satisfactory by the overwhelming majority of the residents of East St. Louis. No doubt this is because so many of them live in freestanding homes that give them more space and privacy than their counterparts in larger cities. The questions of political corruption that upset outsiders are of far less importance to the residents of East St. Louis unless the corruption passes beyond their expectations. Their political culture leads them to expect politicians to behave this way, and hence they are not disturbed when officeholders do.

It is not unreasonable to assume that much of this generally favorable attitude on the part of the local residents has to do with the fact that East

St. Louis is a medium-sized city—indeed, now at the lower end of the scale of medium-sized cities. It is not a large urban ghetto within an even larger metropolis but a civil community in its own right, even if a different kind, even though it is located within a large metropolitan region whose SMSA population exceeds 2 million. By remaining an independent city, it has its share of problems but also its share of advantages, offering a neighborhood-oriented way of life for the locals who reside within it. In an article by Leon Cheres, "In Defense of a Lady," a longtime resident summed up his view of East St. Louis:

> I've been here from the beginning—and I know what a great lady you used to be. I've seen you strut your stuff with the best, and I know that you know how to handle yourself in a crowd. You've made me laugh in my time, a little sad in my time, yet proud in my time that I knew you so well. . . . I've seen your once busy railroad station sing the song of the new people, carrying their hope in cardboard boxes. I watched you make love to prosperity at the turn of a card and the roll of the dice and watched your neon lights blaze into the early light of day.
>
> I crouched in your doorways when the riot came, and I saw the blood and dreams of many of your people run through the meadows of your mind. Yet you sustained, building and re-building, creating and re-creating, doing more than anyone [twice] your size, being just a little better than you really had any right to be.[21]

Apparently this view is more widely held than outsiders are apt to believe.

In many respects Pueblo and Joliet were the most visible examples of change in geohistorical location. Pueblo, spatially the urban backwater of Colorado's eastern slope (the area of the state east of the continental divide) in the past, suddenly found itself at the nexus of the expanding Sun Belt to the southwest and the expanding Front Range megalopolis to the north.[22] While this change did not bring great population growth, it did put Pueblo into a position to secure steady growth opportunities and to attract vital public and private sector investments related to the metropolitan frontier. Puebloans had to work for what they got, but they did manage to acquire a regional state university, which they had been seeking, and several major federal installations, including the Department of Transportation testing center and a major distribution center for United States government documents. A site adjacent to the city was chosen by the developers of Sun City, Arizona, for another planned community. These in turn enabled the civil community to adjust to the decline of its older urban-industrial economic base, including the railroads, Colorado Fuel and Iron, and the state mental hospital.[23]

Joliet, on the other hand, found itself even more drawn into the orbit of the northeastern Illinois metropolitan region, though it continued to successfully resist the encroachment of Chicago (which in any case was losing some of its preeminence in this period).[24] The outer edge of the Chicago suburban frontier entered rural Will County and the Joliet urbanized area during the latter half of the postwar generation. It would have pulled Joliet more into that orbit had not the civil community been able to capitalize on its location at the junction of two major interstate highways to the southwest, which pulled its development in that direction. Joliet's traditional geohistorical predilections to turn southwest away from Chicago as part of its effort to avoid being absorbed into "Chicagoland" was thus reinforced.

The Quad Cities held their own very nicely until the end of the generation. Their geohistorical location at the nexus of the greater Northeast, the greater West, and the greater South, the country's three great spheres, seems to remain unchanged generation after generation, bringing them steady growth and, most important, enabling them to adapt to changing frontiers.[25] During the latter half of the postwar generation, the Illinois shore lost ground to the Iowa side, perhaps a reflection of the overall national shift westward, and the central business districts of all three major cities declined. At the same time, a key characteristic of metropolitan growth in the Quad Cities area in the 1960s and 1970s was the expansion southward, particularly south of Rock Island, into Henry County, particularly around the villages of Milan and Oak Grove. The Quad Cities, with their interstate as well as interlocal dimension, remain the apotheosis of interlocal cooperation among separated jurisdictions.

The cities were the world's largest center of farm implement production throughout the postwar period. Thirteen percent of all employment in the SMSA was in the farm implement industry in 1977. Nevertheless, the industry did not grow quite as fast as total employment in the area over the previous decade. Another sign of impending economic trouble was that the Quad Cities' role as a transportation center decreased between 1967 and 1977, with major declines in air freight traffic and railroad car loadings, both forwarded and received. Railroad passenger service ended in 1978. Barge traffic on the Mississippi River and air passenger traffic were up slightly, but not enough to offset the general decline. Apparently, the Quad Cities' onetime advantage of being located midway between Chicago, Des Moines, St. Louis, and Minneapolis–St. Paul has ceased to be an advantage as freight haulage is organized around more widely separated basing points covering longer distances. Nevertheless, the Quad Cities remain a regional trading center for six counties in Illinois and nine in Iowa and a farm implement manufacturing center for the whole country and indeed the world.

In terms of intended settlement patterns, the Quad Cities region underwent classic suburbanization. The three central cities did not have an annexation program to keep up with the migration outward, hence all three are declining in population, although they remain centers of employment. In the decade 1970–80, Bettendorf did undertake some major annexations, crossing into Leclair and Lincoln townships and annexing other areas around its fringes. Davenport undertook only minor annexing of other areas on its fringes. On the Illinois side, Moline expanded its annexations into Coal Valley Township. Most of the municipalities within Rock Island County added territory through annexation, though Silvis and Milan also detached areas. The standard metropolitan commuting pattern is further complicated by the existence of five significant cities rather than one central place. Already by the mid-1960s some 65 percent of all employed persons in the SMSA worked in a city other than the one they lived in.[26]

Decatur was one of the last of the cities of the prairie to acquire an interstate highway connection, something that has proved vital to full participation in the metropolitan frontier. Today the civil community is linked with Champaign–Urbana to the east by Interstate 74 and Springfield to the west by Interstate 72. On the other hand, it is a sign of the times that U.S. 51, the great north-south artery bisecting the state of Illinois, which passes through the heart of Decatur and is a product of the first generation of highway construction in the United States at the very end of the urban frontier, has fallen into disrepair. U.S. 51 was a two-lane highway throughout the postwar generation, and one of the last state-federal actions of the generation to have an impact on the Decatur civil community was the decision to rebuilt it as a four-lane divided highway, giving the civil community a proper north-south connection.[27] Subsequent implications kept this decision from being carried out, however, and the real consequences of that decision will come only in the next generation.

For quite different reasons, Decatur also managed to adapt its agribusiness and agri-industrial economy to whatever external changes took place.[28] Moreover, like Rockford and Pueblo, it did so while preserving the city's predominance throughout the generation. Whereas the other civil communities are multicentered and even Champaign County is now built around two separate and unequal poles, Champaign–Urbana as the center and Rantoul in the north, virtually all of Macon County relies on employment and service opportunities offered by Decatur. Decatur has had one of the most successful annexation records of any of the cities of the prairie in the second half of the postwar generation, which has further helped to maintain the city's centrality in the civil community. Nevertheless, the city's population is now stagnant and cannot be significantly changed by further annexation.

Decatur's economic base remains tied to agriculture, whether directly through the processing of agricultural produce, through agribusiness, or through the manufacture of farming equipment. Hence by the end of the generation it was beginning to take a downward turn economically, in contrast to Champaign–Urbana. Indeed, the one common dimension of decline among the central urban civil communities noted at the very end of the generation was the decline in the farm implement industry. This was of substantial significance to the Quad Cities, Peoria, and Springfield, where it was the major industry, and to Rockford, where it was of considerable importance. The industry reached its peak at the end of the postwar generation. Its decline at the very end of the generation presaged an uncertain future for those cities' economic base, but its effect was to be felt only in the next generation.

Central Illinois, located as it is in the transition zone between the three geohistorical spheres of the United States, has generally managed to adjust to the country's tipping to the Southwest, even though most of the Near West of which it is a part is losing out as a result of the shift (map 2.1). On the other hand, the two cases chosen as controls in the original study, Duluth and Superior on the one hand and Pueblo on the other, reflect to a pronounced degree the tendencies of their regions, Duluth and Superior losing further ground in terms of geohistorical location and Pueblo gaining ground because of it. These shifts in geohistorical location reflect the continuing frontier process that has shaped the United States.

Toward a Fourth Frontier?

By the mid-1970s the metropolitan frontier had effectively ended for the country as a whole and for most of the cities of the prairie as well. Especially in the aftermath of the Arab oil embargo of 1973–74 and the end of cheap energy, the basis of the metropolitan frontier seemed to have evaporated. People began to think in terms of retrenchment rather than development, of redividing the same pie rather than expanding it. The frontier spirit seemed to go out of America. This is not to say that certain of the phenomena of metropolitanization were not continuing: new subdivisions continued to be built on the peripheries of the urbanized areas, and new shopping centers were being opened. But these had become routine and no longer represented the cutting edge of development and a force for societal change.

Indeed, the events of 1968–76 can be seen as a backlash by those who revolted against the frontier's principal characteristics on behalf of something else that, curiously enough, represented an accentuation of some of those self-same characteristics. All this was magnified by many of the accepted commentators on American life, who had earlier been dubious

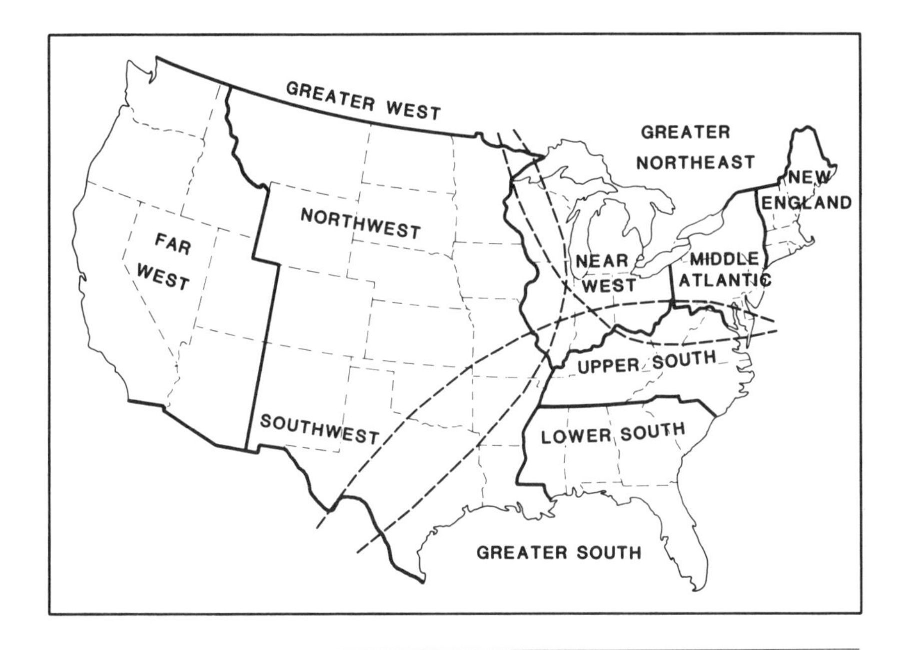

Map 2.1. The geohistorical location of the cities of the prairie.

about the value of the metropolitan frontier but refrained from expressing all their doubts until it became fashionable to do so.

Had this book been published in 1978, it would have ended on a very sober note. Shortly thereafter, however, the outlines of a fourth frontier state began to emerge, a rurban or citybelt-cybernetic frontier in which metropolitan patterns of settlement have given way to megalopolitan ones, that is to say, belts of cities of various sizes, interspersed with areas of rurban development, stretched lineally over hundreds of miles and tied together by a new cybernetically based communications network, computerized in every dimension.[29] By the beginning of the 1980s the United States was stepping out onto a new frontier.

The impact of the citybelt-cybernetic frontier on the cities of the prairie will be explored in the next round of this study, but even as early as the middle years of the metropolitan frontier, the medium-sized cities of central Illinois and their smaller counterparts showed signs of being among the first to enter that stage of development.[30] The area from Danville on the Indiana border westward to Peoria and from Kankakee southward to Springfield already constituted something of a dispersed minimegalopolis in which the various nodes—Champaign-Urbana, Danville, Decatur, Bloomington-Normal, Kankakee, Peoria, Pekin, and Springfield—each played a specialized role of its own, providing some service for the whole. Thus Springfield served as the state government center. The state university was located in Champaign-Urbana, and there was a teachers college in Normal. Danville offered a concentration of illicit services and Peoria a medical complex. These and other services were available to and utilized by people from the whole region.

This pattern intensified in the latter half of the postwar generation. Bloomington-Normal became a medium-sized metropolitan area in its own right. The completion of the interstate highway network has made travel between these various nodes even easier and has transformed the locational dimensions of economic development in the region, thus laying the groundwork for an early midwestern expression of the citybelt-cybernetic frontier.

On the other hand, the same central Illinois civil communities, and their other Illinois sisters, are in economic trouble as a result of the shifting frontiers. All made the transition from the urban-industrial to the metropolitan-technological frontier with relative ease because of an appropriate manufacturing base—the agricultural equipment industry and in Rockford the machine tool industry as well—and a proper role in their region's transportation network. The decline of the former and the transformation of the latter are putting them in the same situation Duluth and Superior found themselves in at the close of the urban frontier. By the earlier 1980s, the manufacturing cities of Illinois and Iowa were suffering very high unemployment, and only Champaign-Urbana and to a lesser extent Springfield seemed to be making the transition to the new frontier with few difficulties.

Pueblo, on the other hand, which was still a freestanding civil community during the first half of the postwar generation, during the second half became the southern anchor of a Front Range citybelt stretching northward to Fort Collins or even Cheyenne, Wyoming.[31] We already began to pick up patterns of interaction in the second stage of the study, including a consciousness of what was happening on the part of urban and regional planners in the area and those who utilize their work. Thus it too was being pulled onto the new frontier.

An interesting consequence of this has been the transformation of the rivalry between Pueblo and Colorado Springs. Until the mid-1960s the two neighboring cities were locked in an equal competition. Colorado Springs, nestled at the base of Pike's Peak, was a little gem, just approaching medium size, with picture-book qualities. Founded as a resort town a century ago, it was settled by a heavy influx of Yankees and those who sought a Yankee style of life. Pueblo, by contrast, was still "Pewtown" for people from Colorado Springs and the rest of the state, the site of ugly steel mills, situated in a region of minimum natural beauty and heavily populated by southern Europeans and Mexicans with no "style."

Then, as the tides of migration from the Sun Belt engulfed the region, the population of Colorado Springs tripled in a decade, bringing with it the tackiness of rapid development, while Pueblo continued to grow slowly and simultaneously underwent an internal renaissance. No observer would suggest that by the end of the generation Colorado Springs had lost all its advantages over Pueblo, but as far as Puebloans were concerned, they no longer felt inferior to their sister city to the north. As a sign of the times, increasing numbers of people were settling at the northern edge of the Pueblo civil community and commuting to work in Colorado Springs rather than living in that increasingly overdeveloped, underplanned area. For Pueblo, geohistorical location combined with a special measure of civic spirit, will, and leadership had opened a new frontier—perhaps the best yet.

3. Political Culture and the Geology of Local Politics

One of the central purposes of the Cities of the Prairie study is to map and monitor sources, manifestations, and effects of subcultural variations in the local political arena. The first study identified significant relationships between political culture, ethnicity, and religion and between those three factors and three geohistorical factors: sectionalism, migration, and the frontier. In the restudy we were able to monitor and analyze the dynamics of change in the cultural geology of the cities of the prairie and its political consequences.

Approaches to the Study of Political Culture

The study of political culture in its contemporary form goes back some thirty years. In a sense its emergence in the 1950s represented a reemergence of what was once defined in the study of political science as "national character," substantially refined and certainly more hesitant, skeptical, and cautious.

The "national character" approach had run into problems both methodologically and politically. Racist applications of its premises, which were features of the last generation of the nineteenth century and the first generation of the twentieth and reached their apogee in the Nazi era, made all generalizations about nations, peoples, and groups suspect. Yet however suspect such generalizations might be, the questions they addressed remain enduring ones. Hence it became impossible to continue the study of political science and simply ignore those questions because the way they were treated in previous years was so questionable.

The emergence of the study of political culture represented an attempt to come to grips with the modalities (to use Alex Inkeles' term) one finds within enduring political communities, which seem to have their roots in the very character, or social psychology, of the members of those communities.[1] It seeks to do so in a way that avoids the overgeneralization that leads to stereotyped conclusions, whether favorable or unfavorable to the particular group involved, and at the same time does not underplay these factors when we consider institutional and other behavioral dimensions of political life.

Two general approaches to the study of political culture have emerged. One, the school Gabriel Almond pioneered grew out of the study of comparative politics. Almond and his colleagues, Lucian Pye, Sidney Verba, C. Bingham Powell, and others, have tended to focus on "macro" cultural manifestations of an essentially nationwide character, and only from time to time have they tried to explore the subtleties within the nations they have studied. They have developed methods that have been quite useful in exposing and addressing such "macro" questions.[2]

The other school, which the original Cities of the Prairie project pioneered, grew out of the study of state and local politics. It represented an attempt to understand the more subtle subcultural distinctions within the American polity in order to develop an overarching view of American civil society. It was based on a theory designed to deal with the most local and specific manifestations of political cultural differences.

The first approach emerged as an attempt to transcend the limitations of earlier institutional and behavioral studies and to give a comparative dimension to those studies that would allow for greater subtlety of international comparison. The second approach emerged in response to the kinds of glowing generalities about the American character that used to be written to describe the United States as a whole. In such books the American character is delineated by lists of traits, generally positive (i.e., Americans are optimistic, forward-looking, energetic, pragmatic, and whatever). These long lists were not necessarily erroneous, but as propositions they were not systematically organized or tested in any way. As the study of American civil society passed into a more rigorous phase, this kind of treatment seemed increasingly inadequate to many students of American civilization, who began to look for ways to systematically test these propositions or, if they thought they had some merit, to refine them and clarify the subtleties.

The Cities and American Political Subcultures

American political subcultures arose out of very real sociocultural differences (ethnic, racial, linguistic, and religious) among the peoples who came to the United States over the years, differences that date back to the very beginnings of settlement in British North America and to the Old World before that. Such differences are to be found within what are commonly conceived to be single nationality groups as often as among them. The New England commonwealths, for example, were developed primarily by English settlers from East Anglia, whereas Englishmen of different backgrounds and apparently from different regions created the "private city" of Philadelphia and the southern patriarchal county and plantation system.[3]

Because the various ethnic and religious groups that came to this country tended to congregate in their own settlements and because as they or their descendants moved westward they continued to settle together, the political patterns they bore with them are today distributed geographically. Indeed, it is the geographical distribution of political cultures as modified by local conditions that has laid the foundations for American sectionalism.

Fifteen demographic-culture streams settled the continent: three "native streams" (Yankee, Middle Atlantic, southern); seven "European streams" (English, Scottish, Jewish, Irish, Continental—including Germans, central Europeans under German influence, French, and Belgians—eastern European, and Mediterranean); two "Canadian streams" (French and Anglo); and three "excluded streams" (Afro-American, Hispanic, and Oriental). Those streams, in themselves relatively clear-cut, have left residues of population in various places to become the human equivalent of geological strata. As they settled in the same locations, sometimes side by side, sometimes overlapping, and frequently on top of one another, they created structured cultural mixtures. Sorting out these mixtures for any one locality, in an attempt to portray the overall patterning of political cultures in that locale, requires a kind of human or cultural "geology" that adds another dimension to the problem.

The earlier study demonstrated that American political culture is actually a synthesis of three major political subcultures that jointly inhabit the country, existing side by side or even overlapping, labeled *individualistic, moralistic,* and *traditionalistic.*

The *individualistic political culture* emphasizes the conception of the democratic order as a marketplace. In its view, government is instituted for strictly utilitarian reasons, to handle those functions demanded by the people it is created to serve. A government need not have any direct concern with questions of the "good society" except insofar as it may be used to advance some common conception of the good society formulated outside the political arena just as it serves other functions. Since the individualistic political culture emphasizes the centrality of private concerns, it places a premium on limiting community intervention—whether governmental or nongovernmental—into private activities to the minimum necessary to keep the marketplace in proper working order. In general, government action is to be restricted to those areas, primarily in the economic realm, that encourage private initiative and widespread access to the marketplace.

The *moralistic political culture* emphasizes conception of the commonwealth as the basis for democratic government. Politics, to the moralistic political culture, is considered one of the great activities of man in his search for the good society—a struggle for power, it is true, but also an effort to exercise power for the betterment of the commonwealth. Consequently, in the moralistic political culture, both the general public and the politicians conceive of politics as a public activity centered on some notion of the public good and properly devoted to the advancement of the public interest. Good government, then, is measured by the degree to which it promotes the public good and in terms of the honesty, selflessness, and commitment to the public welfare of those who govern.

The *traditionalistic political culture* is rooted in an ambivalent attitude toward the marketplace coupled with a paternalistic and elitist conception of the commonwealth. It reflects an older, precommercial attitude that accepts a substantially hierarchical society as part of the ordered nature of things, authorizing and expecting those at the top of the social structure to take a special and dominant role in government. Like its moralistic counterpart, the traditionalistic political culture accepts government as an actor with a positive role in the community, but it tries to limit that role to securing the continued maintenance of the existing social order. To do so, it functions to confine real political power to a relatively small and self-perpetuating group drawn from an established elite who often inherit their "right" to govern through family ties or social position. Accordingly, social and family ties are paramount in a traditionalistic political culture, even more than personal ties are important in the individualistic culture where, after all is said and done, a person's first responsibility is to himself. At the same time, those who do not have a definite role to play in politics are not expected to be even minimally active as citizens. In many cases, they are not even expected to vote. Like the individualistic political culture, those active in politics are expected to benefit personally from their activity though not necessarily by direct pecuniary gain.

While all three are of nationwide proportions, each subculture is at the same time strongly tied to specific sections of the country, reflecting the streams of migration that have carried different peoples across the continent in more or less orderly patterns.[4] Figure 3.1 portrays the three political subcultures in their various modifications, showing their relation to one another and the location of each of the cities of the prairie in relation to them.

Since the first study, only Duluth has incurred any notable change in its political culture, becoming even more uniformly moralistic as the traditionalistic segments of the immigrant generation of southern Europeans who settled in that civil community have gone the way of all flesh, with no augmentation through migration to replace them. The other civil communities

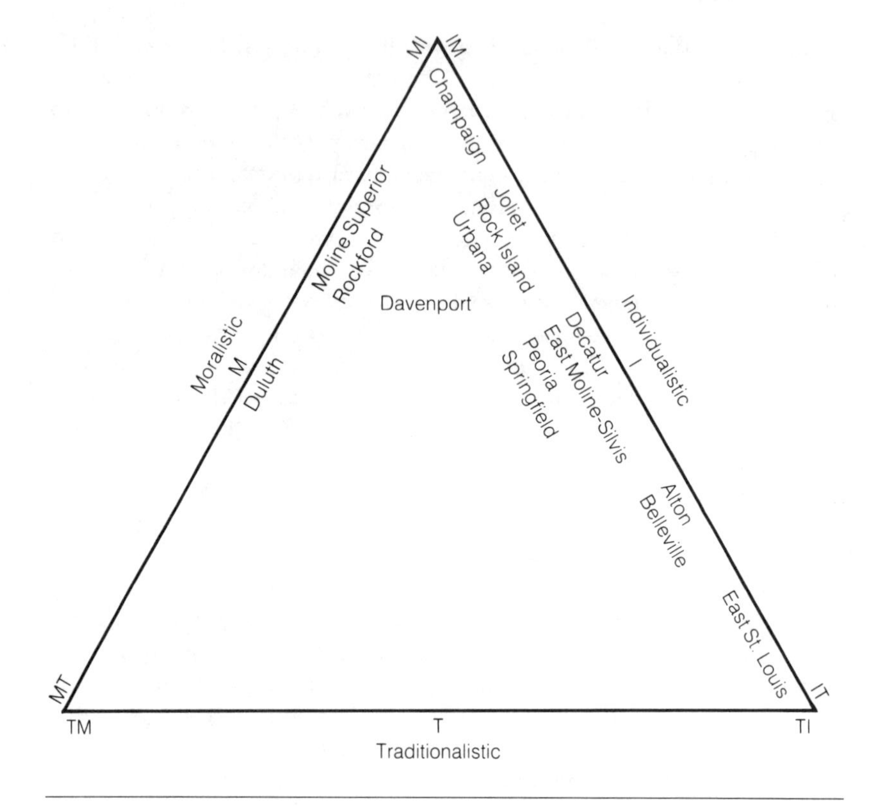

Fig. 3.1. The political cultures of the cities of the prairie.

have remained essentially in place, either because the local populations have remained unchanged or because the migrations that have reached them have reinforced existing tendencies. As figure 3.1 makes clear, most of the civil communities fall on the individualistic side of the triangle. There are some notable clusters; for example, Rock Island, Davenport, and Moline form a kind of subtriangle at the intersection of the individualistic and moralistic political subcultures, while Alton, Belleville, and East St. Louis form a cluster at the intersection of the individualistic and traditionalistic subcultures. Duluth is the most moralistic, while Decatur, Peoria, and Springfield are the most purely individualistic. Champaign and Urbana have a moralistic dimension because the university brings in a transient moralistic population that leaves a small permanent residue. Pueblo is the most balanced of all the cities of the prairie. Rockford remains the most deviant city in Illinois and maintains that deviance by virtue of its governmental buffer zones, which, as will be noted below, began to be penetrated by the end of the postwar generation.

The various sequences of migration in each locale have determined the particular layering of its cultural geology. Those variables found to be important to this process include the political generation and subcultural orientation of the group(s) of first settlement; the temporal and cultural distance between the first and second groups of settlers; the length of single-group domination and intergroup competition, usually characterized by variants of either the "mixed" or "two cities" models; and the subsequent patterning of intrametropolitan migration and settlement. At the same time, even as the strata were being deposited over generations and centuries, externally generated events such as depressions, wars, and internal cultural conflicts caused upheavals that altered the relative position of the various groups in the community. Beyond that, the passage of time and the impact of new events have eroded some cultural patterns, intensified others, and modified still others to make each local situation even more complex.

These migrational streams passed over the land in "waves," generation by generation. Five successive waves can be identified in the greater West. The first came with the first generation of permanent American settlement, approximately 1815 and 1847. They were principally native streams embracing the initial settlers. In the second generation (1848–76) there was the first large-scale European migration, including the English, Scottish, Jewish, Irish, and Continental streams. The third generation (1877–1916) brought the arrival of the last of the European streams and the first large-scale settlement of the "excluded" streams. Between 1917 and 1947 there was a generation's interregnum, separating the first era of growth in the community from the second, which began with the fifth generation (1948–76), linked to the opening and development of the metropolitan frontier.

Excluded Streams, Civil Rights, and Political Culture

The so-called revival of ethnicity sharpens our understanding of the relation between ethnicity and political culture. The original study suggested that political culture becomes almost the last active remnant of ethnicity for many ethnic groups that have lost either overt ethnic consciousness or, if they retain that, consistently distinctive ethnic behavior.[5] New England Yankees, for example, represent an ethnic group, as it were, that no longer seems aware of its ethnic distinctiveness but which expresses itself through its moralistic political culture. At the same time, the links that were formed between Yankees and Scandinavians and the conflicts between Yankees and

Irish reveal how in one case political cultural similarities overcame ethnic differences whereas in another case such differences reinforced ethnic hostility.

What Americans witnessed in the latter half of the postwar generation was not the reemergence of ethnicity in the United States but the last stand of ethnic separatism for certain ethnic groups. It was parallel to what happened in the 1880s and 1890s for the northern European ethnic groups of the time—the Dutch, the Scots, the Germans, the Welsh—who, just at the threshold of their being assimilated into what was to become known as WASP society, initiated a resurgence of ethnic claims and ethnic associations. A whole literature emerged in the last generation of the nineteenth century dealing with contributions of these groups to the building of America. What they were saying, in effect, was that those of the English-descended "establishment" who think that the United States was founded by the English should look back and see that it was just as much founded by Welsh, Scots, Dutch, and Germans.

After a very brief period, in part because of the influx of new ethnic groups that made ethnicity somewhat foreign and in part because of processes indigenous to American society, those groups virtually ceased to exist as overt ethnic communities; they were assimilated into American society on more equal terms. The same thing happened to southern and eastern European ethnic groups in the late 1960s and early 1970s. The ethnic revival of those years was the last step in the process of their full integration into American society—on the basis of equality and not as second-class communities. As at the turn of the century, this process was intensified by the influx of new, unintegrated groups, especially Hispanics, who sharpened the contrast between real ethnics and former ethnics, as it were. The political arena serves as a major vehicle for integrating each set of ethnic groups in turn, in part through finding common political cultural links with parallel groups.

During the second half of the postwar generation, there was a radical change in the relations among the streams that shape American political culture. One of the main points made in *Cities of the Prairie* was that the scholarly and journalistic attention given to power struggles over strictly local activities such as the revival of the central business district or off-street parking—a central feature of most of the conventional studies of local power—missed the point. The real issues were not necessarily those to which the local powerholders addressed themselves, but were the issues that had transcendent importance and long-range implications, of which desegregation was no doubt the foremost. So it turned out to be in the second half of the postwar generation, when the vital importance of that issue became clear to all. It must be said that the communities rose to the occasion, some generously and others minimally, with significant change occurring in all, even if it was insufficient in some. In a dramatic demonstration of the accuracy of the thesis presented in *Cities of the Prairie,* the hitherto excluded streams ceased to be excluded and were incorporated into the polity in an active way,[6] to eliminate the "two cities" into which all American civil communities had hitherto been divided. Indeed, it is that dimension of the civil rights revolution that brought the most significant transformation in all the cities of the prairie and in the United States as a whole in the latter half of the postwar generation.

Some of the various ways that transformation was effected are documented in the following pages. What seems clear from all of them is that blacks and Hispanics secured political integration in the cities of the prairie even where other forms of integration proceeded more slowly. Residential integration was perhaps slowest of all, and school integration was a matter of alternating conflict and accommodation.

Rockford's confrontation with the civil rights movement was relatively easy except for the school busing controversy. The Human Relations Commission, in the 1950s a weak body, was transformed into the Department of Human Resources, with a full professional staff. Its community action program came to embrace all the "in" issues of the late 1960s and 1970s, ranging from special services for the Spanish-speaking population to energy conservation. The department also administered equal employment programs with enforcement responsibilities within the city government and advisory services for the private sector.[7]

As befits a civil community with a moralistic political culture, school policies have been major issues in Rockford's history and were intense in the latter half of the postwar generation. Not unexpectedly, those controversies involved moral and ideological dimensions far more than was common in the other Illinois cities. For example, as late as 1950 the Rockford school district did not permit the employment of married women as teachers. That rule was changed only when the state legislature banned such discrimination that year.

In 1964 Rockford voted to establish a separate elected board of education. Until that time the school board had been appointed by the city council. The new board took office to face major controversies over desegregation of the schools and busing to achieve racial integration. Since the school district includes suburban areas outside the city limits, the school board became an arena of confrontation. A conservative group, the Community Education Committee, became a quasi-party to contest school elections and managed to gain control of the board, where it maintained its opposition to busing.

Negotiations continued until 1976, when a voluntary integration plan was worked out and received reluctant state approval, though in the state's eyes it did not go far enough. The program was appropriately Rockfordian, emphasizing centers of excellence and alternative education programs to which parents could send their children wherever they happened to live within the district. During the 1977–78 school year, the first year the program was in full operation, well over 10 percent of the students enrolled in the system participated. The plan was designed to provide programs not only for the academically talented and those with special interest in science, mathematics, and the fine arts, but for nonmotivated children as well.

Springfield was also the subject of a desegregation suit that ended the city's patterns of segregation. Although the schools were overcrowded in the 1960s, declining enrollment in the 1970s reversed the situation. School boundaries had to be changed, grades realigned, and the teaching staff reduced.[8]

Rock Island school district 41 was one of the thirteen districts in the state cited for failing to conform to Illinois Office of Education desegregation guidelines adopted in 1971. The desegregation problem was concentrated in the city's four junior high schools. The school district did not accept state intervention easily, and it fought against state pressure throughout the remainder of the postwar generation.[9]

Moline faced minor desegregation problems in 1977 when a small group of parents sought to realign some attendance boundaries that involved East Moline, so as to bring their children into the Moline school district. The complexities of the desegregation effort were made manifest when the state sought to pressure the Moline school district to "mainstream" the 144 students of Hispanic origin among the schools throughout the district rather than allowing them to be concentrated in the one school that had a bilingual education program. The school district contended that the bilingual program was preferable to mainstreaming, and in September 1977 it secured a court injunction against the change.[10]

In school integration, as in so many other things, East St. Louis is the exception to the pattern. Because of the heavy black population, school district 189 was integrated even at the beginning of this period but was subject to intense racial strife. Uniformed police had to patrol school corridors to keep even a semblance of order. Then in October 1977 the courts granted permission to the neighborhood containing many of the remaining white children to detach itself from that school district and join a neighboring district that was predominantly white. Although this brought enrollment in District 189 to more than 90 percent black, it did reduce racial conflict to the point where police officers could be withdrawn.[11]

Perhaps the most successful transformation of an excluded stream into an integrated one occurred in Pueblo, where a very large Hispanic minority, which made several modest efforts to assert itself even during the first half of the postwar generation, though with limited success, crossed the threshold into full participation in the life and politics of the civil community, integrating residential patterns as well as political institutions. The transformation of the Pueblo civil community is another manifestation of its character as an exceptional polity. Pueblo's renaissance was already visible at the time of the first study. Since then it has been even more successful. The cornerstone of that renaissance was full participation of the citizenry in the civic and political life of the civil community. Even its institutions were rearranged to accommodate these changes.[12]

Not only were the Hispanics as a group integrated into Pueblo's political system, but the Orientals, whose position may have been somewhat equivocal at the beginning of the generation, also completed the process of integration. By the mid-1970s Pueblo's mayor was a dentist of Japanese descent. Both ethnically and professionally, he belonged to groups that are rarely found in public positions in any part of the United States. In that sense his candidacy, which was taken for granted, and his election without any stir are signs of the completion of the integration of the "two cities" that was a dominant feature of the postwar generation.

The formerly excluded streams have integrated into their political culture environments in the cities of the prairie—most easily into the traditionalistic and individualistic environments, less easily into the moralistic. Integration into the last has occurred only when the population from the excluded streams has been small enough to assimilate culturally into the majority. In the main, however, the civil communities with substantial populations from the formerly excluded streams are also those dominated by the individualistic political subculture, hence the relative ease of integration. Again East St. Louis is a case in point. Almost since its founding, its local political culture has been a synthesis of traditionalistic and individualistic elements. Blacks and Hispanics moving into the community have simply fit into the local pattern.[13]

On the other hand, the "ethnic revival" that was characteristic of the United States in the late 1960s and early 1970s did not affect political culture in any significant way, because even before that, when overt ethnicity was quiescent, its political impact was a reality. In general the ethnic revival had relatively little effect in the cities of the prairie. Those cities with clearly distinguishable ethnic groups, such as Duluth, Superior, Rockford, and Moline, always had a relatively high degree of ethnic consciousness, not only among the very distinctive Scandinavians but also among the Yankees, certainly relative to the consciousness of Yankee heritage in other parts of the country settled by sons of migrant New Englanders, perhaps as a kind of counterpoint to the ethnicity of the Scandinavians, Germans, Italians, and others. At the same time, ethnic consciousness may have become slightly sharpened among the younger generation in all the cities, slowing down the disappearance of ethnic identity in these communities.

Overall, the percentage of visible ethnics declined with the decline in the percentage foreign-born and of foreign stock in the cities (table 3.1). Nevertheless, a certain trickle of migrants from Europe continued to settle in the cities of the prairie, generally following the earlier migration routes. Peoria, for example, retains its drawing power for German immigrants. One out of every four Peorians traces his or her roots to Germany, and Germans

Table 3.1. Visible Ethnicity in the Cities of the Prairie, 1960 and 1970

Civil Community	Percentage Foreign-Born		Percentage of Foreign/Mixed Parentage		Total Foreign Stock		Leading Country of Origin, 1970 (%)
	1970	1960	1970	1960	1970	1960	
Alton[a]	1.4	1.8	5.3	6.7	6.6	8.5	GE 29.5[c]
Belleville[a]	1.7	2.3	8.7	11.0	10.4	13.3	GE 38.5
Champaign[a]	2.5	2.9	5.8	8.7	8.3	11.6	GE 17.0
Davenport[a]	2.1	2.9	9.4	13.5	11.5	16.4	GE 39.9
Decatur[b]	1.3	1.4	4.9	6.0	6.4	7.4	GE 37.1
Duluth[a]	5.2	8.9	22.6	27.9	27.8	36.8	S 20.5
East St. Louis[a]	1.0	2.1	3.5	6.1	4.5	8.2	GE 15.3
Joliet[b]	3.4	5.3	15.9	21.0	23.1	26.3	IT 14.0
Moline[a]	4.3	5.9	15.8	18.3	20.1	24.2	S 25.8
Peoria[b]	1.8	2.4	7.6	9.7	10.8	12.1	GE 24.8
Pueblo[b]	2.4	3.9	11.4	13.5	13.7	17.4	M 20.8
Rockford[b]	4.2	6.1	13.0	17.2	19.6	23.3	S 31.7
Rock Island[a]	2.3	3.7	10.9	14.1	13.2	17.8	GE 20.6
Springfield[b]	2.2	3.2	9.5	11.2	12.3	14.4	GE 22.1
Superior[a]	3.7	7.2	22.1	27.5	25.8	34.7	S 20.2
Urbana[a]	5.7	4.5	7.7	8.2	13.4	12.7	GE 10.8

Sources: 1970 figures, U.S. Bureau of the Census, *General Social and Economic Characteristics, State Statistics; County and City Data Book, 1977;* 1960 figures, Daniel J. Elazar, *Cities of the Prairie: The Metropolitan Frontier and American Politics* (New York: Basic Books, 1970), p. 188.

[a]City.

[b]Urbanized area.

[c]GE = Germany; S = Sweden; IT = Italy; M = Mexico.

continue to make up the largest ethnic group in the civil community even though the city's overt German character, more visible in the days of the urban-industrial frontier, has continued to diminish.[14] In the same way, Rockford continues to attract Scandinavians, particularly Swedes. At the other end of the scale, except for the issue of black integration, ethnicity is not a contributory factor in the local politics of Champaign–Urbana. Whatever residual ethnic dimensions remained in the first half of the postwar generation were further dissipated in the face of the "town/gown" division, which has become more prominent on the local political scene.

The Quad Cities offer a good example of the pattern in the latter half of the generation. They remained ethnically diverse, especially on the Illinois side, but the ethnic composition of the civil communities changed. The earlier ethnic groups continued their integration into the common civil community, moving out of the old ethnic neighborhoods and achieving spatial as well as social and political integration. Their places were taken by communities that were once excluded but that also have acquired a share in the local polity. Indeed, the second half of the postwar generation was dominated by the struggle of the immediately preceding wave of immigrants.

At the time of the first study, the black population of the Quad Cities was relatively small. During the 1960s it increased dramatically, particularly in Rock Island, which developed an expanded black neighborhood in its West End, traditionally the city's minority ethnic neighborhood. One result of this is that Rock Island's black population exceeded 10 percent by 1970, with the West End two-thirds black. Given the lack of effective mechanisms for resisting outside encroachment, the neighborhood was subject to exploitation by the city's real estate establishment. Redlining by housing mortgage institutions was a known factor throughout the period and no doubt persisted until the end of the generation. Zoning variances were granted with ease, eroding the neighborhood's residential character. The city fire department kept in practice by burning down houses there under controlled conditions. The only park in the neighborhood was used as a dump for debris from the construction of Illinois Highway 199, which passed through the area. An extensive program of condemnation and demolition of substandard houses did not involve any replacement, thereby reducing the available housing stock. The neighborhood public schools became increasingly segregated along racial lines. All of the foregoing contributed to the usual social pathologies.

Some of the worst of these problems were mitigated somewhat by the Model Cities program that functioned between 1968 and 1973. Unfortunately the program could not capitalize on an organized local leadership, since none existed, and programs initiated by the residents faltered. As a result, the city government's departments took over the program and provided whatever direction it had.

By the end of the generation Davenport and East Moline each had significant concentrations of blacks as well. Moline had a concentration of Mexican-Americans, and the older, established Mexican-American community continued to exist in the East Moline–Silvis area. Native Americans also migrated in significant numbers to the Quad Cities area during that period. They established a Quad City intertribal council with a cultural center in Rock Island and an annual Sauk–Fox powwow held at Black Rock State Park. The Mexican-American community continued to function through the GI Forum, which emphasized education and employment opportunities for its constituency. A bilingual educational program for Spanish-speaking children was introduced into the Moline school system.

Housing for minority groups remained a major problem in the Quad Cities. In Rock Island, local action groups such as Project Now and the Catholic Inter-Racial Council worked for an effective fair housing ordinance, accompanied by proper enforcement mechanisms. Such an ordinance was adopted and a fair housing commission appointed, which improved matters somewhat, but the problem remained. The Rock Island Housing Authority did make one effort to disperse the concentration of blacks in one neighborhood by constructing a housing project on the East Side, but it was not done with proper care or sufficient facilities for families with large children, and the project only exacerbated tensions while failing to provide much improvement for the people who moved into the units.

A similar effort by the Prince Hall Masons and Order of Eastern Star Village, Incorporated, which led to the construction of 150 low-cost apartment units along the Rock River in southwestern Rock Island in the late 1960s, also was less than successful. Poor maintenance and poor relations between the sponsoring group and the tenants led to serious troubles in the mid-1970s, so much so that the United States Department of Housing and Urban Development, which had guaranteed the loan for the project's construction, threatened to foreclose in 1977. This led to the appointment of the Moline Housing Authority as manager of the Rock Island project in December of that year, bringing an improvement in the situation. Nonwhite minorities in the Quad Cities were slower to initiate a struggle for their rights than those in most of the other cities of the prairie. Even as late as the inauguration of the Model Cities program, there was little in the way of an organized black community. The National Association for the Advancement of Colored People had a very small membership; there was no chapter of the Urban League in the area. Militant groups were almost unknown. Perhaps the closest the city came to violence in this period was interracial conflict in Rock

Island High School in the 1970s, which abated after programs were introduced to combat it or perhaps because of the general decline in black militancy throughout the United States. The churches remained the major organizational framework for blacks, and they tended to abstain from participation in local politics; hence the Quad Cities remained somewhat anomalous, since they were bypassed by the civil rights movement of the 1960s. On the other hand, the cities did adjust to the changing circumstances with a minimum of militancy, though the existing white establishment kept control over the pace of events.[15]

The migration of blacks to the North essentially stopped in the latter half of the postwar generation. Countrywide, a reverse migration of modest proportions began. The South became a more open society and one of the focal points of Sun Belt development, drawing back some of its native sons and daughters who had left to seek opportunity elsewhere.

The black populations of the cities of the prairie continued to increase in most places, but not nearly in the proportions of the first half of the generation (table 3.2). Peoria's black population continued to grow after 1970 at a rate exceeding that of any other of the cities of the prairie, including East St. Louis. In 1970–80 there was an almost 50 percent increase in the number of blacks in the city of Peoria, making it second only to East St. Louis in total black population.

It may well be that a kind of demographic homeostasis has been reached within most of the cities of the prairie, even with regard to the place of blacks within their respective civil communities. The assumption is that the black role will grow but in an evolutionary way. The one exception to this may well be in Madison and St. Clair counties, where the tangle of municipalities within the common metropolitan area, coupled with a modest continuing influx of blacks, has established a moving line of black/white confrontation that is likely to continue to exist.

On the other hand, Brooklyn, one of the cities within the Madison–St. Clair counties region, has remained all black. One of the historic black enclaves within America's major metropolitan areas that developed in the late nineteenth to early twentieth century, Brooklyn's primary development took place before 1950. Its maximum population has always hovered around 2,500. It remained a backwater in the wake of the great postwar black migration. Nevertheless, it has continued to develop as part of the general movement toward the suburbanization of blacks that began after 1960. Thus, 36.1 percent of its housing stock was built between 1960 and 1970 — a sign of its continued development or redevelopment. Unfortunately, it has been limited by a location that does not give it room to expand.[16]

A very different situation prevails with regard to the Hispanic popu-

Table 3.2. Cities of the Prairie: Black Population, 1950–80

Civil Community	1950	1960	1970	1980
Champaign County	4,553	6,770	10,635	14,661
Champaign	3,118	4,520	5,310	7,557
Urbana	699	1,253	499	350
Douglas County	53	31	89	114
Superior	44	21	36	—[a]
Macon County	3,438	5,949	9,849	13,785
Decatur	3,438	5,949	9,841	14,112
Madison County	9,532	11,933	12,945	14,236
Alton	3,842	4,944	6,403	7,176
Granite City	12	55	—	—
Peoria County	6,276	10,157	14,806	21,528
Peoria	5,646	9,584	14,712	20,717
Pueblo County	1,714	2,026	2,070	2,254
Pueblo	1,441	2,026	1,954	2,034
Rock Island County	2,426	4,290	7,303	9,811
Moline	42	338	455	457
Rock Island	156	2,754	5,038	7,055
St. Clair County	34,566		63,408	73,651
Belleville	196	195	261	752
East St. Louis	27,555	36,338	48,308	52,751
St. Louis County	383	624	1,051	961
Duluth	334	565	1,024	928
Sangamon County	4,479	5,923	7,841	11,400
Springfield	4,285	5,632	7,651	10,960
Scott County	1,150	1,886	4,179	6,620
Davenport	1,120	1,778	4,099	6,296
Tazewell County	38	14	—	208
Pekin	0	3	0	—
Will County	5,886	11,915	16,970	31,480
Joliet	1,950	4,638	9,459	15,591
Winnebago County	3,882	8,574	15,842	21,042
Rockford	2,499	5,323	15,169	18,163

Source: 1950 and 1960 figures, Daniel J. Elazar, *Cities of the Prairie: The Metropolitan Frontier and American Politics* (New York: Basic Books, 1970), pp. 182–83; 1970 figures, U.S. Bureau of the Census, *General Social and Economic Characteristics,* Illinois, Minnesota, Iowa, Wisconsin, and Colorado (Washington, D.C.: Government Printing Office, 1970); 1980 figures, U.S. Bureau of the Census, *County and City Data Book, 1983* (Washington, D.C.: Government Printing Office, 1983).

[a]Dash means blacks constituted less than 0.5 percent of the population.

lation. One of the dimensions of the "westernization" of the cities of the prairie and the United States as a whole was the growth of a Spanish-speaking minority of Mexican origin. Indeed, at the time of the writing of *Cities of the Prairie* such minorities were to be found mostly in the cities along the Mississippi or west of it. Since then there has been a steady migration of Mexicans eastward so that today most of the other cities of the prairie have Hispanic populations as well, and growing ones at that (table 3.3). The implications of this new migration are not likely to be felt until sometime during the new generation.

With all of this there remain significant continuities that reflect the cultural patterns established earlier. Take, for example, relative educational achievement. While the median school years completed and the percentage completing high school have risen in all the cities of the prairie, even East St. Louis (table 3.4), nevertheless, with minor exceptions, the ranking of the cities remains as it was in 1960. Urbana and Champaign, with their large university population, expectedly lead the pack. They are followed by the cities dominated by the moralistic culture. In the middle are the civil communities dominated by the individualistic culture, and the traditionalistic ones bring up the rear.

Looking at some of the anomalies in the table, Springfield as state capital remains slightly higher in rank than its cultural position would predict. Pueblo and Peoria have moved up to the top of the individualistic grouping, in both cases reflecting the relative decline of traditionalistic elements in their populations. Alton, on the other hand, has dropped to near the bottom, reflecting the increase in such elements through in-migration. Rockford is the only real anomaly in the table, probably because of its still relatively large foreign-born/foreign-stock population, and it has moved up closer to its expected position.

The Political Cultural Patterns Maintained

The continued mapping of all of these patterns was one of the principal tasks of our study. Since the original study's presentation of what has become known as the Elazar political cultural typology was the outgrowth of comprehensive empirical study, we were interested in searching out any political cultural changes that may have occurred in the second half of the postwar generation.[17] In fact we found no significant ones simply because population change in cities of the prairie was very moderate and generally followed earlier migrational patterns. Even the population shifts that did take place occurred within the context of existing political cultural patterns.

Table 3.3. Cities of the Prairie: Hispanic Population, 1970–80

Civil Community	1970	1980
Champaign County	2,060	2,404
Champaign	468	581
Urbana	*[a]	720
Douglas County	—[b]	*
Superior	*	—
Macon County	859	745
Decatur	814	941
Madison County	2,193	2,495
Alton	*	*
Granite City	*	774
Peoria County	1,829	2,472
Peoria	1,143	1,726
Pueblo County	37,088	41,631
Pueblo	31,493	35,590
Rock Island County	4,642	7,209
Moline	1,988	2,286
Rock Island	702	1,411
St. Clair County	3,847	3,391
Belleville	565	*
East St. Louis	632	518
St. Louis County	696	775
Duluth	*	—
Sangamon County	720	1,008
Springfield	459	996
Scott County	2,267	3,553
Davenport	1,969	2,859
Tazewell County	532	808
Pekin	*	*
Will County	7,312	13,778
Joliet	3,252	6,237
Winnebago County	3,169	5,399
Rockford	2,211	4,486

Source: U.S. Bureau of the Census, *County and City Data Book, 1977, 1983* (Washington, D.C.: Government Printing Office, 1977, 1983).

[a]Asterisk indicates data not shown where population is under 400.

[b]Dash means Hispanics constituted less than 0.5 percent of the population.

Table 3.4. Cities of the Prairie: Relative Educational Achievement, 1960 and 1970

City	Median School Years Completed		Percentage Twenty-Five Years or Older with Less Than Five Years Schooling	Percentage that Completed High School or More	
	1970	1960	(1970)	1970	1960
Urbana	13.7	12.8	1.6	76.1	66.7
Champaign	12.8	12.4	2.1	72.7	60.3
Duluth	12.3	11.5	2.5	58.9	46.5
Davenport	12.2	11.4	1.9	55.7	45.4
Moline	12.2	11.4	2.1	59.1	46.4
Rock Island	12.2	11.4	2.6	55.6	45.7
Springfield	12.2	11.1	3.3	57.0	44.3
Superior	12.2	11.3	2.5	58.3	45.3
Peoria	12.2	10.5	2.9	55.6	40.0
Decatur	12.1	11.1	2.7	52.9	43.7
Pueblo	12.1	10.6	6.2	52.0	40.8
Rockford	12.1	11.0	3.9	53.2	43.1
Joliet	12.0	10.9	4.1	49.7	42.1
Belleville	11.6	9.8	3.3	47.2	34.6
Alton	11.4	10.2	5.1	45.8	38.7
East St. Louis	9.4	8.7	11.6	29.4	23.2

Sources: 1970 figures, U.S. Bureau of the Census, *General Social and Economic Characteristics, 1970*—Illinois, Iowa, Minnesota, Wisconsin, and Colorado; U.S. Bureau of the Census, *County and City Data Book, 1977;* 1960 figures, Daniel J. Elazar, *Cities of the Prairie: The Metropolitan Frontier and American Politics* (New York: Basic, Books, 1970), p. 273.

Thus, for example, East St. Louis, long a rather venal synthesis of the individualistic and traditionalist subcultures, became even more so as a result of population change. East St. Louis politics underwent a certain kind of transformation toward the end of the postwar generation. Mayor Alvin G. Fields, the dominant figure in city politics from 1951 to 1971, whose Irish-dominated machine controlled city and to some extent county politics as well during those years, was replaced by a reform administration headed by James E. Williams, Sr., who was in turn replaced in 1975 by William E. Mason, the politicians' choice. Fields died that same year, leaving the city's political organization up for grabs at the generation's end.

The demise of the Fields machine ended a dynasty that had controlled

East St. Louis since shortly after World War I—that is, through the interwar and postwar generations. The blacks did not even begin to challenge this machine until the middle of the postwar generation, and it was not until 1967 that the Fields ticket, which included one black, was opposed by an all-black slate, even though whites by then constituted no more than one-third of the population. The extent of Fields's control can be seen by the fact that even in the face of that challenge his group secured 75 percent of the vote. By the end of the 1960s, however, the situation was changing. Not only was the percentage of blacks growing, but the middle class in the city was entirely black. The latter group had an interest in fostering some kind of improvement and was minimally dependent on the machine.

The fall of the Fields organization between 1967 and 1971 reflected the middle-class blacks' efforts but, more important, resulted from the intervention of bankers concerned about the city's deepening fiscal crisis. By the early 1960s it had become apparent to the bankers that the city, long on the edge of bankruptcy, was allowing the Fields machine to skim off too much money. They forced Fields to hire a professional administrator in 1963 to bring some level of managerial efficiency to city hall. The administrator, himself a former city manager, actively pursued federal and state programs, bringing in new revenues that satisfied the bankers without seriously interfering with the machine's prerogatives.

The programs themselves, however, began to transform the face of the city. A new class of professional planners and administrators was introduced into city affairs to manage the model city's urban renewal and antipoverty programs. Thus federal and to a lesser extent state involvement led to the creation of a local cadre of people interested in some measure of reform, at least to advance the civil rights and participation of the black population. Since the funds they had available were not controlled by the machine politicians yet soon came to compose the bulk of the city budget, the machine was further weakened.

When all of this was combined with the new surge of investigations, indictments, and even convictions for illegal activities, Fields and his colleagues realized that their end was near. In 1971 all but one of them decided against running for reelection. Only the black incumbent, Calvert, himself a representative of the machine, stayed in the arena to run for mayor. In the ensuing primary he and another black emerged as the runoff candidates, ensuring that East St. Louis would have a black mayor for the first time.

Calvert was not a continuation of the Fields regime, since he and the outgoing mayor had been strong opponents, but he was a machine politician, and the time had come for a reform victory. James E. Williams, Sr., the reform candidate and executive director of the local Legal Aid Society, upset Calvert in the runoff election. He was a reformer through and through, entirely dissociated from the machine and from the local political establishment. His major backing came from the reform elements in the community and others interested in getting rid of the machine, including the governor of Illinois, a Republican who promised additional state facilities in East St. Louis if Williams were elected. Williams succeeded in carrying two other candidates into office with him, both young men, one white and one black. The other two commissioners, also one white and one black, were from the old machine and had been on Calvert's slate.

Unfortunately Williams, like many reformers, lacked Fields's political experience and skills. Hence, after an initial honeymoon he lost power to the other commissioners, who functioned in the manner of the old-style politicians. Unable to serve as a broker between factions, Williams was essentially paralyzed, and the governance of the city was immobilized. As a consequence, the reform movement initiated a referendum to change the city's governmental structure from the commission to the aldermanic form. The change was voted in November 1972, with wide public support, to take effect after the 1975 municipal elections. Under the new system, the city was divided into nine wards, with two aldermen to be elected from each, and the mayor, city treasurer, and city clerk were to be elected citywide. Partisan elections were introduced to replace the nonpartisan system that enabled the machine to dominate both the Democratic and the Republican parties locally.

Mayor Williams ran for reelection in 1975 as an independent to avoid having to make deals with either of the political parties. The two commissioners who had been aligned with him in the 1971 elections joined his opponent, William E. Mason, superintendent of the East St. Louis school system, a popular politician who, because of his Ph.D. in education, also seemed to be one of the new breed of black leaders. Mason inherited what remained of the Fields organization and had strong party support. Williams was supported by the media but had no organization, and the other two candidates on his ticket were relative unknowns. Even so, he lost by only 800 votes out of 12,000 cast.[18]

Despite his efforts to improve the city's image, Mayor Mason practiced the old politics. Within a year he was being accused of supporting members of his administration who had been convicted of bribery, violation of the gambling laws, official misconduct, extortion and racketeering, nepotism, mismanagement, and misappropriation of federal funds—the usual pattern for East St. Louis politicians. Administration of the federal Comprehensive Employment and Training Act (CETA) was transferred from the city to the county as a result of mishandling, but Mason supported his people and even raised their salaries.

In the wake of the 1977 elections there were charges of large-scale voting fraud. The St. Clair County state's attorney estimated that 10 percent of the votes cast were questionable. A number of election judges were found guilty of misconduct, and in 1978 a new board of commissioners was appointed by the circuit court. A door-to-door canvass of East St. Louis voters revealed that 25 percent of those registered had to be stricken from the voting lists. As a result of this, by the end of the generation Mason himself was being challenged. He was defeated in the 1979 mayoralty elections by a twenty-seven-year-old state official from a respected East St. Louis family who had returned home to try to refurbish the reform movement.

In East St. Louis all local governments are of the same mold. Between 1975 and 1977, board members and key employees of School District 189 were convicted of bribery and extortion, marking the fourth or fifth generation in which such convictions had been obtained in connection with the district. The school district had a $4 million deficit at the time and had been subject to five teacher strikes over the previous decade. So pervasive was the corruption in the school district that among those convicted in 1975 was a former nun who was a school board member and her new husband who had been a security guard in the district. In sum, while locals may argue whether things are better or worse, the change is that now there is more attention paid to the extreme manifestations of venality (assassination attempts, for example) than there used to be. This in turn has to do more with the changing federal and state roles in searching out local corruption than with changing local expectations.

Rockford has been able to preserve a local political culture that is very different from the statewide synthesis in connection with its local politics, but only by maintaining the buffer zone between state and local political affairs that it had created earlier, utilizing municipal, town, and special district governments as the repositories and expressions of the local culture. Rockford has preserved its moralistic political subculture locally through Rockford Township and the governments within it, while utilizing Winnebago County as a buffer zone that mixes both local moralistic elements and the individualistic elements of the statewide synthesis. Nevertheless, the statewide synthesis not only is very real but has a tendency to be pervasive, to permeate all aspects of state political life, unless appropriate institutional barriers have been erected to limit its spread in certain places. In chapter 4 we will see how it has even begun to break Rockford's barriers.

One of the by-products of the strong moralistic political culture in Rockford was the emergence of a strong John Birch Society chapter in the 1960s, a phenomenon generally rare in the cities of the prairie. Duluth, which is equally moralistic, would not be prone to such an occurrence, while the individualistic civil communities do not take ideology seriously enough to encourage such forms of expression. Perhaps because of its location in Illinois, which brought it central as well as northern European migration, Rockford has an extremist element in its population.

The climax of John Birch activity in Rockford came in the chapter's full-scale attack on the public school system in 1969 for being too liberal and permissive. They succeeded in forcing the resignation of the superintendent of schools (who was almost immediately appointed to head the school system in San Francisco). The attack foundered in the society's follow-up, an assault on one of the city's most respected teachers, and the organization was never the same afterward.

The argument has been made that political cultural change was initiated in Urbana when a reform group, drawing heavily from the university community, gained control of the city government.[19] However, there is no evidence that the desire for a more activist city government, more responsive to groups than those comprising the business community, is a sign of cultural differences, since most of the activists seem to be from regions in which the same individualistic political culture is dominant. The change is more than a result of the assertiveness of interest groups with newfound strength in the community, who also reflect a generational difference in style and expectations.

It can be said, however, that the development of a politics of demonstrations, principally in Champaign and Urbana, does mark a change in political style, though it seems to have been a relatively transient one. Demonstrations as a means of political expression began at the University of Illinois in the early 1960s with protests by a peripheral group against the Reserve Officers Training Corps program on the university campus and more serious protests against racial discrimination in downtown Champaign. Such protests escalated during the course of the civil rights revolution and the anti–Vietnam War campaign in the late 1960s but had virtually disappeared by the mid-1970s. Demonstrations did become legitimized during that period, something that was clearly not the case before 1968, and they still do occur, not only in Champaign–Urbana. But they have once again become relatively peripheral to the political process, even if no longer treated as illegitimate.

In fact, despite general upheaval among Americans in the 1960s, which at least peripherally affected the cities of the prairie, the cities seem to have avoided most of the changes in political style that were spreading around the country at that time. None of our case studies suggest any significant changes in political style on the part of those who became active in a continuous way during the period.

Issues in the Study of Political Culture

The issues that stand before us at this juncture are those of refinement, of more systematic study, and of dealing with methodological problems that have arisen. The past decade or so has brought attempts to operationalize certain basic concepts or theories of political culture, attempts that have taken a variety of forms, some meeting with greater success and some with less.[20] Two kinds of problems are particularly important in this context. One is interpretation. How does one interpret data in a way that elucidates the systematic exploration of political culture? The second is a problem of measurement. The design of instruments has reflected, it seems to me, questions of interpretation.

For one thing, there has been the perhaps natural attempt to take the political cultural theories this study has proposed and place them on a continuum, applying techniques of measurement that have been used most effectively in political science in many ways in the past two decades. The very success of the technique leads to the attempt to use it for almost any phenomenon. Sometimes this is easily enough done; at other times it is problematic. While most of the studies using a continuum have produced better results than expected, they still are deficient. One of the theoretical products of the resurvey was an improved model for conceptualizing the three political subcultures for statistical analysis.

Graphically, a more accurate model is three-sided, as portrayed in figure 3.1. By using a triangular model, it is possible to measure multiple interrelationships and the intersections between subcultures—to identify "fields" (in the physical sense), indicate where they overlap, and distinguish between pure types and modifications in more than one direction. This kind of model also makes it possible to do some of the work toward bridging the gap between the two schools, because it offers the possibility of interjecting a variety of cultural orientations without having to change the model itself. Although such a model requires more sophisticated statistical techniques than the simple continuum, such techniques are readily available. This question of refinement and systematic study, of interpretation and measurement, deserves serious attention from those who use political culture measures.

A second question deserving attention is what issues ought to be studied or can profitably be studied, utilizing political cultural models or dimensions. One of the problems in operationalization is the very difficult one of grappling with the fact that different people do the same things for different reasons. The original study discussed examples of this with regard to the adoption of the council-manager plan and nonpartisan elections in the local arena, suggesting that in individualistic settings they represented an effort to take politics out of government, whereas in moralistic ones they represented an effort to make local politics more effective by separating local elections from the state and national political parties.[21] There are many other actions that if measured as outputs would seem to negate the differences between political subcultures but that when examined more thoroughly reflect different policy choices and intentions.

At any given time and place there are relatively few policy or program options available. Thus the policy choices of different groups are likely to resemble each other on the formal level more often than not. Developing ways to understand the different reasons people do what are apparently the same things is a key to the systematic study of political culture. This probably makes impossible the kinds of simple correlations that have frequently been used to study the role of political culture in such matters. This is not to deny that many things can be correlated in relatively simple fashion, but in many cases where simple correlations have been used they do not tell us very much. Worse, they may lead us into error in that they may suggest a weak result when deeper explanatory dimensions could be tapped if another level of analysis were added.

A second problem is that not enough attention has been paid to certain other sources of data—for example, the study of political rhetoric, which, though it has not been a particularly popular branch of political science for many years, is of great use for understanding a political culture and its subcultural nuances. The political cultural study of political rhetoric would be somewhat different from any of the traditional ways such rhetoric has been studied, since it would look for orientations to political action rather than direct ideological expression.

One of the earliest studies of political rhetoric undertaken at the Center for the Study of Federalism compared the New Deal rhetoric of three United States senators coming from states representative of the three archetypal subcultural models—they included Senator Cummings of Iowa—and all considered progressives with regard to New Deal legislation.[22] We examined the records of the Senate to determine how the senators justified their positions in support of this legislation in the debates. We found clear differences between them, reflecting their different subcultural orientations. The senator from the traditionalistic subculture kept saying that the measures would restore the great American tradition; the senator from the individualistic political subculture invariably said they would help guarantee that the marketplace would continue to function; and the moralistic senator said the measures would bring America closer to fulfilling its ideals.

Several years later we analyzed the reporting and commentary on Watergate and once again found that political subculture made a difference.

When the scandal broke, traditionalistic people generally were reluctant to doubt the president because of his standing as an authoritative figure and their willingness to accept his right to act. But in the end most turned on Nixon for breaking the traditional rules of the political game. Individualistic types generally took the position that, though Nixon's dirty tricks were not that original, he deserved to be punished for being dumb enough to get caught. The moralistic ones reacted most strongly against the president from the first, rejecting the notion that any public official could be allowed to do such things. This picture could be obtained simply by reading newspaper interviews with the "man in the street" throughout the Watergate years.

Similarly, whatever its other problems, the present presidential primary system offers a good way to test political subcultural responses to candidates, something that was absent under the previous system of selecting presidential nominees. The self-selection of primary candidates generally ensures the involvement of products of the various political subcultures in their various manifestations, at least in the early stages of the presidential race. Hence the state-by-state primary results frequently reveal subcultural dispositions. At the same time, the number of candidates can be used as a control to distinguish between political culture and other elements influencing voting patterns. Once the two major-party candidates are chosen for the general elections, other factors come into play and, except on rare occasions, reduce the influence of political culture to a very minor one.[23]

In the 1980 primaries, for example, it is notable that John Anderson, from archetypally moralistic Rockford, scored best in the moralistic states or among moralistic populations in mixed states. Teddy Kennedy, like his brothers, scored best in individualistic states or among individualistic populations in mixed ones. John Connelly's clearly traditionalistic style and Texas markings served him poorly outside the South. (While it was suggested that other factors, such as the prior strength of Ronald Reagan, affected him even on what was presumed to be his home ground in the South, the general cultural differences between Texas and other southern states like South Carolina no doubt had an impact.)

Political subcultural differences were first noticeable in the 1968 Democratic presidential primaries when Eugene McCarthy, from moralistic Minnesota, faced Robert Kennedy, who had found his political base in individualistic New York. Both candidates gained supporters on the basis of their opposition to incumbent President Lyndon B. Johnson and "his" Vietnam War. But the appeal of each was clearly to a different political subculture, as the results of the primaries revealed. McCarthy did extremely well in the moralistic states and Kennedy in the individualistic ones. In the mixed states the results were extremely close, and only then were other factors sometimes decisive.

In the 1976 primary elections, Morris Udall of Arizona captured the lion's share of the moralistic vote in the Democratic primaries as John Anderson did among Republicans in 1980. While Jimmy Carter managed to do better than any other Democratic candidate in the primaries, a curious point about him, which may tell us something about where the American people are going, is that he was able to project the image of a man who had no clear-cut class or cultural identification. It is not that he represented the section whose label he bore. He was—and is—almost indistinguishable, almost unidentifiable culturally on the overt level. Table 3.5 represents the results of those primary elections in the counties of the cities of the prairie.

Another set of issues that should help in the refinement and systematic study of political culture has to do with the relation between political culture and one-issue politics. For example, there is a shift among those groups and in those areas noted for their moralistic orientation, from a moralistic stance against certain kinds of behavior to an equally fervid moralistic endorsement of the freedom to engage in such behavior. If abortion was considered immoral forty, or even twenty, years ago, today those moralistic people who support the right to freely choose abortion tend to view anybody who favors limitations on abortion as, in a sense, rejecting the true faith. Recognition of homosexual rights presents the same kind of fervid response. While the cities of the prairie were less disturbed by these issues than some of the larger metropolitan areas or sister cities along the east and west coasts, still we found considerable evidence of this process.

Table 3.5. Presidential Primary Results in the Counties of the Cities of the Prairie, 1968–80

	1968 Preference[a]			
	Democratic			
County	Johnson	Humphrey	Kennedy	McCarthy
Champaign	3	23	12	172
Macon	1	14	3	19
Madison	5	50	28	136
Peoria	22	207	58	182
Rock Island	—	—	—	—
Sangamon	13	173	117	203
St. Clair	—	—	—	—
Will	—	—	—	—
Winnebago	3	31	21	77
Douglas	4,213	114	471	5,269

Table 3.5. Continued.

County	1968 Preference Republican: Nixon	Reagan	Rockefeller
Champaign	191	31	91
Macon	58	8	18
Madison	199	19	40
Peoria	1,571	253	335
Rock Island	–	–	–
Sangamon	2,064	131	266
St. Clair	–	–	–
Will	–	–	–
Winnebago	1,160	115	90
Douglas	3,329	369	85

	1972 Preference Democratic: McCarthy	Muskie	McGovern[b]	Humphrey[b]	Wallace[b]
Champaign	7,697	6,633	315	100	307
Macon	3,631	5,895	39	69	112
Madison	7,491	16,689	–	–	–
Peoria	4,855	11,598	574	228	699
Rock Island	3,676	7,403	–	–	–
Sangamon	4,929	13,411	61	35	129
St. Clair	8,603	14,975	–	–	–
Will	5,389	10,124	120	55	451
Winnebago	6,649	12,190	97	71	170
Douglas	132	1,654	2,139	4,509	2,254

	Republican: Nixon[b]	McCloskey[b]
Champaign	48	2
Macon	23	1
Madison	–	–
Peoria	610	–
Rock Island	–	–
Sangamon	42	3
St. Clair	–	–

Table 3.5. Continued.

	Republican	
	Nixon[b]	McCloskey[b]
Will	82	2
Winnebago	23	–
Douglas	1,958	66

	1976 Preference				
	Democratic			Republican	
	Wallace	Carter	Udall	Reagan	Ford
Champaign	1,908	7,369	–	5,598	9,362
Macon	3,137	8,492	–	3,919	5,025
Madison	14,764	14,103	–	3,958	4,461
Peoria	5,536	10,291	–	7,861	12,447
Rock Island	4,357	9,106	–	3,846	5,381
Sangamon	6,878	13,890	–	5,908	11,136
St. Clair	10,715	13,331	–	4,179	5,278
Will	8,074	11,300	–	8,976	9,851
Winnebago	7,154	13,494	–	8,976	9,851
Douglas	1,166	2,295	4,934	1,639	2,454

	1980 Preference				
	Democratic			Republican	
	Carter	Kennedy	Anderson	Bush	Reagan
Champaign	4,623	2,230	9,888	3,384	9,228
Macon	6,487	2,685	2,728	2,774	7,484
Madison	16,620	7,817	2,896	1,177	10,257
Peoria	9,978	3,486	7,953	4,839	15,564
Rock Island	9,247	3,486	4,592	2,552	6,640
Sangamon	12,375	6,087	5,850	4,915	14,152
St. Clair	17,116	9,223	2,576	1,498	9,520
Will	11,607	5,878	8,154	3,469	15,235
Winnebago	11,607	5,878	8,154	3,469	15,235
Douglas	3,209	2,315	2,441	1,304	2,124

[a]In 1968, in Illinois, only write-in votes were recorded to express presidential preference. Colorado, Iowa, and Minnesota do not have presidential primaries.
[b]Write-in candidates on the Illinois ballot.

This kind of 180-degree turn in terms of the definition of rights and wrongs should not obscure the effect of cultural predispositions on the way a particular stance is held and expressed. Attitudes change as styles change; what remains is the moralistic fervor with which a particular attitude is embraced. In examining the three subcultural dimensions, it is necessary to distinguish clearly between the prevalent position on an issue and the way the issue is embraced. On the other hand, there is also the problem of real cultural change. I have already suggested that it is possible to have general cultural change without political cultural change and vice versa. The one-issue questions may be good ones for clarifying this distinction.

A third issue is the differential effect of new campaign techniques. We may ask whether what has worked in California, in its kind of mass society, will work in Minnesota and Wisconsin, or even in the large eastern states. There is some evidence that they will not work in the cities of the prairie, where campaign styles remained much what they were in the 1950s. Duluth's politics continued to rest on "amateurs," and in East St. Louis, as has been indicated, politics continued to be the preserve of "professionals" in the worst sense of the term. Although Rockford introduced national party labels into local elections in the late 1960s (see chap. 4), the kind of people attracted to local politics in that civil community remained the same, as did its campaign style. So too with the other civil communities, each in its own way. Even Champaign and Urbana maintained their differences, assimilating the new elements that got involved in local politics to the older patterns as the price of success. Thus reformers from individualistic backgrounds did better in local politics than those from moralistic backgrounds.

On another level, one of the postulates of a great deal of our work has been that there is a close relation between religion, ethnicity, and political culture. We are now in a period of heightened religious consciousness for large numbers of people in the world—not only Americans—that has both traditional and new dimensions and real political impact. The original study made the point that Protestant fundamentalists in the civil communities studied generally remained aloof from politics—including local politics—representing as they did an apolitical millennialist strand in American society. In the 1970s this began to change on the national scene. The changes that began to occur came too late to be visible in this study. Nor it is entirely clear that fundamentalists have become as involved in local politics as in national affairs, but the trend is an important one that we hope to address in the third round.

These developments may well include some dimensions of political as well as religious change. Now this may be change within a framework that is as old as humanity, but for the moment it involves the creation of new religious groups and new sets of values that are attached to religious groups. As in the past, new religions have become exponents of new cultural packages—value packages—while revived religious ties involve a restoration of older values, previously abandoned. This gives us an opportunity to examine what some of us have suggested is extremely important; namely, the role of religion as a primary force in inducing cultural—including political cultural—change.

4. Continuing the Generational Rhythm

Although generations do not begin and end like stage plays with the curtain going up and down, often there are decisive events that mark the crossing of a generational boundary. In that light it is possible to view the years 1976–77 as marking the end of the postwar generation and the beginning of a new one.[1] The postwar generation had opened some thirty years earlier, between 1946 and 1949, with the consolidation and reorganization of the surviving New Deal programs and the shifting of American policy from a reluctant and minimal involvement in world affairs to full-scale interventionism. In addition, those years also saw the enactment of the federal legislation that laid the groundwork for defining and meeting the issues of the new generation. Throughout the 1950s that agenda was clarified, and devices for meeting it were developed. In the sphere of intergovernmental relations alone, the Eisenhower years were years of transformation from the practice of enacting a few broad-based federal grant-in-aid programs, established at the beginning of the previous generation and reaching its apogee during the New Deal, to one of many narrowly based programs designed to respond to smaller constituencies. This new pattern was to become the most pronounced aspect of the federal grant system during the postwar generation, and it provoked a strong negative response.[2]

During the 1950s the country passed through the cycle of critical elections that set its political direction for the rest of the generation. Dwight D. Eisenhower's 1952 presidential victory was a personal triumph that left the majority Democratic coalition intact. In 1956, however, he carried traditional Democratic strongholds and seriously weakened the Democratic party. John F. Kennedy managed to reintegrate the Democratic majority coalition with his victory in 1960, and Lyndon Johnson consolidated it in his 1964 landslide.

Johnson's "Great Society" represented the culmination of the domestic response to the postwar generation, just as his Vietnam venture represented the climax of America's foreign interventionism. Both led to reactions in the last decade of the generation that involved both the consolidation of the new realities and retrenchment and redirection.

The generation's culminating events began in 1973 with the Arab oil embargo and the Watergate scandal. The first ended the economic basis of America's postwar prosperity and completed the shift in the power position of the United States begun as a result of the Vietnam War. The second cast into disrepute the "imperial presidency" that had emerged in the course of the postwar generation. Richard Nixon's resignation and Gerald Ford's successful if apparently bumbling efforts at restoring national harmony brought the generation to a close.

Jimmy Carter's presidential victory in 1976 represented the first step into a new generation. Carter was the outsider, antiestablishment and anti-Washington, apparently facing up to the new problems of energy infrastructure that would be the focal problem of the national government in the new generation. Although he was able to accomplish little else, he did initiate the federal government retrenchment that was to become the major feature of his successor's administration.

Carter's own weaknesses prevented him from giving the generation a good start and paved the way for the election of Ronald Reagan, another champion of the outsiders, albeit one who on the surface was out of tune with the generational change. Reagan had been born at the very close of the historical era of the nineteenth century and had come of age before World War II. While there is much in his administration that seems to be a last hurrah for that America, he is also the spearhead of a dedicated group of young conservatives who belong to the new generation now moving into positions of power. Thus Americans are just at the beginning of the process of defining the new agenda and determining how it will be dealt with.

In the interim, the cities of the prairie have coped with the generational rhythm, each in its own way in light of its geohistorical location. We have already reviewed some of their responses to the frontier changes. In the following pages we will look at their responses to directly constitutional and political matters.

Changes in Constitutional Design

One of the most prominent features of American constitutionalism is the idea that constitutions are designed by the people they serve, who exercise a special kind of political decision making in the process—what Vincent Ostrom and others have referred to as constitutional choice.[3] The exercise of constitutional choice has been one of the constant elements in the political life of the cities of the prairie, on the formal plane through the adoption or alteration of municipal charters or their equivalent, or the modification of charter provisions, and less formally through a variety of planning and programming devices.

When local constitution making takes the form of adopting or changing city and county charters, it is most easily visible. However, even where formal charters are not part of the local constitutional framework, there are constitutional acts that can be recognized as such. Charles M. Haar has written extensively on the adoption of a city plan as a constitutional act.[4] In the Cities of the Prairie study we have always taken a broad view of constitution making because the subject brings us back to the essence of the political. However much extrapolitical forces may influence particular constitution-making situations or constitutional acts, ultimately both involve directly political expressions and political choices.

To be legitimate, constitution making requires consent. Constitutional legitimacy is not a commitment that can be coerced, even though people can be forced to obey a particular regime if the rulers possess sufficient power. Consensual legitimacy is utterly necessary if a constitution is to have real meaning and to last. The very fact that while rule can be imposed by force, constitutions can exist as meaningful instruments only by consent demonstrates that constitution making is the preeminent political act. In the cities of the prairie, as in American society as a whole, we have seen how the integration of the "two cities" and, finally, the excluded streams into the body politic became necessary at some point if the constitutional system was to retain its legitimacy. Indeed, this outcome was brought about because claims based upon fundamental constitutional principles were denied to significant segments of the population.

A constitution is also a political artifact. That is why making constitutions combines science and art. Crafting a constitution entails identifying basic principles of constitutional design and the technologies derived from them as well as the needs of a particular body politic. These must be matched by a group of skilled artisans.

Every constitution is first of all a frame of government, delineating the basic structure, institutions, and procedures of the polity. But properly understood, constitutions are not only frames but also "power maps," to use Ivo Duchacek's term; that is to say, they reflect the socioeconomic realities of the distribution of political power in the polities served.[5] A constitution that does not sufficiently reflect and accommodate socioeconomic power realities remains a dead letter.

Constitutions also have a third dimension in that they reflect, explicitly or implicitly, the moral principles underlying polities or regimes. Although the moral underpinnings of some constitutions may be confined to virtually unenforceable code words or phrases in the preamble or declaration of rights, they need not be written down at all to have a reality and power of their

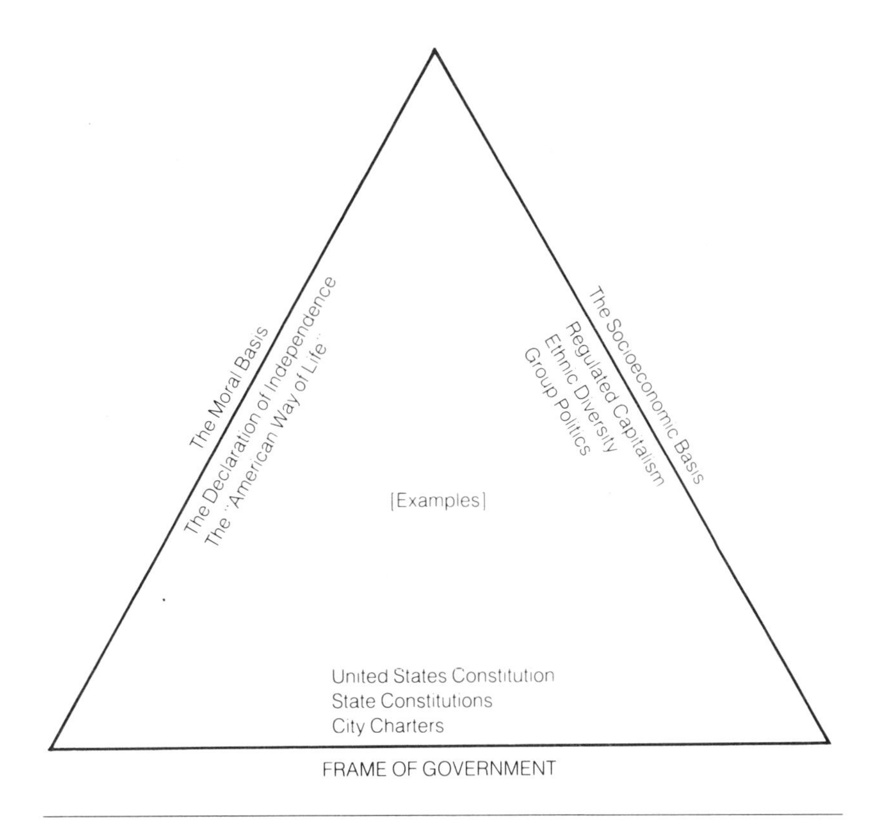

Fig. 4.1. The three dimensions of a constitution.

own that serves to limit, undergird, and direct ordinary political behavior. At the very least, they embrace the rules of the political game; often they express far more. In every case, the moral basis of the constitution is an expression of the political culture of the polity it serves.

These are, in fact, the three dimensions of constitutionalism recognized as such by Aristotle and by clear-minded students of the subject ever since.[6] They can be presented as forming a triangular relationship like that portrayed in figure 4.1.

In light of the foregoing model, constitutional change in the cities of the prairie can be seen as involving governmental structural change—that is to say, changes in the frame of government; changes in the socioeconomic basis of the polity; and changes in community norms and the rules of the game—in the moral basis of the polity.

The most visible constitutional changes in the cities of the prairie were formal changes in government structure that were introduced in the first half of the postwar generation as part of the adjustment of local government to the metropolitan frontier. At the same time, as emphasized in the original study, even farther-reaching changes occurred in connection with the socioeconomic distribution of power and the moral basis of the civil community through the merger of the "two cities." Continuing that thrust, constitutional changes in the latter half of the generation were of two kinds: structural changes designed to correct overzealous actions in the first half, and the integration of the excluded streams into the local bodies politic.[7]

In the case of the first, the reforms of the first half of the generation emphasized the councils elected entirely at large to break the control of "bosses" or "parochial interests" in city hall. This in turn virtually disfranchised the "locals" to the advantage of the "cosmopolitans," who had initiated the reforms in good faith but sooner or later came to realize the impact of their unanticipated consequences in this area.[8] Efforts to correct this situation led, in a number of the cities, to a change in the municipal charter to provide for a mixture of district and at-large elections so as to give locals as well as cosmopolitans a chance to gain municipal office.

Cosmopolitans regard the community as a total entity and maintain connections and involvements across all of it. While their cosmopolitanism is first defined in relation to a particular local community, after they develop a cosmopolitan outlook toward the local community they almost invariably also take a cosmopolitan view of the larger world of which that community is a part. Locals, on the other hand, are persons whose involvement and connections are confined to a small segment of the total community—a neighborhood, a particular social group, organization, or club—and do not extend to the community as a whole, except indirectly. Moreover, their perceptions of the larger world are also quite limited, based as they are on localistic involvements.

Everybody, it might be said, is either a cosmopolitan or a local. To a very real extent this is a natural social division. Yet all cosmopolitans have clearly localistic needs and seek more intimate ties than are afforded by connections to the community in the abstract or even to a set of institutions, which must inevitably be depersonalized to some degree. Moreover, locals can be mobilized for essentially cosmopolitan purposes when the purposes strike home. Thus every community needs institutions devoted to serving both cosmopolitan and local needs, plus the local needs of cosmopolitans and the cosmopolitan needs of locals.[9]

The struggle over the form of the city's government remained a dominant issue in Peoria throughout the generation. After council-manager government was instituted in 1953 as the centerpiece of the reform of Peoria politics, the issue was not stilled. The city's locals and their political leaders felt disfranchised by the change and initiated three subsequent attempts to restore the aldermanic system, on the grounds that the at-large character of council elections and the managerial thrust of city-manager government excluded them from a proper voice in city affairs. The cosmopolitans in turn consistently supported the council-manager system. The first attempt to return to aldermanic government was made in 1959 and failed by a three-to-two margin. The generation's final effort was made in 1973. In the end, a compromise was reached whereby city council elections continued to be nonpartisan, with five councilmen elected from single-member districts and three selected at large. Candidates may or may not specify their party affiliations. The Quad Cities, on the other hand, witnessed only the most modest change in the structure of their city government in the latter half of the postwar generation.

Decatur voters also challenged the council-manager system in a 1979 referendum, for the same reasons. Although the city manager was retained, a local person was appointed to fill the position, with the understanding that he would be more responsive to local mores. All told, however, Decatur retained one of the simplest frames of government of any of the cities of the prairie, in keeping with its rather straightforward socioeconomic distributions of power and interest in the political game.

Rock Island was the only one of the Quad Cities to have adopted council-manager government in the 1950s. As in every other case, the idea was supported by the cosmopolitans and opposed by the locals. In the latter half of the postwar generation, three attempts were made to change the council-manager system. The first referendum, held in April 1963, resulted in overwhelming approval for the system, with 62 percent of the electorate voting to retain it, a considerably larger proportion than voted for its adoption in 1952. The breakdown of the vote showed the cosmopolitans strongly in favor and the locals strongly against.

A second effort was initiated in 1971 by a coalition of the Rock Island County Taxpayers Association and Local 1309 of the United Auto Workers Union, both representatives of the locals. They argued that blacks, the poor, the elderly, and workers were underrepresented on the city council because of the at-large election system and that only the aldermanic form of government would provide proper representation for all groups in the city. They were opposed by an ad hoc group, Citizens for Council-Manager Government, composed of the cosmopolitan establishment. Once again, nearly two-thirds of the voters supported the existing system, and the referendum was defeated, with the polarization even more intense than in 1963.

Opponents of the council-manager system tried a more modest effort in 1975, seeking only to introduce district elections for the city council, while retaining the city manager. This too was defeated, since opponents of the change were able to present the idea of returning to district elections as a first step toward destroying the council-manager system itself. The incumbent city manager was popular and well respected, and a black had been elected to the city council and another to the school board, thereby weakening the argument that there was no representation for minorities. Again the vote was two to one for the existing system. In 1977 Rock Island took a further step toward managerial governance by making its city clerk and city treasurer appointive rather than elective positions.

Moline, on the other hand, considered a shift from its mayor-aldermanic government to the council-manager system in the 1960s, but that referendum was roundly defeated. In 1972 Moline established the office of city administrator within the framework of its mayor-aldermanic system. East Moline, which did adopt the council-manager system during that period, quickly abandoned it after a rather negative experience. In sum, by the end of the generation the status quo more or less prevailed in local government structure.

Springfield continued under its commission form of government. In the 1950s an effort was made to replace it with a strong mayoral system, but it too was defeated at the polls by the established political network, which remained in place at generation's end.

A major change took place in the counties of Illinois and Iowa as a result of the United States Supreme Court reapportionment decisions and the introduction of equal or scaled representation of townships on the county boards and apportionment strictly by population. In Illinois the new state constitution adopted in 1970 provided for equal apportionment by population in the counties. Thus every one of the civil communities in those states was subject to the same form of change, which made a real difference in that it enabled the cities to gain control of the county boards where they had not yet been able to do so. This meant that heretofore conservative county governments shifted toward a more positive view of government activity, reinforced by the availability of new federal and state aid, including general revenue sharing.

In some cases—Champaign County, for example—the change was seen locally as a veritable revolution, since the county board had been a particularly strong bastion of the old political conservatism and patronage politics.[10]

The Winnebago County Board was also reapportioned under the new requirements, ending a system of township representation that had existed since 1848. The new board had twenty-eight members, elected from districts based strictly on population. The immediate consequence of the change was to shift control of the board from the Republican to the Democratic party. In the first elections under the new system in 1972, twelve of the twenty-eight board members elected were Democrats. Two years later the Democrats won a majority, which they held for the rest of the decade.

In a parallel arena, the Rockford school district underwent a major constitutional change in 1969 when it was mandated by the state to absorb all the smaller school districts in the city. This transformed the district's politics by introducing a city/suburban split that became particularly acute in connection with the busing issue.[11]

Land-use planning was another constitutional concern widespread in the civil communities. In a nationwide survey conducted at the end of the postwar generation, the small and medium-sized cities of the north-central states, which include all the cities of the prairie but Pueblo, ranked land-use planning even higher than housing in their list of perceived planning needs. This is in all likelihood a reflection of the constitutional importance of land-use control and the fact that this remains perhaps the last bastion of relatively exclusive local powers in matters of constitutional import. In every other sphere of local government, state and federal intervention in setting or mandating standards has become the norm, while land use remains almost exclusively a local matter.

The constitutional dimension of land-use control should be clear. The determination of a community's land use is a major exercise in constitutional choice. Indeed, housing and economic development and water and sewage are either extensions of land-use planning or closely related to it. The latter is particularly important in most of the cities of the prairie because of their particular character as Grand Prairie oases, where drainage and sewage become keys to local development.[12] Our case studies reveal the realities of this dimension of local constitutional choice time after time.

Land use and housing rank either first or second in planning needs for all of the survey sample. However, in declining cities or those with minimal population growth, housing planning is ranked even more important than land-use planning, no doubt because the need to repair a deteriorating housing stock has become more important than redeveloping land per se, although in fact the two are effectively the same in such circumstances. In growing cities, land-use planning as such becomes more important because of the expansion taking place.

Similarly, economic development planning becomes most important for declining or barely growing cities and somewhat less important for those growing faster, where economic development is already bringing the population into flux. The faster-growing cities also were more concerned with planning for environmental protection and recreation than the others. All told, land planning was the first-priority planning need across the board, a fact confirmed by our case studies. In every case the constitutional dimension of planning should be clear.

Some constitutional changes are accomplished by less overt means. The key to strengthening the executive branch of Rockford City government was strengthening the office of mayor by giving the mayor fiscal control over municipal affairs. The effort took a decade, culminating in 1977 when the mayor was empowered to appoint a professional comptroller with the advice and consent of the city council, who would be responsible to him and would manage an integrated municipal financial structure. The comptroller was given a staff of five accountants and fourteen technicians. The mayor became responsible for preparing the city's operating and capital budgets by establishing policy guidelines for the department heads, who submit their budget requests to him. The requests are passed on to the city council only after mayoral review and integration into two documents. Council approval comes after budget review by the planning and finance committee.

Perhaps the most dramatic constitutional change in any of the communities was the establishment of the Pueblo Council of Governments (COG).[13] Barely known outside Pueblo, it is one of the most successful examples anywhere of voluntary political integration of the government institutions of the civil community. Although it could have happened only in Pueblo or in similar civil communities (Lincoln, Nebraska, is an example of a comparable successful effort), it is no less successful because of that. It demonstrates the power of voluntary action in the right circumstances, where key figures and forces in the civil community have made the commitment to work together and to either persuade or "jawbone" others to join with them.

Pueblo's COG is equally important for what it indicates about how institutions prescribed by outside governments for all civil communities can adapt to the particular needs and unique conditions of a specific civil community. It has been emphasized that local governments, to be successful in federal systems, must function to acquire outside aid for local needs, to adapt external actions and services to local norms and conditions, to experiment with governance, to initiate new public programs, and to serve as a means through which the local population may have an effective voice in government decisions affecting them.[14] The Pueblo case shows how strong that power remains within the federal system, even in light of the efforts to centralize control in federal hands during the latter half of the postwar generation. The COG was a regionalizing device forced upon metropolitan areas throughout the United States by the federal government as a condition of federal aid. In most cases it was adapted locally in such a way as to do the least damage to existing political institutions and power networks. In Pueblo it was taken as a device that could be used to strengthen the civil community. What developed did so utterly without federal prodding—perhaps even without Washington's knowledge. Other communities found ways to take the federal money and run; Pueblo found ways to take the same federal money and build.

Pueblo is the easy case in the sense that what it was doing before the introduction of the COG was leading in the precise direction the originators of the COG idea wished to move. Champaign-Urbana is a harder case. There, federal pressure was applied through the COG device to encourage consolidation of the two cities. The effort failed totally; the power of the locality functioning as a civil community outweighed the ability of the federal government to move it in directions it did not want to go.[15]

If major constitutional change was sporadic in the second half of the postwar generation, the continuing dynamics of constitutional choice suffered no diminution. Referenda of all kinds continued to be a staple of the local electoral diet, allowing the various local publics direct constitutional choice on traditional referendum issues. School taxes continued to be a major issue, although success in securing tax increases declined precipitously in the latter half of the generation.

In addition, the Vietnam War brought efforts in various parts of the United States to introduce national policy questions into the local referendum process, at least to get expressions of local public opinion. Once that was done, life-style questions such as the legalization of marijuana were also put on the ballot in some localities. The cities of the prairie were not prominent in either of these trends, which were most prevalent in medium-sized cities, a class where the referendum as a popular device is more widely used than in large cities, with university cities such as Berkeley, California, and Madison, Wisconsin, being the most prominent.

The new role of the ballot as a vehicle for providing constitutional choice has not been treated fully enough in the Cities of the Prairie study, in part because there has been a pronounced increase in its use only recently. Before the late 1960s the referendum was mainly a device for introducing governmental structural changes, altering the local tax base, or authorizing local bond issues. These important subjects continue to dominate the referendum process, but in the latter half of the generation the process was opened up to become a populist vehicle for checking or guiding the people's representatives. American constitutionalism was always *popular* in character; it remains to be seen what will be the consequences of its turning *populist.*

Constitutional Design, the Party System, and Democracy

Related to this new populism was another significant dimension of constitutional design: the transformation of the civic and constitutional basis of the civil community. While Pueblo's example was the most extensive, it was by no means the only one. The broadening of the base of civic participation throughout the cities had the effect of bringing about constitutional change by introducing groups hitherto absent from local and civic processes. Similar phenomena were occurring throughout the United States, but in medium-sized cities the size of the formerly excluded populations was large enough to have an impact, while the size of the place was small enough so that communication among activists remained face to face. Therefore it was easier to open doors to newcomers.

Despite the pressures from the outside to expand the role of government, the civil community seems to have responded in traditional ways. East St. Louis, Pueblo, and Duluth remained civil communities in which government was expected to play an active role, albeit in very different ways, while Champaign–Urbana and Decatur expected government's role to be minimal.

It already has been noted that government in East St. Louis is the major source of stable employment. In addition to School District 189, the park district and the East Side Levee and Sanitary District were major local sources of patronage. For example, during World War II guards were hired by the latter to protect the pumps and levees from sabotage. By the 1960s their number had grown to twice the wartime level. In 1976 the levee district, which services Madison and St. Clair counties, was restructured and placed under the control of the two county boards. A reflection of the demise of the Fields machine, this change was merely a means of shifting control over the patronage. Two years later the Metro-East sanitary district, as the restructured levee district was now known, was in the headlines again for a patronage scandal.

Local government labor costs in East St. Louis have grown at an annual rate of 12 percent since 1965. The city's per capita expenditure for police increased 315 percent from 1960 to 1972 compared with 142 percent in other Illinois cities of comparable size. Per capita costs for fire protection increased 192 percent compared with 106 percent during the same period, and expenses for street maintenance increased three times more than those of comparable cities. All this reflects the character of local politics and the machine's use of city revenue to increase the salaries of its patronage employees.

East St. Louis's dependence upon government is also reflected in the fact that approximately 25 percent of its residential stock consists of public housing—totaling more than 3,500 units, probably the largest percentage of any city in the country. At that, there is a waiting list for entry into those projects. In 1975 East St. Louis issued building permits for sixty-one single-family residences and one apartment building; only the apartment building and two of the residences were to be privately owned. The remainder were part of the public housing system.[16]

In Rockford the antigovernment ideology remained as strong and clearly articulated as ever for most of the generation, though toward the end, after the death of its primary spokesman and catalyst, Rockford began to take a less absolutist position with regard to federal aid, no longer rejecting it outright but accepting it case by case. At midpoint in the postwar generation, Benjamin Schleicher, who had been elected mayor of Rockford in 1957 on the All-Rockford Party ticket, essentially a Republican-dominated group, was entrenched in office.[17] He was to serve sixteen consecutive years as mayor, the longest tenure of any mayor in Rockford's history. During Schleicher's first term, at the time of the first Cities of the Prairie study, he was quite dependent on the inner circle of the All-Rockford Party. During his second term, however, most of those who had played key roles in his 1957 victory dropped out of active political life, and he consolidated his own power sufficiently to win a third term under the All-Rockford Party label.

By that time his former supporters had decided to organize as Republicans, and they appealed to him to disband the All-Rockford Party and join the local GOP. Schleicher refused, and in the 1967 off-year elections he lost control of the city council to the Republicans, who elected eight aldermen. Even though he was a registered Republican, Schleicher was kept out of the Republican caucuses. This in turn led him to break with the chamber of commerce, the major backer of the GOP and the leader of the opposition to the city's use of federal funds, the central plank of the All-Rockford Party platform since the mid-1950s.

The mayor reactivated the Rockford Housing Authority, which had been dormant for more than a decade, and secured close to $30 million in federal funds for low-cost housing for the poor and the elderly. He introduced the first scattered-site housing program of its kind in the nation, constructing one- and two-family homes on vacant lots throughout the city and providing nearly ten thousand low-cost housing units through the city-federal program. Nevertheless, by 1969, when he decided to seek a fourth term, Mayor Schleicher did disband the All-Rockford Party and ran for reelection as a Republican.

Schleicher was opposed by a coalition of Democrats and conservative

Republicans. The campaign essentially revived Rockford's traditional three-way political battle between Democrats and the progressive and conservative wings of the Republican party, which went back to the turn of the century and had continued until Schleicher's initial victory in 1957 under the sponsorship of the conservatives. Schleicher won a fourth term, but when he tried for a fifth term in 1973 he was defeated by Robert McGaw, running on the Democratic ticket, who managed to beat Schleicher in most of the latter's strongholds.

Benjamin Schleicher dominated Rockford city politics in the postwar generation. His election in 1957 signaled the end of the progressive-cum-socialist regime in city hall that had dominated the interwar generation, and his defeat in 1973 marked the true introduction of national party labels and mainstream partisan politics into the Rockford civil community. McGaw was not a Democrat of convenience, as Schleicher had become a Republican of convenience for municipal electoral purposes. He was involved in the rebuilding of the Democratic party locally.

During Schleicher's tenure, Rockford moved from a clean but conservative approach to government to one supportive of undiluted local autonomy, including the rejection of federal aid for local improvements, then to an acquiescence to the changed circumstances of intergovernmental relations and finance in the United States. Mayor Schleicher changed the direction of his administration reluctantly, and only by breaking with his former supporters. While the struggle for change was internal for Rockford, it was also a product of the Great Society. In that respect Rockford changed even more than the central Illinois cities of the prairie, because it started with a position further from the thrust of intergovernmental relations as they had developed since the New Deal.

Rockford had managed to preserve much of its integrity and autonomy by that position; hence the change was a real one. Perhaps it was only a convergence of forces that led the city not only to accept federal aid in the late 1960s but also to reintroduce Republican and Democratic party labels and the organizations that came with them into municipal politics. In essence, the latter half of the postwar generation saw Rockford's cocoon crumble. From now on the civil community must be part of the larger political system in a way it had not been since the beginning of the Progressive Era when the local progressive Republicans broke with the national Republican party and when its city fathers simultaneously opted to build distance between Rockford, Chicago, and the rest of the state through political mechanisms. The impact of this transformation will be known only in the coming generation.

McGaw's victory was followed two years later by a Democratic majority on the city council. The victory itself was the result of the Democrats' success in weaning the Rockford progressives away from the Republican party. The roots of that shift can be traced to the 1964 Goldwater debacle.

In the 1950s, despite a certain hesitation, the progressives had joined with the conservatives to be part of the All-Rockford party challenge to the remnants of the old socialist group that had dominated city hall since 1921. They did so not because of disillusionment with the ideas of the socialists, but because the latter had become obsolete in their refusal to address the emerging issues of the postwar generation, which the conservatives—more accurately neoconservatives—were willing to do, in their way. The conservatives, however, were so strongly ideological in their orientation that they were among the first to jump on Goldwater's bandwagon prior to the 1964 presidential elections. This in itself led to a polarization within Republican ranks that might have survived had Goldwater not suffered so disastrous a defeat at the hands of Lyndon Baines Johnson. The electoral defeat of the conservatives' candidate at the hands of a progressive Democrat reawakened old sentiments among the Rockford progressives, including Mayor Schleicher. Meanwhile, the regular Winnebago Republican party organization, which was naturally conservative in the more traditional sense, had won victories in the Winnebago County elections, filling the county courthouse with county politicians who had always been something of an anathema to the progressive forces in the civil community. This "courthouse gang" came to be even more important in Republican party circles after the death of the executive director of the Rockford Chamber of Commerce, who was the initiator of the ideological conservative movement in the city. Progressives found they had no place to go within the GOP. As a result, the rank and file crossed over to the Democrats.

The Swedish-American vote, the core of Republican strength, in Rockford as it was throughout the middle border until the New Deal, for the first time in a century went to the Democrats in a local election. This crossover first became evident in the 1971 municipal elections and continued in the county arena in 1972 with the election of twelve Democrats to the new county board. Although the Republicans retained control with sixty members, the tide had clearly turned. Two years later the Democrats took control of the county board and elected the county chairman.

McGaw was reelected mayor in 1977, but his party was able to hold on to only half the city council seats. Two years later they lost control of the county board. Nevertheless, by the end of the generation the Democratic party was obviously a serious force in Rockford politics.

Reflecting its moralistic political culture and long-held commitment to the efficacy of politics, Rockford has never sought to bring about political change by changing the structure of its city government. The city retains the same system of government it has had since its incorporation in 1852. Major structural changes in the past increased the terms of office of the mayor and aldermen to two years in 1881 and to four in 1937 and made the position of mayor full-time in 1921. After the adoption of the Illinois constitution of 1970, with its home-rule provisions, the city charter was finally amended to expand the power of the mayor. In sum, a secular trend toward strengthening the office of mayor is the major structural change that has taken place.

Robert McGaw was the first strong mayor elected under the new city charter provisions. He was the first to be able to build an administrative staff for his office and establish his control over the annual budget and municipal finances generally, removing those responsibilities from the office of city clerk. McGaw was a catalyst for a number of local projects, including the fiscal and administrative reorganization of the city government, concentrating fiscal and budgetary control in the hands of the mayor, the rehabilitation of the city's waterworks, a major urban redevelopment program for the central business district, and a major bridge reconstruction program. McGaw's package for the central business district/urban redevelopment program involved a $29 million downtown civic center for which he obtained state funds, state and federal office buildings in the redevelopment area, and a city-county public safety building planned to cost $15 million.

Although the projects themselves were useful for Rockford, as in other cities they did not halt central business district decline, since they could not substantially affect the structural reasons for it, any more than other projects had done elsewhere. Still, the increase in the power of the office of mayor was the culmination of the postwar reform effort. In that sense it paralleled the return to partisan elections in the municipal arena.

At the beginning of the postwar generation in 1952 Rockford's two daily newspapers, the *Register Republic* and the *Star,* had been sold by ultraconservative Ruth Hanna McCormick (of the Chicago *Tribune* family) to E. Kenneth Todd, who turned both papers into strong local forces, giving heavy coverage to local and state government affairs in both the news columns and the editorial pages. Under Todd, the two papers played a significant role in the postwar transformation of Rockford. In 1967, however, Todd sold the papers to the Gannett chain, which immediately proceeded to reduce the papers' involvement in political affairs and turned them toward a more bland coverage of news trivia. After a 1970 newspaper strike, the importation of a new publisher by the Gannett chain completed the transformation of a once hard-hitting political press into a bland daily magazine, with a subsequent loss of subscribers so severe that the two papers were merged into one, the *Register-Star,* in 1978.

In the meantime three new weekly newspapers took up the slack, flourishing in Rockford's climate, where citizens are interested in local public affairs. The daily's one concession to this climate was a series of "investigative" reports of presumed local corruption that — given the Rockford political culture, where politicians must be further above reproach than Caesar's wife — did lead to some public officials' resigning or being defeated at the polls. Although the print media in Rockford have a long history of local involvement, for good or for ill, the electronic media have never had even a fraction of their impact.

Champaign-Urbana's situation was far less ideological and more a matter of tradition. Thus, as Rozann Rothman points out in chapter 7, it was possible for a reform group in Urbana to press for a large, somewhat expanded local government role, but reaction to outside government intervention remained much the same throughout the period. The two cities turned to federal aid reluctantly, and then only in the late 1960s and early 1970s when it was well-nigh forced on them by circumstances.

Politics in Springfield continued much as it had throughout the postwar generation. The city retained its commission from the government, and elections remained nonpartisan. Each city commissioner organizes his own following, and elections are hard fought. Although the candidates seek the support of the regular parties, the parties themselves never compete against one another in their endorsements. Instead, they sometimes unite to maintain the political status quo against reform elements. One reason for this bipartisanship is the patronage the commissioners dispense, in an openly political way.

Since commissioners are elected at large, blacks cannot achieve credible candidacy, much less election, but they can sometimes use their voting strength to influence the outcome of an election and gain some of their political ends. Unfortunately for them, the overall turnout for local elections in Springfield during the latter part of the generation has been quite high, averaging two-thirds of the eligible voters, while the black turnout is considerably lower.

The Springfield Chamber of Commerce remains the most powerful single interest group in the civil community, but not even it can claim to be the only voice of businessmen with local interests. Labor unions, on the other hand, are correspondingly weak, which is not surprising given the lack of a local industrial base. In general, cleavages in the city are not very sharp, and alliances are easily formed across the usual lines of division because of common community interests.

The mass media have some influence on Springfield politics. In 1974 the two semi-independent daily newspapers, both owned by the Copley chain, were merged to form the *State General Register,* today the only daily paper published in Springfield. It provides reasonable local coverage, but nothing exceptional. The local National Broadcasting Company affiliate does provide local news coverage at a reasonable level, but it is the public radio station affiliated with Sangamon State University that does the best job in that respect.[18]

Local politics in the Quad Cities area also remained much the same in the second half of the generation as in the first. Rock Island County remained Democratic throughout the 1960s and 1970s, although congressional redistricting in the 1960s put it into a district with so many Republican voters that it lost its ability to elect a Democrat to Congress. The township remained the basis of party organization in both Rock Island and Moline. Rock Island remains more state oriented and Moline more insular in politics, as in the past and for the same reasons. Organized labor remained more community oriented than in many other communities, supporting school referenda and United Way drives as well as endorsing local candidates for office.[19]

The range of issues that preoccupied Peoria in the latter half of the postwar generation reflected the kinds of questions which come before medium-sized civil communities. We have already noted that one continuing issue is government structural reform, whether to keep the council-manager system. Another structural issue, albeit of a different character, was annexation; like government structural change, this reshapes the configurations of local politics. So, for example, the annexation of Ridgewoods Township in the early 1960s, with its cosmopolitan population, in all likelihood made the difference in the struggle in the retention of council-manager government and, conversely, the passage of school finance referenda. In Peoria between 1956 and 1975 there were five unsuccessful attempts to raise school taxes. Despite the support of the more cosmopolitan sectors of the city's population, the locals turned out in large numbers to oppose such tax increases. Finally, in November 1975 the issue was presented to the voters on a special ballot. An extraordinarily high voter turnout of 54 percent—the largest ever recorded for such a referendum—approved the tax increase.

It was relatively easy to annex the township; it was far more difficult to merge the Ridgewoods community high school district with Peoria School District 150. The same people who wanted to be part of the city of Peoria for other purposes wanted to retain a substantial measure of autonomy for the high school but, at the same time, did not want to pay the extra taxes necessary to do so. In the end, annexation could be effected only along with the merger of the school districts. Both were completed in 1964. What was characteristic of this issue, as of most others in Peoria, was that the economic leadership represented by the Peoria business community and Peoria's Association of Commerce took the lead in promoting the issue but had to conciliate a whole range of other interests before it could succeed in its efforts.[20]

The division between cosmopolitans and locals remained the principal continuing division in local politics in the cities of the prairie, manifested in issue after issue. The only cleavage to challenge it was that which coalesced around matters of racial equality in those communities where the nonwhite population was growing and politically active.

As throughout the country, there was a tendency in the cities of the prairie for the political party structures to be weakened, although again the picture differs from community to community and does not seem to have included changes as radical as those that took place in the national or state arenas. Since the Democratic and Republican parties were already in a weakened position in the cities of the prairie, it is not surprising that they remained weak in an era when the major party ties were loosening throughout the country. On the other hand, there is no particular evidence that they have weakened further. In Rockford and Duluth they even became stronger. The decline of partisan politics in the cities of the prairie took place at the beginning of the postwar generation and simply persisted through its second half, when a similar weakening of major party attachments and organizational frameworks took place in the state and national arenas.

More precisely, the cities of the prairie fall into two categories—those in which partisan politics is a basic fact of life throughout the civil community's government institutions and those in which the local governments in the civil community are nonpartisan, with partisan politics confined to the more peripheral governments. Most of the changes that took place affected the former through the opening of party ranks and leadership positions to new groups and forces, on one hand, and through the decline of the power of party organizations on the other. Many of these changes were the result of court-mandated redistricting and acceptance of new party rules promulgated by the national party organizations—that is to say, constitutional changes rather than the dynamics of the normal political process. In the latter case there has been relatively little change in the organization of political life, though there seems to have been a substantial turnover in leadership in the fourteen years between completion of fieldwork for the first and second studies.

The first study documented the way the cities of the prairie were notably free of power structures in the conventional sense of the term. The restudy reinforces that conclusion. The turnover of those involved in local affairs in itself keeps power from being very structured in those civil communities.

Some might see Pueblo as having a power structure of sorts, since the group that moved into a controlling position about 1960 remained dominant through the mid-1970s, but that was in great part due to its ability to broaden the base of political activists and integrate everybody or very nearly everybody into a comprehensive and very open network rather than because it was able to form an oligarchy or even sought to do so. Stephen Schechter discusses this in greater detail in chapter 6. By the end of the 1970s its members too were beginning to retire from public affairs. Similarly, the groups competing for power in Duluth remained more or less intact during the period, though with significant changes in personnel. The combination of continuity and change that was a feature of Rockford politics has been described in some depth, with changes among the activists noted.

The greatest changes occurred in those nonpartisan systems that reflected business-oriented reform, in which politics was a one-time activity for the reformers, designed to achieve a particular constitutional change, or something akin to it, and then allow politics to take its course, on the assumption that the new order would be self-executing. In such cases reformers would get involved for brief periods and then withdraw from political life. Peoria, Springfield, and Decatur are good examples of this.

The issue of continuity and change in the local power system is one of the central questions in community studies, one the "snapshot" approach cannot answer. Examining the question over time, as is done in this study, we can draw some tentative conclusions. All in all, the greatest continuity was maintained by the more democratic local regimes. The more institutionalized the broad base, the greater the continuity. Perhaps that explains why traditional partisan politics is almost as continuous, since it has institutionalization, though without the broad base. The least continuity is to be found in the sporadic activities of middle-class reformers who intervene for a specific purpose and believe that changes in formal constitutional structures alone will gain the desired ends.

Issues and Controversies

The principal policy issues confronting the cities of the prairie in the latter half of the postwar generation were those that had a countrywide dimension and were initially generated from outside their boundaries. Probably the most important single issue was civil rights, which involved a wide range of specific questions including school desegregation, neighborhood desegregation and redevelopment, employment opportunities, and political participation, all of which had constitutional implications for each civil community. While it may be that specific efforts to attend to these problems were the result of outside pressures, for the most part local citizens were responsible for their local manifestations. As has been the case throughout American history, such issues reflect not some "inside/outside" dichotomy but, rather, a mixture of forces.

While it would be difficult to say that any of the cities of the prairie played a role in shaping the direction of the civil rights movement nationally, in each community people did what had to be done in order to make changes locally. In many cases the local "establishment" responded to local demands for change in order to avoid the outside pressure it anticipated. The case studies of school desegregation in Champaign–Urbana and Decatur emphasize this aspect of the issue.[21] On the other hand, in Pueblo what was done to improve housing for the Hispanic population was entirely local, sui generis in its scope, and innovative in character, even it if went unnoticed outside Pueblo and, for that matter, in many quarters within the civil community. Although Pueblo was the exception and public housing was generally stimulated from the outside, even so each civil community directed its public housing efforts more or less on its own terms. In the Quad Cities, public housing in Moline, which dates back to the 1950s, has been principally for the elderly. This is somewhat less true in Rock Island and Davenport, though still the bulk of public housing in the Quad Cities area is directed toward the elderly rather than toward minorities. Davenport had not introduced a public housing program at the time of the first study. For it, the introduction of public housing in the second half of the postwar generation marked a real change in policy. Rock Island's public housing dates back to World War II when the Rock Island Housing Authority was established to build housing for war workers. Approximately half of its 912 rental units in six housing projects are designed specifically for the elderly. A major facet of Rockford's public housing program, on the other hand, was its homesteading project. Under that program the Rockford Housing Authority used federal funds to purchase deteriorated buildings and for a nominal sum transfer them to individual families under a certain income level who committed themselves to renovate them.

A set of issues that more clearly reflected the "inside/outside" dichotomy involved coping with the growing number of state and federal mandates. Most of these mandates were strictly products of outside decisions. Here the local problem was how to adapt to those mandates with the minimum of change, unless the mandate triggered some internal constellation of forces that sought greater change and was able to gain local support for it. New state mandates were most visible in matters of elementary and secondary education, and federal mandates were most visible in civil rights matters.[22]

The policy issue with the most local character continued to be economic development. Even so, the necessity to actively seek economic development grows out of each civil community's integration within the regional, national, and international economies of the larger world, which regularly bring changes of one kind or another to the local economies and must be confronted. In the period under discussion here, the situation for many of the cities was like that described for Joliet in chapter 9: it was necessary to run hard simply to stay in place. Jobs were disappearing because of external pressures, at a rate that made local efforts at job creation merely a question of trying to keep even. Although local efforts were self-generated and no one from outside pushed the civil communities to do anything in that direction, the necessity clearly grew out of external pressures. If there was any change in the period, it seems to have been a movement from economic development efforts based on optimistic projections of growth to equally intensive efforts based on realistic assessments of the need to work hard simply to remain stable.

After 1964 the impact of the Great Society and the New Federalism represented a new set of outside-generated issues, some requiring local action to make them relevant and others, like revenue sharing, affecting each civil community willy-nilly. Here again the difference from community to community was vital. Some civil communities sought every federal dollar they could obtain, while others so thoroughly avoided federal entanglements that revenue sharing remained almost the only significant source of federal funds to come their way. Several of the case studies that follow suggest the differential effect of those federal initiatives. By the end of the generation, both Great Society programs and Nixon's New Federalism programs had reached their peak and were either stabilized and integrated into the community or declining and being phased out.

5. Federalism versus Managerialism in the Civil Community

The Cities of the Prairie, the Great Society, and Local Autonomy

As in every previous frontier stage, government played a major role in the advance of the metropolitan frontier. Even in the so-called laissez-faire periods of American history, government—local, state, and federal—helped provide the infrastructure for the unfolding of each frontier stage. In every case the pattern was similar. During the early years of the particular frontier, government activity was directed toward building an infrastructure, designed to help along, rather than interfere with, the natural course of the frontier. Only later, toward the end of the frontier stage, did government try to redress some of the imbalances generated in the process, as human activities invariably generate imbalances.

Although the same pattern of action was followed in the course of the metropolitan frontier, the collapsing of the time frame into a single generation has had serious consequences. In many respects the public works projects and social programs of the New Deal helped lay the foundations for the metropolitan frontier, building needed public facilities and creating appropriate social protections that provided a jumping-off point for postwar developments. Then, from the late 1940s to the early 1960s, the states and localities expanded that infrastructure—in some cases with federal assistance (for highways, health facilities, and aviation, in particular; urban planning and redevelopment, somewhat less; higher education, even less) and in other cases, such as elementary and secondary education, without such assistance. Then came the massive federal intervention of the mid-1960s, ostensibly to redress imbalances. In the last analysis, however, as a result of certain pressures generated from other quarters, federal intervention began to interfere with the frontier process and not simply correct the problems created by it.[1]

In sum, the Great Society programs were ambivalent in character and ambiguous in effect. On one hand, they represented a response to the metropolitan frontier similar to earlier bursts of federal activity. On the other hand, they tried to redirect the metropolitan frontier away from its natural course. In that attempt they moved away from the proper role of government in a frontier society; that is, to help the frontier processes along, nudging them back into correct paths only when they seem absolutely unable to stay there by themselves, but basically providing the infrastructure for the frontier to work its own social transformation.

Our return to the cities of the prairie a decade after the original study, in the wake of the Great Society and the other upheavals of the late 1960s, reaffirmed earlier findings that the local polity is still the best framework within which to preserve local autonomy. Moreover, the data clearly indicate that it is possible to preserve considerable local autonomy, even in a period of intense federal activity, by utilizing the governmental mechanisms of the civil community, especially when the civil community unites to utilize them. This was demonstrated in case after case, whether in cities like Pueblo, which sought to ride the crest of change and be in the vanguard; like Duluth, which had so very few options in bringing up the rear that in seeking change for the better it usually found that the changes made things worse; or like Decatur, which sought to avoid almost all change except that minimum needed in order not to change by standing still. All our field researchers reported that the communities they studied did indeed weather the period without losing their character or even being substantially budged from that character, even where they had to open up to changes initiated from the outside.

This was not accomplished without a struggle—one that reflected the nationwide contest between various forces and principles of governmental organization and reform. It was a struggle that took place on two levels: in the relationships between each civil community, its state, and the federal government on one hand, and between the civil community and its metropolitan area on the other.

The thrust of American government from the beginning of the twentieth century until now has been toward greater centralization within a hierarchical model.[2] This is in no small part the result of reformers' efforts, conscious or unconscious, to transfer to government the mode of organization big business had adopted a generation earlier. The great entrepreneurs who built their enterprises after the Civil War and Reconstruction maintained tight personal control at the top. Their model, transferred to the government realm, led to an emphasis on a very powerful president responsible for setting policy and administering it through an elaborate bureaucratic structure responsible to him. Congress was judged by how rapidly it provided the legislation and funds the president requested. Some state governors and legislatures were expected to develop the same relationships, and then the model was applied to cities as well. Present dissatisfactions with this model in the national arena have their source in the widespread feeling that presidential power has run away with itself in both foreign and domestic spheres, while the administrative pyramid has become too large to be controlled from the top yet too broad to be controlled at any other point.

By the time American reformers and political leaders were leading the country into centralized hierarchical arrangements, business intellectuals were beginning to question the efficacy of tight pyramids in organizing complex enterprises. Their answer was to keep the pyramid but to loosen it, through decentralization. After World War II, while government rolled on toward more hierarchy, business moved to implement the decentralization model. In the late 1960s—a generation later—that model entered the governmental arena in the form of Richard Nixon's New Federalism, which was designed to be an answer to the problem of overcentralization or too much hierarchy.

In the New Federalism the pyramid model was retained and strengthened, but the emphasis was on decentralizing operations within it. From regional arrangements within the federal government to the delegation to the states and localities of authority to enforce federal standards, it represented a new thrust toward decentralization. Unfortunately, all the good intentions of the Nixon administration notwithstanding, the overall result was a series of administrative efforts that increased federal dominance over the states and localities in crucial policy and program areas (ostensibly balanced by the decentralization of administrative powers over those areas), and an effort to radically expand the president's powers over the funding of all federal and cooperative programs. The ambivalent approach of the Nixon administration was continued in a bipartisan way in the Ford and Carter years. But pyramids, tight or loose, are not the way of American government, deep down. From the very first, the American government system was organized as a matrix, not a hierarchy; a noncentralized political system in which the powers were not allocated by "levels" but divided among different arenas—federal, state, and local. The original model of American federalism was closely related to the market model of many small enterprises of approximately equal size, functioning within a relatively restricted framework: the model of American commerce before the industrial revolution and the one that influenced the original shape of American government under the Constitution.

Figure 5.1 graphically portrays the basis of American government organization from its original perspective. It reflects the fundamental distribution of powers among multiple centers across the matrix, not the devolution of powers from a single center down through a pyramid. Each cell in the matrix represents an independent political actor and an arena for political action. Some cells are larger and some smaller, and the powers assigned

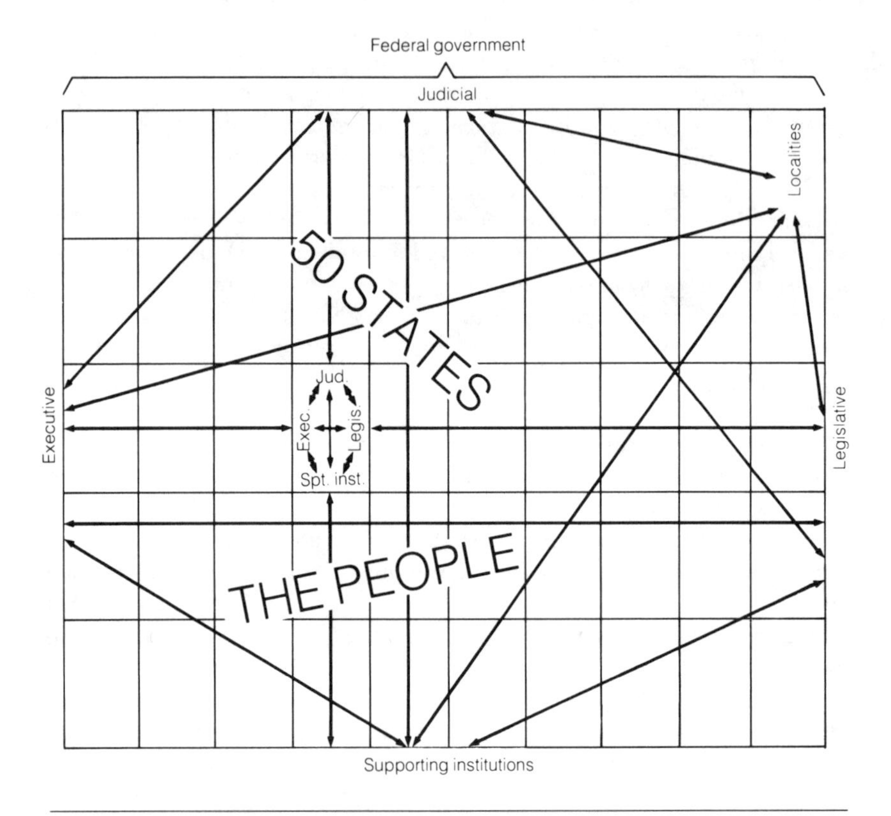

Fig. 5.1. The American government matrix: interacting power centers of general, state, and local governments.

to each may reflect that difference, but none is "higher" or "lower" in importance than any other. The matrix model also clearly delineates the separation of powers among coequal branches of government (executive, legislative, judicial) within each cell. That matrix describes what we call federalism.

Federal democracy is the authentic American contribution to democratic thought and republican government. Its conception represents a synthesis of the Puritan idea of the covenant relationship as the foundation of all proper human society and the constitutional ideas of English "natural rights" school of the seventeenth and early eighteenth centuries. The covenant idea (*foedus,* the Latin root of the word "federal," means covenant or compact), which the Puritans took from the Bible, demands a different kind of political relationship (and perhaps, in the long run, a different kind of human relationship) from that emphasized by theories of mass democracy that have attracted many adherents since the French Revolution. It emphasizes partnership between individuals, groups, and governments in the pursuit of justice, cooperative relationships that make the partnership real, and negotiation among the partners as the basis for sharing power. The Lockean understanding of the political compact as the basis for civil society represents a secularized version of the covenant principle. It is the synthesis of the two forms that undergirds the original American political vision.

To return to the image with which we began, decentralization implies hierarchy, a pyramid of governments with gradations of power flowing down from the top. It is an image used by public figures serving on all planes of government almost as a matter of course, without any thought as to its larger implications. But it is a misleading image that distorts reality. It took the development of the most recent technology, the technology of the space frontier, to open the eyes of some of us to the limits of a hierarchical approach to government. The technology of the space frontier—of the world of cybernetics—is based on the principle that efficiency comes from two sources: a good communications network and a certain amount of redundancy. Redundancy in literary English is usually interpreted to mean useless overlapping, or what American administrative reformers like to refer to as "duplication," a word no longer neutral in the American government lexicon. To the cyberneticist, however, redundancy is a means of providing "fail safe" mechanisms to keep things working, on the assumption that errors will occur in any system and that the continued operation of the system, whether a machine or an organization, requires that there be other channels for the communications and other forces able to initiate and respond to various actions.

The theory and experience of the new technology, in a word, stand in direct contradiction to earlier notions of duplication. Put differently, technology has begun to imitate the Constitution of the United States by following principles that our founders applied to government in the eighteenth century. The founders of this federal republic, taking due cognizance of what they understood to be a "new science of politics," created a political system based upon the very principles that now animate the new technology. That system was not a pyramid, with channels for giving orders from the top to the bottom, but a matrix of authoritative government units within a framework provided by the Constitution. This matrix combined a national or general government that could make authoritative decisions, especially on so-called boundary questions, with state governments equally authoritative within their areas of constitutional competence. The whole system was based upon the federal principle of redundancy—of having more than one authoritative body responsible for the conduct of the government and capable of exercising its responsibilities.

This study has emphasized that the multiple centers of the American federal matrix are not separated unto themselves. They are bound together within a network of distributed powers with lines of communication and decision making that force them to interact. It is not the need for interaction, or common action, that is special here; it is the form and character of that interaction—sharing through bargaining, or negotiated cooperation rather than directive or concern—that is uniquely the property of the matrix arrangement. When, two generations ago, much needed to be done for the nation as a whole and only the federal government seemed to have sufficient size and resources to ensure that what was done was done more or less equitably for citizens in all parts of the land, it was easy for the pyramid model to win wide acceptance and for governors and governed alike to operate according to it. In due time, however, the pyramid approach was carried to its logical conclusion. The President of the United States somehow was placed at its apex and the Congress a level below him. The states became "middle managers" in the system. Local governments became vehicles for the "delivery of services" rather than points of civic involvement.

Finally, presidents began to believe their press notices. The results were the debacles of the 1960s and 1970s when, parallel to the developments discussed here, one president brought us into an undeclared war that became one of the costliest in our history and led to public revulsion manifested even in the nation's streets, and another president brought us to Watergate.

The notion of the American system as pyramidal was reinforced by a convergence of Jacobin views of the polity and managerialist views of its administration, both of which gained currency in the United States in the late nineteenth century and became dominant in the twentieth. The Jacobin model of polity has power concentrated in a single center that is more or less influenced by its periphery (fig. 5.2). Centralization is the organizational expression of Jacobinism, which distrusts dispersed power because of the European historical experience out of which it grew, in which localism was synonymous with support for the prerevolutionary powerholders. Jacobinism was brought to the United States in the mid-nineteenth century as a form of liberalism. Beginning as a theoretical critique of the compact theory of the state (i.e., an attack on the theoretical basis of federalism), in the course of a generation it became linked with the new nationalism of the late nineteenth century in the development of a practical program of expanded national government activity. Woodrow Wilson then gave it a more Americanized form by suggesting that Congress was the natural center of all political power.

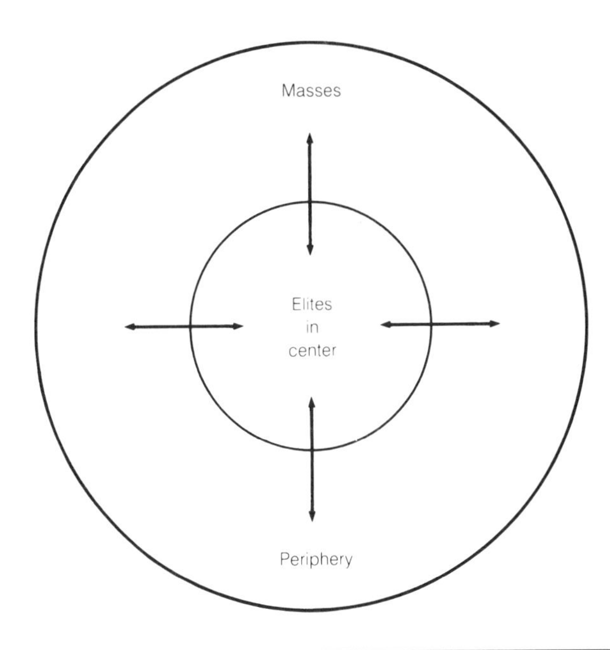

Fig. 5.2. The Jacobin model.

Managerialism is an organizational response to the industrial revolution, in many respects typically American but with strong roots in the military and bureaucratic traditions of Prussia and France. Politically, managerialism represents an effort to democratize (or, perhaps more accurately, republicanize) autocracy, whether in the immediate sense of the autocracy of the great entrepreneurs who built and ruled the new industrial corporations, or in the older sense of imperial autocracy. In both cases the founders can be considered "conquerors" who ruled autocratically and, in the end, unsatisfactorily, given changing times. The introduction of managerial structures was a means of transforming autocratic rule without formally altering the hierarchical institutional structures built by the founders. In both cases the proponents of managerial techniques could argue that what they proposed was politically neutral and hence not a threat to the existing system. In fact, as new generations of managers emerged, and as management became a career in its own right, managerialism itself became an ideology.

The pyramid structure (figure 5.3) is a key feature of managerialism. It goes without saying that the top must be the most important level and the place where decisions are made about which level does what. Since proponents of managerialism never called it that and, indeed, believed that they were advocating a politically neutral means of increasing efficiency, the

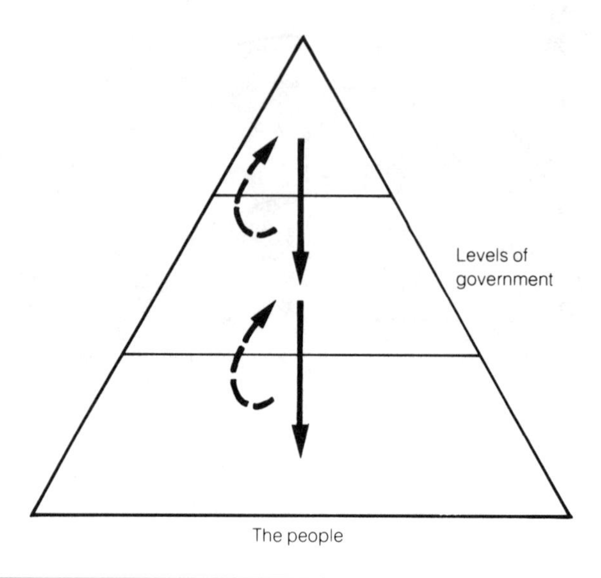

Fig. 5.3. The managerial pyramid.

implications of its spread in the United States are just now beginning to be recognized. In fact managerialism, for all its practical orientation and sincere commitment to neutrality in such matters, does reflect a political position as well, one no less real for not being articulated as such. Originally conceived to be only a technique, in a scientific age committed to the relativity of ends it was transformed by some into a potential vehicle for secular salvation, one that offered a right process in place of a teleology.

In the course of the twentieth century, these three approaches have had to be related to one another in the conduct of American government as a practical matter. What resulted were two separate syntheses that are fundamentally in conflict. That conflict remained submerged as long as it did not affect the pursuit of immediate common goals. Today the conflict is emerging as the old goals must be replaced by new ones that are intimately related to one approach or another.

In ideas, the synthesis was between Jacobinism and managerialism, both of which reflected the twentieth-century thrust toward the centralization of power and were useful in justifying the increase in the velocity of government and its centralization during the past two generations. The synthesis itself grew out of (1) the managerial dimension of Progressivism, which saw in the new techniques of management a means of making government more efficient and economical; (2) Jacobin influences on the liberal intellectuals, generally in their Marxian form, which led them not only to advocate strong centralized government but to reconceptualize social and political life in terms of the center/periphery model; and (3) the practical experiences of the interwar generation, which, confronted by two total wars and an unprecedented depression, increasingly turned to government for direction and control and at the same time became somewhat disillusioned with inherited political ideas, at least in the versions they received (which they did not know differed from the original).

In practice, on the other hand, the synthesis was between managerialism and federalism, reflecting both the realities of American politics and the continuation of fondly supported traditional principles. That synthesis grew out of (1) the communitarian dimension of Progressivism, which sought to restore America's sense of community that was so threatened in an industrial age, as well as to improve the efficiency of its governmental system; (2) the practical experiences of the interwar generation, which led to the need to introduce management techniques and bureaucratic organization into most government institutions yet were unable to bring about any fundamental change in the structure of the federal system even where articulate groups were willing to promote change; and (3) those institutional and political constraints that required the adaptation of managerial devices and ideas to a multicentered federal system whose politics remained noncentralized and that functioned through the separation of powers and a continued reliance on checks and balances.

At first the potential conflict between the two syntheses was avoided because activists were pursuing common goals. It was only toward the end of the postwar generation that it became irrepressible. The emergence of that conflict can be traced through three stages. During stage one (1946–64), the practical convergence of the previous generation was maintained and even extended as the federal government reorganized to accommodate congressional and local interests. Increased intergovernmental cooperation and state government reorganization on the federal model were the order of the day. It was at this time that appropriate theories of management, bureaucracy, and intergovernmental relations were developed to account for, explain, and justify the new order of things. Stage two (1964–70) brought a new spirit of federal activity based on a further extension of Jacobin ideas supported by managerial goals. Whether intentional or not, the Great Society programs represented the fulfillment of the Jacobin-managerial synthesis through which Jacobin goals were pursued by intensive utilization of managerial approaches and techniques. This stage saw a redefinition of equality, democracy, and other American values to fit Jacobin prescriptions, coupled with a redefinition of individualism that went beyond any of the three approaches. In both its successes and its failures, the Great Society made thoughtful Americans begin to recognize the limits of both politics and bureaucracy and, in the process, to question the two approaches that saw in the one or the other a source of secular salvation.

The Rise and Decline of Local Managerialism

Thus, another clear-cut conclusion to come out of the resurvey and, for that matter, another way the resurvey elucidates the original study, is the contrast between federalist and managerial models in the civil community. Interlocally as well as intergovernmentally, the federalist model of government is characterized by an institutionalized division of powers that necessitates arrangements for intergovernmental collaboration and other formal means of power sharing. It is the federalist model that accounts for what has been termed (in the language of the managerial model) "fragmentation" of local government in the United States, "fragmentation" that reaches its peak in the states of the cities of the prairie.[3]

The federalist model was described by Alexis de Tocqueville in *Democracy in America* as the normative model of American government. He emphasized its primary manifestation in the local arena through the division of the powers of government among a number of offices or institutions, each with a limited sphere of competence but substantial powers in that sphere. This model, which was characteristic of the New England town from its founding in the seventeenth century, spread throughout much of the United States during the Jacksonian era, the time when local government institutions were established in Illinois, Iowa, Minnesota, and Wisconsin. (Significantly, Colorado, whose institutions were established in the post–Civil War era, never implemented that model as fully as did its sisters immediately to the east.)[4]

The cities of the prairie have hewed to that model with great faithfulness. Even where there presumably were more integrated administrative structures, the pattern of diffused government association with boards and commissions—essentially committees—prevailed. Thus, until the late 1960s the Urbana city council functioned through what were, for all intents and purposes, autonomous committees. The administrative departments submitted their budgets to their respective oversight committees, where they were reviewed, negotiated, and approved, with enactment by the whole city council pro forma. This changed considerably in the 1970s, as a result of the transformation in local politics in the late 1960s described by Rozann Rothman in chapter 7.

Champaign and Urbana, on the other hand, continued to maintain two city governments, twice rejecting proposals for their merger. They also maintained two park districts and two school districts but did share a common sanitary district. All the school and park districts were successful in securing expansion funding through referenda in the 1960s, but they ran into difficulties in the 1970s, reflecting the shifting situation in the country as a whole. Champaign's school district grew from 8,052 students in 1960 to 12,172 in 1970, then declined to 10,443 in 1975. This led to a closing of individual schools, but not to any real interest in consolidating districts, since each offers a means for the citizens of the city it serves to express themselves in educational matters. Champaign reintroduced district elections to the city council in 1972, providing for five councilmen to be elected from districts and three, plus the mayor, at large.

The political differences between the two cities remained real. As Rozann Rothman has put it, "Urbana has a more rooted and cohesive elite and more agreement on the purposes and uses of government. . . . Champaign, in contrast, has a more heterogeneous population; the distinction between rich and poor has been more visible; there has been less agreement on governmental purposes and policies."[5] She concluded that this is reflected in Urbana's retaining the samc form of government since the 1860s whereas Champaign changed to the commission form in 1917, adopted council-manager government in 1959, had a referendum on aldermanic government which failed in 1968, and then modified the council-manager plan in 1972. In short, what Urbana tried to achieve through politics within the same frame of government, Champaign consistently tried to achieve through changing governmental form.

Champaign introduced post–World War II management reforms into its city government decades before Urbana. On the other hand, Champaign was never able to mobilize public participation in local political life in the way Urbana has done through the political process. It is not unfair to conclude that, in the last analysis, Champaign's civic activists were reasonably satisfied while its public remained apathetic, whereas in Urbana the political activists were more frustrated by the local political process. The period of "leaving it to the professionals" may have come to an end in Champaign after the 1973 municipal election, in which an activist majority took control of the city council. The city manager who had established Champaign's solid commitment to professional management resigned in 1974, and his successor was hired on the basis of his greater receptivity to an activist council role.

The organization charts of the two cities reflect the differences between them (figs. 5.4 and 5.5). Like Decatur, those two cases demonstrate that government must be understood in light of the other dimensions of the local constitution and must clearly reflect those dimensions.

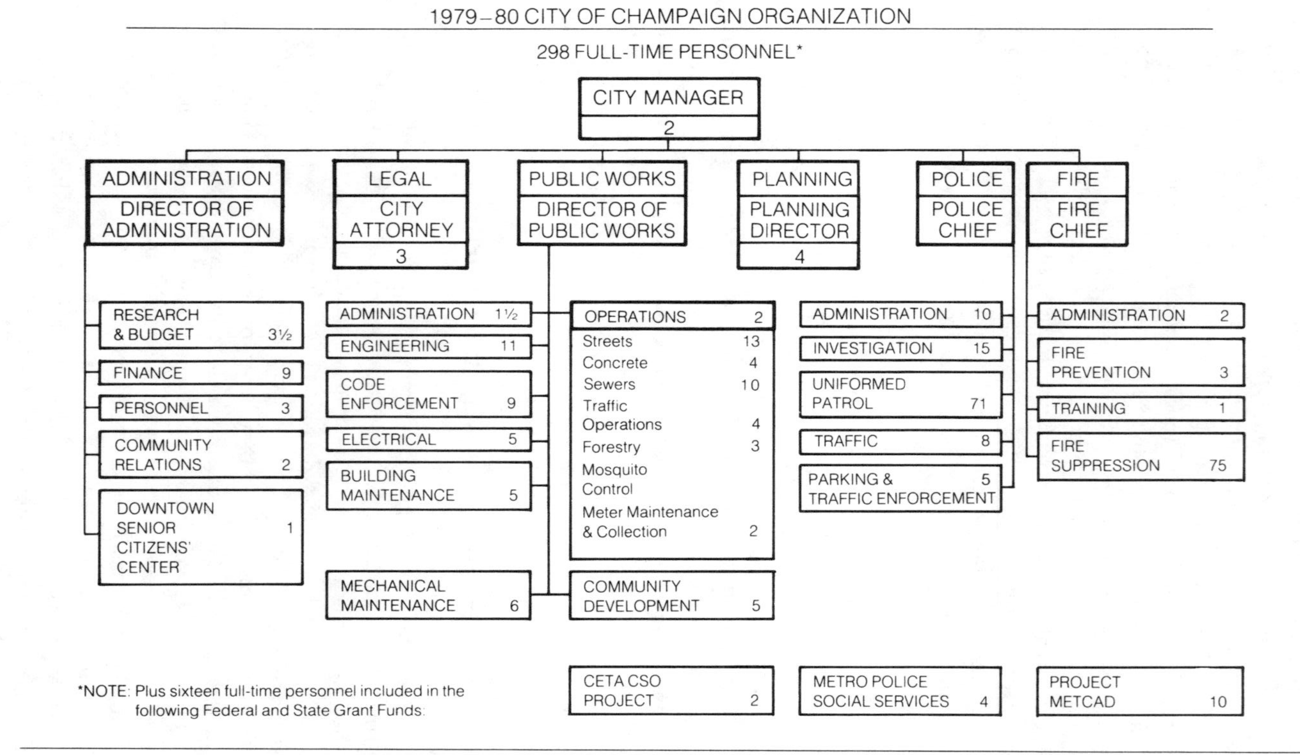

Fig. 5.4. Organization of the city of Champaign. From Rozann Rothman, "Champaign-Urbana: The Politics of Transition," in *The Middle-Size Cities of Illinois,* ed. Daniel Milo Johnson and Rebecca Monroe Veach (Springfield, Ill.: Sangamon State University, 1980), p. 49.

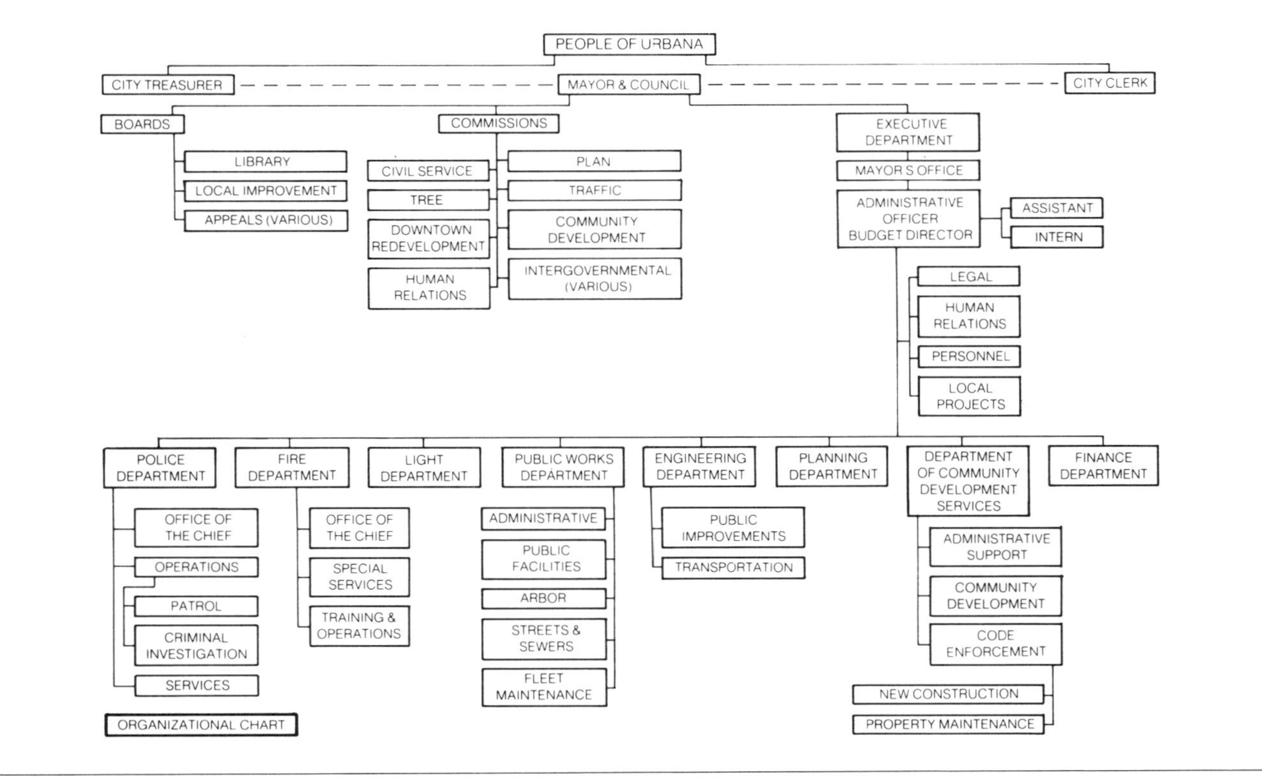

Fig. 5.5. Organization of the city of Urbana. From Rozann Rothman, "Champaign-Urbana: The Politics of Transition," in *The Middle-Size Cities of Illinois,* ed. Daniel Milo Johnson and Rebecca Monroe Veach (Springfield, Ill.: Sangamon State University, 1980), p. 45.

The mayor and city council of Peoria appoint nearly eighty boards or commissions. Five deal with police, fire, local government elections, and electricity and have operating responsibilities. Eleven are advisory boards that make recommendations to the city council for action in concrete fields such as planning, zoning, environmental pollution control, human resources, government ethics, liquor control, and traffic control. Finally, there are the semiautonomous boards that administer institutions such as the Peoria public library, the tuberculosis sanatorium, the municipal band, the public housing authority, the Peoria civic center authority, the downtown redevelopment commission, and the public building commission. While their budgets are subject to city council appropriation, approval of those budgets is automatic, so that they essentially have full governing powers in their own spheres. In addition to these boards and commissions, the city administration itself is organized into seventeen departments or divisions responsible to the city manager and through him to the city council.[6]

The special districts in the Springfield civil community follow the same pattern as those in the rest of Illinois. In addition to the City of Springfield, Springfield Township, and Sangamon County, Springfield has a school district established by charter in 1854, the Lincoln Library District established in 1886, the Springfield Pleasure Driveway and Park District established in 1900, the Springfield Sanitary District established in 1924, and the Springfield Airport Authority established in 1945. In 1966 the Springfield Area Vocational School District was established. The community college district and civic auditorium authority came into existence a year later, and the mass transit district was established in 1968.

All told, a typical Springfield resident pays taxes to and is served by a dozen independent and semi-independent governments with taxing powers, only one of which, the library district, has boundaries coterminous with those of the city. This in turn leads to twenty-nine different tax rate combinations levied against property within the city's boundaries, depending on the district where a particular piece of property is situated.

Voters in the immediate civil community elect fifty officials to the various boards, authorities, and commissions, and another fifty-five are appointed to membership on others. Coordination among these many different units and jurisdictions is through negotiation because there is no single body capable of coordinating among them. The negotiating system seems to work, since controversies among units are rare. Under the commission system of government, the five commissioner-led departments are also semi-independent, de facto, because each commissioner drafts his own budget and hires his own staff, with the city council as a whole simply ratifying his choices on the basis of mutuality.

There is some overlapping of functions. For example, though the civil community is served by independent park districts, the City of Springfield maintains its own park and recreational playground programs administered through two separate city departments. The park district handles the large parks, and the city administers the smaller parks and neighborhood recreation areas. On the other hand, the city council retains power over zoning, contracts, disbursements, regulation of taverns, and street improvements. Planning remains essentially in the hands of the planning commission, whose influence continued to be very limited through the end of the postwar generation. Symbolically, at one point the city council voted to remove the planning commission from space it rented in city hall, although the vote was later reversed.[7]

Another example of the multiple-jurisdictions approach and the local commitment to that approach is to be found in the Rockford civil community. In 1977, seventy-two separate taxes were levied in Winnebago County. Property owners in the city of Rockford were assessed in nine different government units including Winnebago County, Rockford Township, the City of Rockford, the Rockford Park District, the Rockford Sanitary District, the Greater Rockford Airport Authority, the Winnebago County Forest Preserve District, Rockford School District 205, and Rock Valley College District 511.

Various efforts to consolidate functional agencies with overlapping jurisdictions have had minimal success. The city, township, and county health departments were merged into a single health department, but consolidation of fire districts into a countywide unit failed. Instead, however, there developed a substantial cooperative fire-fighting program based on interlocal agreements that has succeeded admirably in accomplishing the same goals.

Efforts were made during this period to eliminate Rockford Township government, but these did not succeed. Since the township is essentially the protective membrane between the civil community and the county government, it is not hard to understand why that has proved difficult. Since the introduction of federal revenue sharing, which includes an automatic distribution to every township, the issue has been dropped. As in so many other cases, in the last analysis federal action reinforces the existing order of things at least as much as it changes it.

In a clear display of how a civil community can link its several governments with a common interest, Rockford combined the City of Rockford, Rockford Township, and Winnebago County to work together in law enforcement, stimulated by the availability of federal revenue sharing funds. The three governments pooled their allocations for crime control and then their law enforcement services to the public. By coordinating and dividing responsibilities, they eliminated unnecessary duplication while retaining the tripartite structure of the local police services.

The Rockford Park District and Winnebago County Forest Preserve District also remained independent governmental units within the Rockford civil community, but they expanded their scope in the latter part of the generation. The park district in particular has taken on a series of cooperative relationships with various other public bodies, particularly public nongovernment institutions, to eliminate duplication and provide better support for a wide range of recreational services. Thus Rockford's Natural History Museum, the Rockford Museum Center and Midway Village, and the Tinker Swiss Cottage are now operated by the park district in cooperation with the citizens' groups that had previously maintained them. Here too the thrust is toward cooperative interlocal agreements—in this case linking government and civic bodies—rather than amalgamation or consolidation. Such arrangements are accurate manifestations of the civil community concept at work and represent ways the concept offers a real alternative to centralist and hierarchical approaches to governance and public service.[8]

One result of this situation is that the city government of Rockford in fact is something less than the general-purpose government it was constituted to be. Rather, it has become a limited multipurpose authority whose primary responsibility is public safety (police) and whose second principal function is constructing and maintaining sanitation arrangements. The city budget reflects this clearly, as indicated in table 5.1. Rockford, in this respect, is like all the other cities of the prairie and, indeed, all American cities except perhaps a few of the largest ones. This was one of the conclusions of the original study. Despite general revenue sharing, block grants, A-95 consultation procedures, and similar federal government initiatives to strengthen general-purpose local governments, it still stands, as true as ever.

The Quad Cities' metropolitan area is the epitome of the system of multiple jurisdictions, with 108 separate units of local government straddling two states, including three counties, forty-seven cities, twenty-six school districts, forty-two townships, plus library districts, airport districts, and transportation districts. Barely metropolitanized Henry County leads with a total of eighty-six separate local government units, most the products of earlier rural times. Rock Island County has seventy-two and Scott County a mere thirty. The list does not count the many city and county boards and commissions with varying degrees of independence as in Peoria. At the same time, these local governments are tied together by over 250 interjurisdictional agreements, dealing with thirty-eight specific categories of services, including fire, civil defense, planning, airport, library, food inspection, milk inspection, water pollution, and sanitary landfill.[9]

Table 5.1. Rockford Government Expenditures by Function, 1978

General government	$ 3,748,135
Public safety	15,507,685
Streets, alleys, and bridges	5,830,577
Community development	396,877
Sanitation and sewers	1,988,340
Transportation	200,929
Culture and recreation	1,538,079
Public health/welfare	31,221
Interest/other	394,373
Capital outlay	4,073,721
Debt service	
Bond principal	1,015,000
Bond interest	440,920

Source: Daniel Milo Johnson and Rebecca Monroe Veach, eds., *The Middle-Size Cities of Illinois: Their People, Politics and Quality of Life* (Springfield, Ill.: Sangamon State University, 1980). Reprinted with permission of the Center for the Study of Middle-Size Cities, Sangamon State University.

Nevertheless, the postwar generation witnessed a series of efforts to impose a new model on local government in those civil communities, the managerial model. These efforts took three forms. The first was the introduction of professional managers into previously citizen-directed bodies. The second was securing the institutional changes appropriate to accomplish the first. Thus, for example, functions that were under the jurisdiction of boards and commissions were reorganized under line departments structured hierarchically, at least in theory. Most important of all, efforts were made to change the very system of municipal government from the mayor-aldermanic or commission forms to council-manager government, in order to introduce "businesslike" (the code word for managerial) principles and practices into local government. The council-manager plan was presented in terms of the managerial ideology throughout, as were the other institutional changes.

The third step involved an effort to consolidate separate governing bodies either within a single government or within a common overarching framework. This took two forms: internal reorganization of city and county governments to strengthen chief executives' control over the administrative departments along hierarchical lines, and merger of governments—cities, cities and counties, school districts—in each metropolitan area. Included in this thrust was a principaled opposition to the creation of new special districts.

The first step met with considerable success, reflecting as it did the necessity for more centralized and professional leadership in fields requiring technical knowledge for their mastery and full-time commitment for their administration. The second succeeded partially, in the sense that most of the cities of the prairie adopted the council-manager plan and those that did not instituted managerial assistants for their mayors in an effort to achieve the same professional level of administration without sacrificing the primacy of political decision making. The distinction is important, since the latter course of action was indisputably consistent with the federalist principles whereas the former was intended to replace them.

By the latter half of the generation, then, the changes that could be seen in the realm of local administration involved a movement toward less technocratization and a broadening of the base of expertise. During the first half of the generation, leaders in many civil communities showed strong interest in strengthening technocratic government. The spread of the city manager plan throughout most of the cities of the prairie exemplified that trend. City manager government was initially represented to be more technocratic in character than it turned out to be. Indeed, it was promoted as the way to introduce expert management into municipal affairs. Moreover, Illinois law makes the managerial dimension of council-manager government explicit. If a city chooses to adopt that form of government, it must give the city manager control of the personnel system and the budgetary process as well as responsibility for administrative oversight and policy innovation. The one political control on the manager is the city council, which can hire and fire him and, of course, must approve all his budgetary and policy proposals.

Even during the first half of the generation it became apparent that local government was at its foundation a matter of politics, not management. City managers themselves became political actors of the first order.

It was precisely in those communities where broad-based democratic government was the norm, such as Duluth and Rockford, that the city manager plan was not accepted. In Pueblo, as the base broadened, the city manager increasingly became one among many local specialists. This indeed was the trend. The discovery that local government was not simply a matter of management did not contradict the general trend toward the increased employment of experts to serve the civil community. Quite the contrary, as civil communities became more sophisticated, they sought more expertise, even while abandoning earlier efforts to put the decision-making power into the hands of experts. Thus the number of specialists employed by the cities tended to increase during this period, with the result that the role of any particular specialist became less pronounced, unless the force of his personality managed to gain him special status *ad personam.*

By the end of the generation, the council-manager system was being modified in city after city through the introduction of district elections to the council, a clear repudiation of the presumed businesslike neutrality of council-manager government and the rediscovery of the political dimension of governing. Moreover, in some civil communities the city manager was being chosen from among locals on a political basis (in either the narrow or the broad sense) in order to make certain the position would be tied in with local politics rather than turned over to an outside professional whose primary commitments would be to his profession and who would be moving from city to city as opportunities for professional achievement presented themselves.

The third step did not succeed in any of the metropolitan areas of the cities of the prairie. The proposed merger of Champaign and Urbana, brought to referendum by a coalition of academics and "cosmopolitan" reformers spearheaded by the League of Women Voters as a pure expression of managerialism, failed early in the generation. Not until the early 1970s was it possible to raise the issue again.

The second effort at merger grew out of a general push toward greater interlocal cooperation in the early 1970s. In 1976 the two city councils created a joint Study Commission on Intergovernmental Cooperation with members from both cities, the special districts, and the university. After two years of work without attracting significant public interest, it recommended a merger of the two cities on the grounds of efficiency. Its recommendations rapidly sank out of sight, as a result of sheer indifference as well as opposition. A public opinion poll taken at the time revealed that less than a third of the population thought such a merger would improve the quality of public services, and less than a fifth believed a merger would lead to greater government efficiency. About as many thought it would worsen matters. Half the citizens thought there would be no change in quality of services or that they would worsen, while 60 percent foresaw no improvement or a lessening of efficiency (table 5.2).[10]

In the other metropolitan areas the issue never reached that stage, though the idea was occasionally broached. Pueblo toyed with the idea of city-county consolidation, but the organization of its Council of Governments achieved the same goals without the struggle that would have been inevitable in a merger move, so the idea was dropped.

Other metropolitan areas worked out their own adjustments to the problems of metropolitan integration. In the Quad Cities metropolitan

Table 5.2. Citizen Opinion on Merger of Champaign and Urbana

Opinion	Percentage	
	Champaign	Urbana
If a merger between Champaign and Urbana took place, do you think that officials of the new government would do:		
What the majority of citizens want	24.6	28.4
What a few more influential citizens want	17.5	28.4
What they themselves think best	24.6	14.8
Refusal	7.0	6.8
NA	0.9	1.1
DADK	25.4	20.5
If a merger of Champaign and Urbana took place, would the quality of public services:		
Improve	28.1	31.8
Worsen	12.3	17.0
No change	40.4	28.4
Refusal	7.0	6.8
NA	0.9	1.1
DADK	11.4	14.8
If a merger of Champaign and Urbana took place, do you think local government offices or officials would handle problems:		
More efficiently	18.4	20.5
Less efficiently	13.2	20.5
In same manner	46.5	37.5
Refusal	7.0	6.8
NA	0.9	1.1
DADK	14.0	13.6

Source: Daniel Milo Johnson and Rebecca Monroe Veach, eds., *The Middle-Size Cities of Illinois: Their People, Politics and Quality of Life* (Springfield, Ill.: Sangamon State University, 1980). Reprinted with permission of the Center for the Study of Middle-Size Cities, Sangamon State University.
Note: Total percentages in each category may not equal 100 due to rounding.

region, the Illinois–Iowa boundary prevented any consideration of merger. Instead, a set of structured interlocal relationships has developed to an extraordinary degree, utilizing semiformal devices. In a study separate from this one, H. Paul Friesma thoroughly examined those relationships in the early 1960s, revealing just how extensive and binding they were.[11] There is every reason to believe that it is precisely because there is no fear of metropolitan consolidation that there has been a readiness to pursue cooperation in a far-reaching way. Official government recognition of the new metropolitan consciousness came with the establishment of the Bi-State Metropolitan Planning Commission in 1966. By and large, however, intermetropolitan activity has been carried on through the public nongovernment sector.

The continued growth of a sense of metropolitanwide concern in the Quad Cities area has been visible in the growth of metropolitanwide cooperation among the local chambers of commerce. Moline's chamber of commerce was reorganized through mergers with those of East Moline, Silvis, and adjacent communities to form the Chamber of Commerce of Upper Rock Island County, taking in the whole east end of the county. It and the others function within the metropolitanwide Council of Chambers of Commerce, which, along with the Associated Industries of the Quad Cities and the Quad Cities Development Group, provides a metropolitanwide network for promoting the region's economic affairs. The latter body, founded in 1959, continues to embrace the great majority of important business and industrial enterprises in the metropolitan area. In the early 1970s it led a drive to increase the industrial park acreage in the region, and 1,800 acres of industrial park space were added between 1972 and 1975, principally in the Davenport area, which has more land available for such uses. It continued to publish the *Quad City Quarterly,* a survey of economic indicators.

The media reflected this metropolitanization as well. The *Davenport Times-Democrat* changed its name to the *Quad Cities Times,* shortly after which the *Rock Island Argus* initiated a Sunday supplement called the *Quad City.* The *Quad City Times* has the largest circulation in the Quad City area. Both the *Argus* and the *Moline Daily Dispatch* continued to publish throughout the latter half of the generation, and weekly newspapers continued to flourish in Bettendorf and East Moline as well as Rock Island. In the beginning of the 1970s a left-wing monthly, *New Times,* was established to feature material of interest to the peace and civil rights movements. It continued to publish through the rest of the decade. In general, the media continued to provide good local coverage without being particularly oriented toward investigative journalism.

Rock Island and Scott County churches have organized a council of churches called Churches United. The United Way is also organized metropolitanwide.[12] On the other hand, as Maren Stein indicates in her study of Decatur (chap. 8), the situation there remained quite the reverse, with each government within the civil community going its own way in virtually every aspect of local government. Efforts to generate interlocal cooperation were consistently rejected. Thus Decatur seems to have retained a dualistic model of intergovernmental relationships more characteristic of the nineteenth century than of the twentieth.[13]

There was some opposition to the establishment of special districts, but invariably the same "cosmopolitans" who supported metropolitan consolidation for reasons of principle supported special districts for airports or parks for reasons of interest—to secure tax revenues for favored public projects. Thus the opposition came from the "locals" who opposed the expenditure as a tax increase and who would have been against consolidation as well.[14]

In the last analysis, federalist principles triumphed over managerial ones in the cities of the prairie because the residents of those civil communities were free to make their own decisions. In choosing the traditional American pattern, however, the local political systems did not reject the idea of better management. They were generally willing to integrate new management techniques, principles, devices, or organizational structures into their federalist frameworks. While their introduction also had to pass through a process of gaining support from generally conservative communities, that was merely a matter of finding ways to incorporate them into existing frameworks. It was only when there was a confrontation with managerialism as an ideology, introduced as a means to transform the local political system, that a conflict took place.

In the first phase of the confrontation between the two, in the 1950s, managerialism won some initial victories in many of the civil communities and seemed to be the wave of the future. Those opposed to "businesslike local government," the code words for the managerial ideology in the United States at the time (and a reflection of how managerialism in the United States grew out of the business community), were generally labeled benighted or corrupt—that is to say, committed to old-style machine politics. While many of the opponents were both, among them were also those who perceived, even if they could not always articulate it, the conflict between the federalist and managerial approaches and chose the former.[15]

It is significant that it was precisely those civil communities that were strongholds of the moralistic political subculture, where politics was considered an efficacious means for civic improvement, that resisted these efforts to take politics out of government and to turn cities into pseudo business corporations. They embraced aspects of the managerial revolution—indeed, they were among the very first to employ specialists in particular fields of government activity and were open to providing political elected heads of government with institutionalized managerial assistance—but they rarely made the mistake of confusing those innovations with a need to eliminate politics. In other words, they did not embrace managerialism as an ideology, probably because they were satisfied with the federal and democratic republicanism within which their polities were already grounded.[16]

It was possible to introduce professional expertise into the federalist style of government without embracing managerialism, precisely because no single expert would do; rather, the multiplicity of experts could be harnessed to the multiplicity of jurisdictions. Needless to say, it did not have to be done that way. Were governmental structures to be centralized, the multiplicity of experts would simply contest for influence within their own closed circle. If, as was and is the case in the cities of thc prairie, the jurisdictions themselves were to remain separate, then the experts were teamed with the representatives of the citizenry to contest with one another. Pueblo is an excellent example of a civil community that was initially moved by the siren song of managerialism and made certain requisite political changes but then pulled back as a result of the influence of experts serving multiple jurisdictions and built a new framework that was politically, civically, and administratively strong.

In some of the other cities there tended to be a greater resistance to the introduction of professionals, in part because of the added cost, in part because it was understood to mean a commitment to more activist government, and in part because the nonprofessionals were reluctant to relinquish power. The last reason was least important, except with regard to functions such as building and zoning regulation, where strong interests had much at stake in maintaining control or at least access. Slowly but surely, however, in even the most reluctant of the cities of the prairie, professionalization was introduced.

In certain functions professional civil servants almost replaced the civic and political leadership, who retreated into the background. In others, building and zoning in particular, the civil servants were completely subordinated to the representatives of the community. The city manager in Joliet, for example, was in the latter category from the first, whereas the Decatur city manager, originally a strong professional with ties to his peer group far stronger than his local commitment, is now in the same situation. The determining factor is whether there are strong interests represented in the political constitution of the council, commission, board, or committee to whom the professional is formally responsible who are reluctant to relinquish power, usually for fear the interests they represent would be damaged.

In the last analysis, federal democracy remained strong even in the face of the challenge of managerialism, not because of overt ideological understanding and commitment, but because of the constellation of local interests in each civil community. Only in those communities substantially influenced by the moralistic political subculture can it be said that more was involved. Even in the others, where city manager government was adopted in a wave of ideological fervor that happened to serve local business interests as well, by the end of the generation the new institutions were modified in the direction of federal democracy. Professional expertise was introduced but was linked to separate boards, commissions, and jurisdictions, and government consolidation generally failed to be accepted in all cases as a result of the combination of ideology and self-interest, even on the part of those elements considered most committed to the reformist, managerial style.

The 1970s: Between Frontiers

By the late 1960s, a combination of factors had caused the initial thrust of the metropolitan frontier to diminish and indeed become routinized. Development continued on the peripheries and in the interstices of the suburban areas in most metropolitan regions. Each new development brought with it the same shakedown period and problems that such development had brought earlier. But outside the Sun Belt, the dynamic atmosphere was gone. Overall, the country had settled into a period of consolidation perhaps not dissimilar to that of the 1920s. The discovery of environmental problems at the same time even led to a new rhetoric, if not ideology, suggesting not only that the period of American growth was at an end, but that growth itself was bad, that Americans should be content with what they have or even less (a view more appealing to the children of the prosperous than to the poor). Only the Sun Belt frontier continued unabated and even expanded, fostering a new sectionalism whose outline, already visible by the early 1960s, began to be filled in with real political content. The result was the emergence of the Frost Belt/Sun Belt conflict, which, like previous sectional conflicts, is clearly frontier-related.

On the other hand, the 1960s thrust of most federal policies continued. Even though many Great Society programs were abandoned, the principles behind them were not. Efforts at greater federal intervention to redirect things in metropolitan regions were just as pronounced, though less successful as they ran into obstacles of one kind or another. Nevertheless, a great deal was accomplished in the federal effort to spread the benefits of the metropolitan frontier around the country.

Perhaps general revenue sharing, more than any other program, is a reflection of this effort. In some respects it can be compared to the land grant college program inaugurated by the Morrill Act of 1862. Up to that time, the federal government had indeed made land grants, but only to the frontier states actually in the process of being settled. This led to a demand from those states that no longer were on the rural-land frontier for their share of that frontier's largesse—namely, free land. So the Morrill Act was passed to give every state a land grant, with the land to be sold and proceeds used to establish a state land grant college. Similarly, general revenue sharing was designed to spread the largesse of the metropolitan-technological frontier (i.e., money from the federal treasury that has the appearance of being free money) not only to those frontier communities marked by entrepreneurial energy and skills and able to gain grants to advance their local ends but for all communities regardless of the level of their grantsmanship. It is an open question whether this has led to more equal results or simply encouraged greater expenditures. By the mid-1970s it was clear that in the wake of the new expenditure levels, the notion of free money was rapidly disappearing.

The solution to the real problems of American cities and metropolitan areas, however, is not to be found in simply increasing federal largesse. It is to be found in re-creating the civil community, with its sense of a local public that is composed of citizens, not consumers, who take an active interest in the health of their community because they understand their stake in it.[17]

The problem of growth is not simply physical; it is how to accommodate newness and transience—that is, the American frontier condition. It is very difficult to deal with that problem in the best of circumstances. On earlier frontiers, when the sense of citizenship and civic pride was part of the common coin of the realm and the lack of externally provided alternatives was apparent to all, civil community could be and was maintained, even by transients. Studies of nineteenth-century communities reveal that their cadres of active citizens were no less susceptible to moving around than are those of today, but they were not distracted by commitments to external corporations or governments and a perception of themselves as consumers rather than citizens.

In a society in which the props of citizenship have been eroded, the problem is intensified. The only solution is building civil community in the cities of the United States—metropolitan or otherwise. Building civil community is a most difficult task, since it involves a revival of citizenship. Norton Long has written extensively about the problem of local citizenship, quite properly suggesting that it is the basis for truly healthy cities.[18]

As correct as Long's analysis may be, it is not likely that classic forms of local citizenship can be revived in the United States. There is no polis in the offing in America, even in healthy cities. At best we can hope for civil community, a community of limited liability based upon a modest sense of citizenship.[19] This is difficult enough, since it means cultivating a renewed will to be citizens rather than consumers. The creation of civil community can reestablish the possibility for properly negotiating with the federal government in matters affecting the city. More important, it will provide a basis for building cities that are not merely service units making consumers happy but political entities that cultivate participating citizens.

In this connection there is much to learn from the cities of the prairie. The passage of those cities onto the metropolitan frontier transformed them from civil communities in which the manners, morals, and institutions of late-nineteenth-century America had survived almost intact well into the postwar generation into civil communities of the twentieth century. These changes are not to be minimized, just as they could not be avoided even by those who wished to do so, but they need not be exaggerated either. Equally impressive is that in 1978 as in 1961 the cities of the prairie seemed capable of confronting and coping with change with the minimum surrender of their vital interests and commitments. Perhaps what is most important of all, considering the radical changes that did take place, for example in the integration of nonwhite minorities, is how many things could be changed that before-the-fact assessments suggested were probably unchangeable without massive outside intervention. That this did not prove true demonstrates both the flexibility of those civil communities and the reality of their existence as civil communities.

In 1976 the post–World War II generation came to an end. Nothing symbolized this better than the election of Jimmy Carter, the first American president to have come of age since World War II, a man who ran on a platform suggesting that the issues of the post–World War II generation were no longer central in American life. As the new generation began, the third stage of the American frontier no longer seemed compelling. At the same time, despite the "limits of growth" rhetoric, there was every sign that a fourth stage was beginning—a rurban-cybernetic frontier generated by the metropolitan-technological frontier, just as the latter had been generated by its predecessor.

The rurban-cybernetic frontier emerged first in the Northeast, as did its predecessors, as the Atlantic coast metropolitan regions merged into one another to form a six-hundred-mile-long megalopolis (the usage is Jean Gottman's)—a matrix of urban, suburban, and exurban settlements in which the older central cities came to share importance if not prominence with smaller places.[20] It was a sign of the times that the computer was conceived at Massachusetts Institute of Technology in Cambridge and developed at IBM in White Plains, two medium-sized cities in the megalopolis that have become special centers in their own right. This in itself is a reflection of the two primary characteristics of the new frontier. The new locus of settlement is in medium-sized and small cities and in the rural interstices of the megalopolis. The spreading use of computer technology in everything from direct dialing of telephone calls throughout the world to microwave ovens is the most direct manifestation of the cybernetic tools that make possible such combinations of rural and urban settlement. In 1979 the newspapers in the Northeast published frequent reports of the revival of the small cities of the first industrial revolution, particularly in New England, as the new frontier engulfed them. Countrywide, the media focused on the shifting of population growth into rural areas. Both phenomena are as much a product of direct dialing as they are of the older American longing for small town or country living. Both reflect the urbanization of the American way of life no matter what life-style is practiced, or where.

Although the Northeast was first, like its predecessors the new rurban-cybernetic frontier is finding its true form in the South and West, where these citybelt matrixes are not being built on the collapse of earlier forms but are developing as an original form. The present Sun Belt frontier—strung out along the Gulf coast, the southwestern desert, and the fringes of the California mountains—is classically megalopolitan in rurban form and cybernetic with its aerospace-related industries and Sun Belt living made possible by air conditioning and the new telecommunications.

It is still too early to delineate with surety all the imperatives or even the propensities of the rurban-cybernetic frontier, but some are already visible. Perhaps most important is the new sectionalism, the reemergence of an older basis of American politics in new form. The urban-industrial frontier brought in its wake a politics of class, reflected at its height in the New Deal and the political realignment of which it was a part. This politics of class attacked the division of urban America into "two cities," the "Protestant" and privileged versus the "ethnic" and denied. It persisted through the metropolitan frontier years in no small measure because even after affluence and influence came to Protestants and ethnics alike, it was reinforced by the transformed politics of race. As blacks moved from the southern backwaters remaining from the old rural-land frontier to the world of the metropolitan frontier, their problems took on an economic dimension previously submerged by the legally enforced caste system.

The politics of class divided the country into liberals and conservatives, a division that most concede has become very blurred in recent years. The blurring of what were once relatively clear-cut differences reflects the emergence of the new frontier, with its new problems and politics revolving once again around "have" and "have-not" sections whose economic interests are often diametrically opposed. Significantly, the emergence of this renewed sectionalism is tied to the end of the economic dominance of the Northeast. The sunbelt/frostbelt division is only one aspect of it; presidential contests have revealed how sharp are East/West divisions as well. The reallocation of House seats in the wake of the 1980 census has sharpened these divisions as they are translated into new power balances in Congress and the Electoral College. These sectional divisions are reflected in life-style differences as well.[21]

The issues associated with what current idiom denominates "life-style" have for the moment contributed to a great weakening of the political party system and single-issue politics. Although these particular manifestations may be less long-lived than conventional wisdom suggests, it is very likely that a continued concern with life-style issues will be a major propensity of the rurban-cybernetic frontier, and at least some resolution of the conflicts associated with those issues will become a major imperative. This problem is intensified in that the rurban dimension, with its emphasis on smaller communities, encourages recrudescence of the kind of territorial democracy that potentially allows different life-styles to flourish without clashing, whereas the cybernetic dimension, with its propensity to foster a global village tied together by telecommunications, works in the opposite direction.

Since this fourth frontier stage is only beginning to emerge, it is not surprising that government policies—federal, state, or local—have barely begun to address it. It is quite true that the federal government's promotion of space exploration from the 1950s on was crucial in opening this new frontier stage. But it was not intended for that purpose in any direct sense. Conscious government efforts to address the problems of the day are still mostly directed to problems of the metropolitan-technological frontier. This is quite natural, for the first task of any new generation is to begin to identify the new problems that will come to dominate its agenda. President Carter took at least a first step in that direction with his announcement of a national Small Community and Rural Development Policy that, despite the older imagery evoked by its name, actually was addressed to the urbanlike needs of the small towns and rural interstices of the new citybelts. In certain respects his policy statement can be likened to the Truman program of the late 1940s, which, though it had little direct impact itself, forecast the national response to the metropolitan-technological frontier half a generation later. When a new generation coincides with the beginnings of a new frontier stage, as in both these cases, the task of agenda building is even greater. The agenda for the new generation and the new frontier has yet to be defined. There is every expectation that much of it will be defined in connection with the state of America's medium-sized civil communities.

Part 2. Case Studies

6. From Industrial City to Metropolitan Civil Community: The Politics of Constitutional Change in Pueblo

Stephen L. Schechter

As there were many reformers, so likewise many reformations; every country proceeding in a particular way and method, according as their national interest, together with their constitution and clime, inclined them; some angrily and with extremity; others calmly and with mediocrity, not rending, but easily dividing the community. (Sir Thomas Browne, *Religio Medici*)

From its inception, Pueblo, Colorado, has had a reputation as the "ugly duckling" of the high plains, unceremoniously plunked down along the banks of the Arkansas River and Fountain Creek in southeastern Colorado. As an unlicensed trading fort operating during the last years of the Rocky Mountain fur trade, Pueblo was described by Francis Parkman as "a wretched species of a fort . . . surrounded by a wall of adobe, miserably cracked and dilapidated," with an assortment of denizens "as mean and miserable as the place itself."[1] As a supply town established in the early days of the Colorado gold rush, Pueblo was visited by Father Jean Baptiste Lamy, bishop of the Santa Fe diocese, who expected from promoters' maps to see a "second New York, with splendid streets and blocks, parks and public gardens." Instead he found "a few miserable huts of frame" with the word "Saloon" scratched in charcoal on one.[2]

In the 1870s, when "General" William Jackson Palmer was considering sites for the steel mill and resort town of his Rocky Mountain railroad empire, Pueblo seemed as natural a setting for the former as Colorado Springs seemed for the latter. Since that time, Pueblo has been promoted as the "Pittsburgh of the West," site of the largest steel plant west of the Mississippi River, and dubbed "Pewtown" by fellow Coloradoans. As late as 1971 Neal R. Peirce wrote: "A purely blue-collar, lunch bucket town, Pueblo presents an overwhelmingly dreary face to the world, even though there is now real hope with a new [U.S.] Department of Transportation test site there and more adequate water supply through the Fryingpan-Arkansas project."[3]

As one travels north from Pueblo, its reputation rapidly expands from "ugly duckling" to "suspect community." By the time one reaches Denver, Pueblo emerges on the seamy side of much of Colorado's history: "desultory" as a trading fort dealing in "Taos lightning"; dominated by "eastern" interests as a company town of the Colorado Fuel and Iron Company; "crime-ridden" and "boss-dominated" as a twentieth-century industrial city; and "culturally impoverished" as a lunch-bucket town that claims Damon Runyon as its favorite son.[4] In the words of a 1968 special report to Governor John A. Love, Pueblo has "a historical posture of 'having been down so long anything is like looking up.'"[5]

Pueblo is different from other Colorado cities, and therein lies the source of its suspect status. That difference was greatest during the fifteen years immediately following World War II. In describing that period, Daniel J. Elazar observed:

> Pueblo is a suspect civil community in the eyes of the rest of the state, particularly in the eyes of northeastern Colorado where the bulk of the political power lies. Its heavy industrial base, until recently a unique phenomenon in the state; its high percentage of Southern, Southern and Eastern European, Afro-American and Hispanic-originated, who make it the state's only Eastern-style "melting pot"; its penchant for political organization and party regularity and the fact that elements held to be "less desirable" by the state's opinion molders are not only represented but actually hold considerable power locally; all tend to make it different and suspect.[6]

Since 1960 many of the socioeconomic differences between Pueblo and other Colorado cities have been narrowed by diversification and retrenchment in Pueblo's economy and by industrialization and immigration patterns in northern Colorado cities. Beginning with the local elections of 1969 and 1971, Pueblo's political system has moved closer to the "progressive-reformist" orientation preferred by northern Coloradoans. Sometime during the late 1970s, one could detect a subtle shift in Pueblo's reputation among northern Coloradoans and state officials from that of a suspect community to that of an underdog struggling against its own nature. Yet even today Pueblo appears to people as a city inexorably pulled by its industrial base and southern exposure toward the corrupting influences of those cities "back east" that so many Coloradoans have fled.

For Pueblo, the injustice in all this is not that its history has been mistold, but that its efforts since 1961 to escape the limits of its past have been largely ignored. For the student of local politics, the implication lies in how those efforts worked and why they succeeded where earlier ones had failed.

In either case, we are directed backward in the search for recurring patterns and turning points in the city's history.

The Culmination of Pueblo's Urban-Industrial Order, 1941–60

On the eve of World War II, Pueblo was a prematurely aging industrial city of approximately 50,000 inhabitants. Though Pueblo had begun to assemble the makings of an urban-industrial community some seventy years earlier, the Pueblo of 1941 had already become an odd amalgam of ripened neglect and youthful incompleteness. The Colorado Fuel and Iron (CF&I) plant had become a neglected element in the Rockefeller empire. The steelworkers' union had not yet been organized, and Philip ("Tiger") Muhic was still assembling the basic elements of his Democratic party machine. City government was tightly restricted by the expectations and charter of a caretaker government. Special improvement districts abounded, yet streets remained unpaved and dust was a serious problem. In all these respects, Pueblo was still operating under the acute conditions of adversity brought on by the depression of 1921 and a devastating flood in that same year.

Comparatively, Pueblo's prewar condition was not unlike other medium-sized cities on the fringes of the prairie-plains economy. Indeed, Pueblo may be considered representative of those cities that had precariously grown to medium size based on a single extractive industry and the urban needs of a chronically depressed hinterland.[7] On the one hand, Pueblo was able to achieve primacy as the urban-industrial center of a large mining and agricultural region from the Arkansas River to the coal mines of southern Colorado. On the other hand, Pueblo remained only one step removed from the acute conditions of economic instability, prolonged depression, and isolation of its hinterland.

For those long-depressed industrial cities like Pueblo that could capitalize on the wartime boom (and many could not),[8] the industrial needs of World War II and the subsequent half-generation of expansion provided a new lease on life. However, wartime and postwar expansion did not fundamentally alter Pueblo's urban-industrial base or the social and political order that had grown up around it. Quite the contrary, the period from World War II to 1960 witnessed the culminating stage of that order.

WARTIME BOOM AND POSTWAR EXPANSION

During the first half of the World War II generation, from 1946 to 1961, Pueblo's economic expansion and population increases seemed to confirm its reputation in northern Colorado as a suspect industrial city "on the move."

Between 1940 and 1960, Pueblo County experienced, even by Colorado standards, a dramatic population increase of almost 75 percent, emerging as a full-fledged metropolitan area of 118,700 inhabitants in 1960. Almost half of the 1950–60 population growth can be accounted for by increases in the Hispanic population and the in-migration of southerners. By 1960, Spanish-surnamed persons accounted for 21.4 percent of the county's population.[9]

For Puebloans, the images and realities of city life pointed in a different direction. Highly stable ethnic neighborhoods and social institutions continued throughout this period to perform a meaningful role in the social and political life of both the city as a whole and the city's most significant ethnic groups: Hispanic, Italian, Slovenian, "Austrian" (including many Slovenians), and German.[10] The city contained a significant proportion of owner-occupied housing—two-thirds of all occupied units in 1960. Equally important, Pueblo maintained the lowest index of Anglo/non-Anglo residential segregation of any city in the Southwest from Texas to California, with the exception of Laredo, Texas.[11]

Much of Pueblo's population growth between 1940 and 1960 was due to a temporary expansion of the city's manufacturing-service employment base. Expansion was brought on by a wartime boom, increased reliance on custodial care at the Colorado State Hospital for the Mentally Ill (situated in Pueblo since 1879), and a rural–small town exodus from economically depressed areas in southern Colorado and northern New Mexico.[12] At the peak of the employment boom, in 1951–52, 40 percent of the city's work force was employed by two principal employers, CF&I and the Pueblo army depot. Furthermore, both institutions were outside city limits and, like the third-largest employer (the state hospital), were absentee controlled and highly dependent on external factors, with their employees tightly restricted from participation in local affairs.

By 1960 the proportion of the work force employed by CF&I and the army depot had dropped to 25 percent; yet Pueblo remained an industrial city, with secondary functions as a regional retail trade and mental health service center. Most of the major employers were still absentee controlled and, in the case of the state hospital and army depot, "custodial" in nature. Approximately 90 percent of all families lived on annual family incomes of less than $10,000—substantially below state and national averages; and there was a relatively small class of approximately 225 families with incomes over $25,000. Less than 10 percent of the work force was engaged in professional and technical occupations. Despite Pueblo's official status as a metropolitan area, the city was still surrounded by an underdeveloped urban fringe area composed of barrios, factories, farms, and prairie.[13] (See map 6.1 and its legend.)

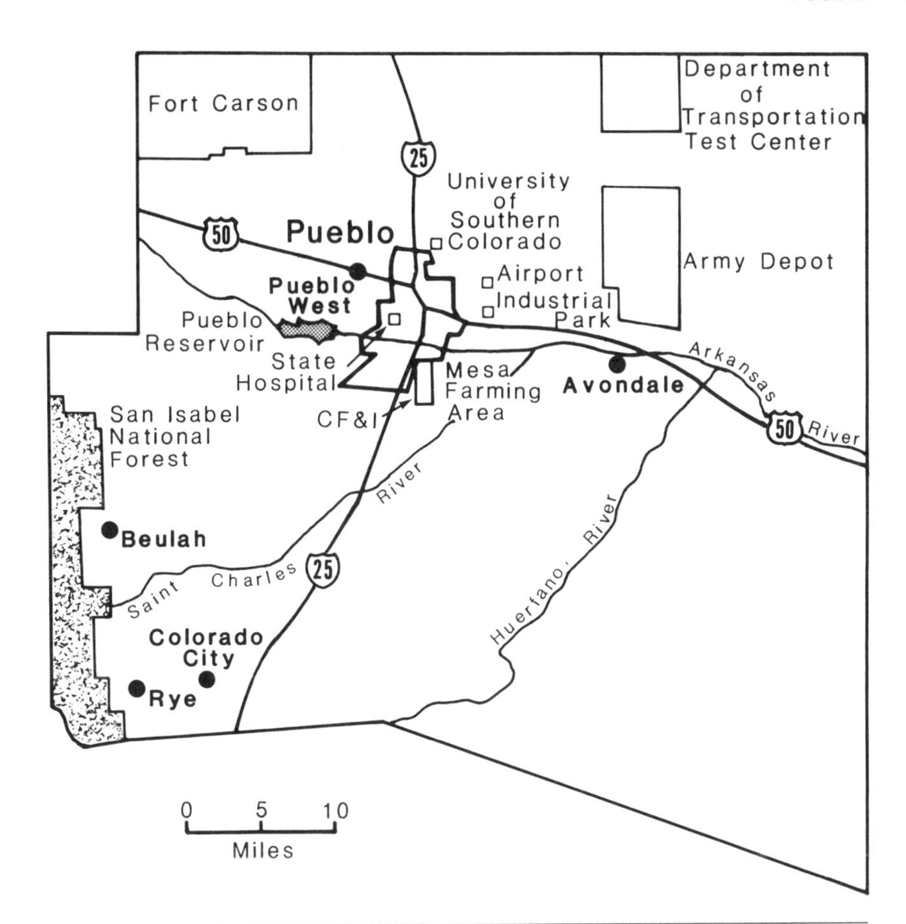

Map 6.1. Pueblo County: major settlements, facilities, and arteries. The following settlements and facilities have been established since 1960: USC (University of Southern Colorado, originally established as Southern Colorado State College in 1963); Pueblo West and Colorado City, both founded as "new towns," the former in 1969; the United States Department of Transportation High Speed Test Center, 1971; the industrial park and United States Documents Center; the Pueblo Reservoir, completed in 1975.

Still, for Puebloans, and for those attracted to Pueblo from its hinterland, the 1940s and 1950s were a time of recovery and expansion. CF&I operations were modernized after Charles Allen, Jr., and Associates acquired control in 1944. The steelworkers' union and the Democratic party had become well-organized vehicles for providing services locally and representing local interests in the state capital. Increases in the money supply and favorable investment conditions triggered a period of private investment and capital improvements. Public finances began to improve, enabling the city to retire its flood recovery debts. And between 1950 and 1960, city population increased by 45 percent, to 91,181.

But recovery and expansion also brought the corrupting influences associated with boom times. A red-light district flourished on Union Avenue with the arrival of the army depot in 1942, and beginning in 1943 United States army police and eager state liquor and health officials initiated a prolonged "cleanup" campaign against it.[14] There also was a relaxed system of "selective arrangements," not atypical in an economy dominated by large institutional interests. The state hospital, for example, was long considered a source of local consultant appointments, patronage jobs, and medical supply contracts.[15] Factories outside the city limits were said to have provided generous gratuities to ensure prompt responses by the city fire department.[16] Finally, there was the "legend," as Neal Peirce reports, that "$50 is the top price to get someone wiped out and the police have been reported to play both sides of the cops and robbers game."[17] Reinforcing this legend was a controversial claim in a special report to the governor of "much cynicism regarding the methods and objectives of the courts and law enforcement agencies of the region and of their presumed connection with the mafia or other powerful interests."[18]

This period of recovery and expansion also witnessed the rise to power of Philip ("Tiger") Muhic as the unrivaled chairman of the Democratic party county committee. As a cigar-chomping Colorado & Wyoming Railroad worker and virtual double for actor Wallace Beery, Muhic embodied the very essence of the "party boss" in the eyes of most Coloradoans long after his death in 1961. For Colorado's gentler citizens, Muhic provided "their first and most convincing demonstration of what 'bossism' can mean in machine politics."[19] Yet Muhic also used a heavy hand to hammer out a place for Pueblo in a state long dominated by the Denver machine.

CHARTER REFORM

Economic recovery, and the new expectations it helped create, challenged the existing caretaker expectations of government and the equilibrium of interests and arrangement that had grown up around them. Throughout the late 1940s and early 1950s, there was a series of unsuccessful efforts to consolidate financing of twenty-eight special improvement districts that had been in arrears since 1938 and were placed under a court-appointed receiver in 1953. Financial problems were compounded by problems of dust and floods caused by a generation of inadequate street paving and sewer facilities.[20]

More important (for those with paved streets) was the issue of charter reform. This issue divided the city for ten years until the adoption of a compromise council-manager municipal charter in 1954, which also empowered the city to levy citywide taxes for special improvements.[21]

The movement for reform began its advance on three local fronts immediately after World War II. On one front, the United Labor League successfully challenged the representational basis of the Republican-dominated "nonpartisan" commission form of government. In 1949, voters approved seven charter amendments proposed by the United Labor League that provided for the adoption of a weak council-manager government with a fourteen-member council, all elected from districts. At the same time, the Civic Taxpayers Improvement Association challenged the inabilities of the system to deliver basic services despite tax increases. Organized in 1945, the association led two unsuccessful petition efforts for a weak manager and nineteen-member council plan in 1945, an unsuccessful drive to block adoption of the 1949 labor-backed amendments, a successful collateral referendum for a charter convention, and an unsuccessful effort to win voter approval for the convention-drafted charter proposal.

Finally, after four years under a system of weak manager and divided council, the chamber of commerce and an assortment of "cosmopolitan-oriented" groups returned to the fray with a proposal for a stronger city manager and a smaller council with all members elected at large. In April 1954 voters approved a new compromise charter, drafted by a committee representative of all factions. The new charter provided for a stronger city manager and a seven-member council, composed of three at-large and four district members and empowered to levy citywide taxes for special improvements.

There is certainly nothing unusual in the mid-1950s adoption of a council-manager form of government. In this respect Pueblo was only following a national fad for municipal reform and the "managerial revolution" behind it. After all, the year of Pueblo's new charter also witnessed the emergence of business administration as the largest single field of undergraduate college enrollment, except for education itself.[22] There also is some evidence that the adoption of city manager governments was most prevalent among that small class of rapidly growing medium-sized cities to which Pueblo belonged. Such cities, according to one line of reasoning, were rapidly reaching a level of urban problems and resources that required the technical skills of a professional manager yet were neither so large nor so small that the need for political representation could not be met by some form of city council.[23] In any case, Pueblo was certainly not catapulted to the cutting edge of the metropolitan frontier by its adoption of a council-manager government in the mid-1950s. While Pueblo was still filling in the interstices of its urban-industrial order, journalists were beginning to herald New Haven's plan for urban *redevelopment* and Toronto's plan for *metropolitan* government as the vanguard of the new frontier.

There is broader significance to Pueblo's prolonged struggle for council-manager government, but it centers less on the national effect of local reforms than on the local reasons for following national fads. Most typically, the adoption of council-manager government is intended to "take politics out of government" and to provide government with the capacity to assume new "unitary" roles of "promoting economic growth" or "providing or securing life's amenities."[24] In Pueblo, the consensus that did exist centered on the notion of imbuing city government with a representational base and a professional bureaucracy that would be better equipped than the existing commissioner government to provide *traditional* services to a rapidly growing population in an equitable and efficient manner. Toward this end, all parties accepted the idea of a legislative council and an executive manager. Few seriously expected city government, however structured, to assume the "promotional" role of the chamber of commerce or the "amenities-providing" role of the county welfare department and existing community organizations; however, some groups may have seen a new government as better able to arbitrate among conflicting interests. In this sense, "Puebloans [were] not interested in depoliticizing their city government, much as they may [have been] interested in professionalizing its bureaucracy."[25] The differences that did emerge were more concerned with the criterion of legislative representation and the extent of the city manager's powers.

The 1954 reform of Pueblo's framework of government, and the very language of debate over its adoption, represented a locally recognized turning point in the city's political history. But the immediate end was not one of political change in the sense of *reconstituting* the civil community around some *new* public consensus or structure of interests. Rather, the reform issues of 1954 triggered long-standing differences between "cosmopolitans" and "locals" over the political question of how best to consolidate the various elements of the existing urban-industrial order for what was believed to be a prolonged period of recovery and expansion.

Toward this end, cosmopolitan-oriented groups (such as the chamber of commerce) held to the belief that consolidation of the existing urban-industrial order could be accomplished with the most "efficiency and economy" by concentrating executive power in the city manager's office and by maintaining the citywide basis of legislative representation that had been nominally in force under the commissioner form of government since 1911. By contrast, localist-oriented groups (such as the Civic Taxpayers Improvement Association and the United Labor League) held to the belief that consolidation of the existing order could be best accomplished by checking the city manager's executive power and by reallocating legislative representation territorially on the basis of existing neighborhoods and sections within the city. The United Labor League won the first round in 1949, when voters adopted the league's plan for a fourteen-member council elected by district. After four years under the excesses of noncentralization, voters approved a compromise charter that contained, for the circumstances, a rather sagacious mixture of centralizing and noncentralizing tendencies that is still basically in force today.

What is particularly interesting about this episode is that the same general pattern of political action exhibited during this period in response to wartime expansion seems to recur throughout Pueblo's political history.

Local Patterns of Political Change

The period of wartime boom and postwar recovery supplies two seemingly contradictory images of Pueblo politics. One is the image of a "suspect community on the make"; the other is the more benign image of a depressed community, too long accustomed to accommodating to adversity. For Pueblo, both images are sustained as the reputation of the one feeds the reality of the other.

The information in table 6.1 provides a schematic view of the historical patterns of challenge and response that Pueblo has faced throughout its development. These patterns are depicted in six stages: (1) a supply town, cumulatively settled on the gold mining frontier (1858–71); (2) an independent center in a cluster of competitive company towns, including South Pueblo and Bessemer, founded by General William Jackson Palmer (1872–94); (3) a consolidated and rapidly growing industrial city, suddenly faced with the internal challenge of sectionalism and political integration (1895–1917); (4) a depressed industrial city, facing the prospect of prolonged economic depression and flood recovery (1920–41); (5) a resuscitated, if not rejuvenated, industrial city in a period of wartime recovery and postwar expansion (1942–60); and (6) a nascent metropolitan center, facing the "no growth" pains of economic diversification and suburbanization (1961–76).

From a distance there is little to distinguish the centenary development of Pueblo's urban-industrial order from national trends of economic change, urbanization, and government reform. In fact the culminating response of each period—town incorporation on the mining frontier, the late-nineteenth-century consolidation of specialized company towns and "frag-

Table 6.1. Development of Pueblo's Urban-Industrial Order

	Foundation (1858–71)	Consolidation (1872–94)	Expansion (1895–1917)	Interregnum (1920–41)	Culmination (1942–60)	Reconstitution (1961–76)
Economic stimulus	Gold rush	Railroad	Industrialization	Depression and flood	Wartime boom	Diversification
Opening gambit	Jefferson Territory movement	Railroad connections; Guggenheim plant		Arkansas River Conservancy District	Army depot; air base	State college; Fryingpan–Arkansas River water diversion project
Settlement pattern	Cumulative settlement	Dispersed settlement	Intensive urbanization	Relative stagnation	Intensive urbanization	Nascent metropolitanism
Initial response	People's courts	New towns, by company and by separation	Ward-based bipartisan system of political "machines"	Administered by special improvement districts	District-based council-manager form of government	Programmatic groups and coalitions
Culminating response	County and town incorporation	Consolidation and annexation	Nonpartisan, commissioner form of government	Attempted fiscal consolidation of improvement districts	"Compromise" council-manager form of government	Council of governments with programmatic commissions *and* governmental powers

Regime tendencies[a]	Organizing polyarchy	Merchant oligarchy Company autocracy	Merchant-industrial oligarchy Unstable party competition	Merchant oligarchy Stable partisan competition	Merchant oligarchy with organized labor opposition Democratic party "machine" rule	Organized polyarchy with occasional government intervention Democratic party "reform" influence
Presidential election[b]						
Average %	No data	50.5	53.0	63.6	72.4	66.1
Maximum %		54.0	59.5	72.5	80.1	70.4
Minimum %		47.0	46.0	54.5	68.2	55.5

[a]Regime traits are meant to indicate tendencies only; though regime changes closely conform to general period changes, this is not meant to indicate clear conformity or causality. For example, the shift from unstable partisan competition (with alternate major party rule, on a frequent basis, modified by influential "third parties") to a more stable pattern of major party competition occurred after the 1924 election and is not solely a product of local factors.
[b]Indicates votes cast in presidential elections as a percentage of eligible voters during each period.

mented" towns into one "imperial" city, the emergence of the party machine and the consequent adoption of a "progressive" and nonpartisan commissioner government, the attempted consolidation of depression-created improvement districts, the mid-1950s adoption of a council-manager government, and even the mid-1970s emergence of a council of governments and advisory commissions—all read like a standard textbook in urban government.

Yet even if we remain with these rather ponderous changes, it is possible to detect a recurring pattern of accommodation and adjustment that represents an important variation on the standard themes of "centralization," "the burden of government," and "loss of community." It is difficult to imagine that Pueblo's variation is typical or characteristic of that class of cities that precariously grew to medium size based on a single industry. On the other hand, it is equally difficult to imagine that the recurring elements of Pueblo's accommodative pattern would occur to such an extent in cities unaccustomed to the politics of adversity. Let us consider some of these elements, focusing first on Pueblo's locational constraints and then on its political responses.

LOCATIONAL CONSTRAINTS AND THE OPENING GAMBIT

For political scientists and city fathers alike, the "opening gambit" can be regarded as the first and most basic mediating factor of politics—interposing itself between, and mixing in due proportions, the capabilities and needs of a particular community. Few cities have escaped getting the short end of the negotiating stick; and, as Oliver Williams and Charles Adrian note, "city government is more handicapped than it was in the nineteenth century as an active recruiter of industry, for the vagaries of industrial location are determined more by economic market considerations than by the character of locally provided services."[26] On the other hand, there is a considerable difference between a city like Colorado Springs, which was founded in no small measure for the entertainment of English railroad investors and now wines and dines generals at the Broadmoor, and a city like Pueblo, accustomed to the short end of the stick. Every Colorado city caught up in the private railroad feuds of the late nineteenth century, or in the urban rivalries over the location of state and federal institutions, has some horror story to tell. Yet few cities (certainly none in Colorado) have grown to Pueblo's scale as a medium-sized city despite being so badly outmaneuvered by private industry and state government.

In part Pueblo's peculiar economic and political position can be traced back to the politics of railroad location. In 1870 General Palmer decided to build his Denver and Rio Grande Railroad south from Denver to El Paso and eventually in a long U (over two hundred miles) through the Royal Gorge to Salida and up the western side of the Rockies. Puebloans were delighted with the prospect of being the southern gateway, and Denver businessmen were equally impressed with the prospect of keeping southern Colorado from the Kansas-oriented railroads. When Palmer threatened to bypass Pueblo, county voters quickly authorized a county bond issue to sweeten the pot. Unfortunately, Palmer quickly broke county bond conditions and moved the railroad depot across the Arkansas River, well beyond the city limits. His land development company then proceeded to build the rival "colony" of South Pueblo around the depot, while another Palmer company established the company town of Bessemer around the new steel plant east of South Pueblo.[27] From these "metropolitan" beginnings, further aggravated by the separation of Central Pueblo from old Pueblo over the issue of taxes and liquor licenses, much of Pueblo's social and political history has centered on questions of political integration, the territorial distribution of power, and sectional identities that still inform the city's political map. The private decisions of individual homeowners and public decisions on zoning have softened these issues by providing a system in which traditional divisions of economic class, ethnicity, and political boundaries would not altogether conform (see map 6.2).

Before the end of the nineteenth century, major shifts in Colorado's economic geography encouraged Denver businessmen, led by David Moffat, to focus their attention on a more direct route west by tunneling through the Rockies to Salt Lake City. For a full generation, Pueblo and other southern Colorado counties—faced with the basic dilemma of losing their strategic position as the southern gateway through the Rockies or jeopardizing their political position in the northern-dominated state legislature—repeatedly blocked Denver's efforts to secure state authorization for the Moffat Tunnel proposal. Then, in June 1921 the flood came, and with it a northern offer Puebloans could not refuse. As David Lavender recounts:

> Weather finally broke the impasse. In June, 1921, unprecedented rains in the mountains sent flood-waters loaded with debris roaring down the Arkansas into Pueblo. Broken gas mains burst into flame, 600 homes were destroyed, and at least 100 persons perished. As the town began to rebuild, hysterical demands arose that reconstruction be tied to flood control works that would prevent a repetition of the tragedy. Yielding to the public, the governor asked a special session of the legislature to consider creating the necessary bonding districts. When legislators from the south reached Denver, they found the northern representatives ready for them. Pueblo would get its flood-control measures *if* a Moffat Tunnel Improvement District was also authorized. The bludgeoning succeeded.[28]

In many respects this bargain finally cleaved a north/south division that still informs many of Colorado's economic, intraparty, and legislative battles. For Pueblo, the immediate needs of recovery, the decline of rail-

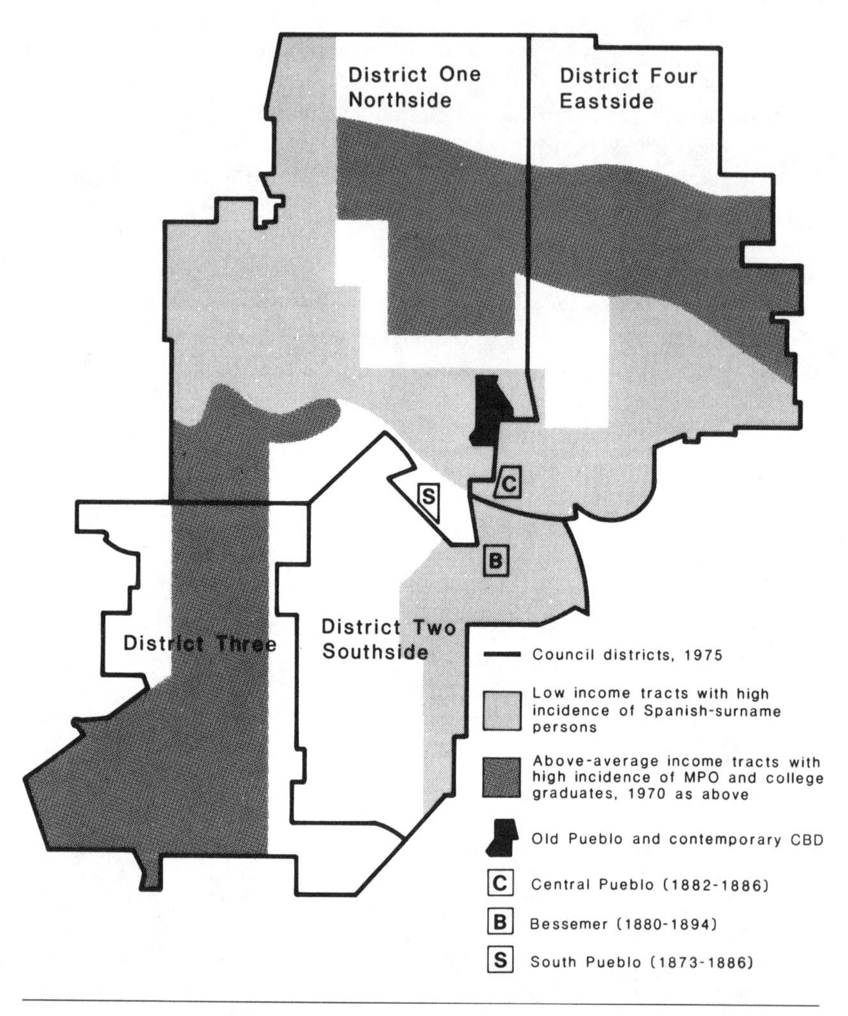

Map 6.2. Pueblo: major political, historical, and socioeconomic sections.

road transportation, the animosities created among state legislators and within the state Democratic party, and the subsequent decline of local influence in state politics all combined to redirect local political attention and energies both inward to the administration of recovery efforts and outward to the United States senatorial careers of men like Alva B. Adams and Edward P. Costigan. To a large extent, Pueblo's role in state politics, as Elazar notes, "has been forced to be obstructionist only, utilizing its bloc of votes in the primary elections against candidates its leadership has opposed."[29] This strategy was most fully developed by the state-oriented Muhic machine.

Today, of course, many of the rough edges of state-local and intraparty negotiations have been smoothed. While Pueblo's wartime and postwar gambits have not been as successful as those of Colorado Springs, the costs endured can now be measured simply in terms of the future dependence on state and federal institutions rather than additionally in terms of the pounds of flesh exacted along the way. Aurora (a Denver suburb) and Colorado Springs even joined forces with Pueblo to obtain congressional authorization for the Fryingpan-Arkansas water diversion project. And though Pueblo's prolonged effort to obtain state authorization for a four-year college is still regarded as a major "political victory," the struggle itself was surprisingly peaceful.

On the other hand, the political effects of Pueblo's prolonged political and economic isolation are still apparent in state political recruitment patterns, which continue to deflect qualified Pueblo candidates from state elective office. Other correlates of isolation include the localist orientation of local political parties; the persistence of Pueblo's political reputation as a "suspect" community, which continues to color the public statements of northern representatives and state press coverage of local politics; the "intangible" political tendencies of a "status-hungry" community that can easily be turned toward a rather buoyant form of boosterism or an intolerance of attempts to "rock the boat"; and the limited negotiating capabilities and orientation of a community that also is composed of those basic elements—absentee-owned institutions, working-class homeowners, and recently arrived "amenities-conscious" professionals—that are least supportive of major public expenditures for promoting economic growth.[30] Today, as one scans the institutional landscape of those state and federal facilities located in Pueblo—including a state hospital originally designed for custodial care and proposed as a site for the state archives, the army depot, and the new documents center—it is not inconceivable that even Pueblo's secondary economic function as a custodial center will continue, albeit reconstituted for the new "technological frontier." In each case Pueblo parlayed her most abundant resource, land, provided more often than not from the dwindling holdings of Pueblo's small class of economic notables (principally the Thatchers).

THE POLITICS OF ACCOMMODATION

Despite persistent locational constraints, Pueblo continues to attract a fresh wave of newcomers each generation, with their own memories of life "back east" (or in the barrio) and their own expectations of life in a western, yet industrial city. In this respect Pueblo departs from the conventional image of an industrial "backwater" and continues to retain certain qualities of the "adolescent" industrial towns of the original mining frontier it has long since outgrown. As David Lavender recounts:

> Like other adolescents, they grew too fast, and although they seemed strong their total orientation toward a single resource made them easily vulnerable. While their first citizens were still trying to determine what they stood for, the towns they yearned to be proud of were captured by outside corporations whose sense of responsibility lay, naturally enough, toward the absentee stockholders who had created them and not toward the localities from which the profits came. . . . If the veins were deep enough to last (and thanks to steadily improving technology some of them have lasted for three quarters of a century), then perhaps a man should adjust his life and his town's life accordingly. But adjust in the light of what values? An urban schizophrenia developed. One element in each of the new towns sought reassurance by trying to make its new home as patterned and as orderly as was any other American city. On the other hand, many residents clung to attitudes bequeathed them by the impatient and careless placer camps. They liked to think of themselves as carrying on the torch of those wild, free (and partly mythical) days when every prospector, no matter how poor, was deemed to be a potential millionaire and free to act accordingly.[31]

Those wild, free (and partly mythical) days are gone, though suggestive evidence points to their lingering effect. According to one comparative study, Pueblo distinctively combines unexpectedly high rates of violent crime and of voter participation.[32] Until recently, it was still possible to observe a reenactment of the "boom town" tensions on the suburban frontier—particularly in Pueblo West, a "new town" developed by McCulloch Properties, Incorporated.[33] More important is the indirect yet persistent way the tensions Lavender describes combine with other local forces and activate Pueblo's particular pattern of accommodation.

If one traces the history of Pueblo's "culminating responses" to each new challenge, indicated in table 6.1, it is possible to distinguish a rather conventional threefold trend of centralization marked by the increasing consolidation of government, the expanding scope of its powers (both territorially and functionally), and the strengthening of the executive branch within government.[34] However, if we take a closer look at the political processes leading up to government reform and the nature of the reform itself, it is also possible to distinguish a more ambivalent, almost federalist pattern of accommodation. Though each period contains its own distinctive set of challenges and responses, the patterning of those responses invariably takes the form of two alternating tendencies: first toward noncentralization but not quite; then toward consolidation but not wholly.[35]

The practical unfolding of this accommodative pattern can be recalled in the post–World War II process of charter reform discussed earlier. Yet this pattern of response had earlier manifestations: (1) in the formal incorporation of those "law and order" functions that had been performed by extragovernmental people's courts and vigilantism for a decade or more; (2) in the consolidation, but not total, of separately flourishing "new towns" through a town-based system of legislative representation and public finance; (3) in the adoption of a commissioner form of government so strongly checked (by initiative, referendum, recall, an independently elected civil service commission, and the prohibition of citywide taxes for special improvements) that it even drew the critical attention of the National Short Ballot Organization;[36] (4) in the establishment of a central Arkansas River conservancy district to meet the future needs of flood control and the concurrent development of twenty-eight special improvement districts to tend to the short-term demands of street paving and flood recovery measures; (5) in the prolonged battle, both in and out of court, over attempts to consolidate the financing of those special improvement districts; and then (6) in the eventual charter reform struggle that dominated much of the first half of the post–World War II generation.

The Emergence of a Metropolitan-Technological Order, 1961–76

With this history in mind, it becomes possible to distinguish the continuities and discontinuities of Pueblo's politics during the second half of the post–World War II generation, from 1961 to 1976. The discontinuities center, at one level, on a variety of social and economic forces that precipitated the collapse of Pueblo's hundred-year-old urban-industrial order and, at another level, on a new brand of community leaders who were able to reconstruct a meaningful community along metropolitan-technological lines. The continuities center on the ways this was achieved.

PUEBLO'S BREAK WITH THE PAST

Between 1960 and 1962, the Pueblo community was forever changed by a series of catalytic events. One event was the presidential election of 1960, which marked the highest voter turnout in Pueblo's history, before or since, and the last campaign of "Tiger" Muhic, who died the following year. Another was the sensibility-awakening case of *The People of the State of Colorado v. Joseph E. Spinuzzi* (1961), in which the district court for Pueblo County found Mr. Spinuzzi not guilty of murdering James D. Scott. Despite eyewitness accounts that Mr. Spinuzzi knelt over Mr. Scott with a gun in his hand, the gun discharged, Mr. Spinuzzi stood up and walked away after placing the gun in his belt, and Mr. Scott was immediately discovered with a bullet hole through the palm of his cupped hand and his left nostril, the court insisted that no one saw the bullet leave the gun.[37]

For the less dramatic, Pueblo's "great change" began in 1961 with decisions made outside the city to modernize two of its largest plants, CF&I and the state hospital. For others it began with the success of two local campaigns, first to obtain state authorization for a four-year college in February 1961, and then to obtain congressional authorization for the Fryingpan-Arkansas project in August 1962. For still others it was the emergence of a "new breed" of leadership, symbolized by the 1960 appointments of a new city manager and the first permanent director of the regional planning commission, and by the 1960 election of Frank Evans to the state assembly. Whatever their mix, the events of the early 1960s precipitated a profound change in Pueblo's economic order and community orientation.

In the early 1960s, Pueblo's economic system shifted from a modified industrial base to a more diversified one. This process was marked by significant decreases in the percentage of the labor force engaged in manufacturing (and its three largest employers) and by significant increases in service sector employment and professional occupations.[38] Yet this economic diversification was precipitated less by a consistent local effort to "escape from industrialism" than by the external decisions of the city's largest employers, variously mediated by local efforts.

As part of the governor's plans to reorganize the mental health field, in 1961 the state hospital began a major effort to sharply increase its professional staff, reduce long-term inpatient care, and decentralize its services. At the same time, CF&I periodically reduced its work force as a result of automation and in 1972 relocated its sales headquarters back to Pueblo after an absence of seventy-eight years. Likewise, the federal government gradually reduced the army depot work force, temporarily upgraded services as part of the Hawk missile conversion program, and subsequently announced massive cutbacks beginning in 1974. Yet largely in response to community efforts, the federal government also located two "high profile" facilities in Pueblo—the Government Printing Office's Documents Distribution Center (whose advertisements have made Pueblo a household name) and the Department of Transportation High Speed Test Center.

These occurrences have had a profound effect on the social and economic character of Pueblo. Unlike the first half of the postwar generation, the period since 1960 has been marked by slow population growth, held to a virtual standstill between 1960 and 1970. At the same time, the proportion of owner-occupied housing units increased to almost 70 percent, and the proportion of the population aged five years or older residing in the same house for five years or more increased to almost 60 percent. Yet, as one can imagine from the shifts in the employment market, this was a time of considerable job insecurity marked by cutbacks in factory and depot jobs, increased unemployment and welfare rolls, a new mix of employment skills with considerable retraining and population turnover, and a near 27 percent increase in the proportion of married women in the work force.

In the period since 1960, there also have been significant structural changes in the social system. During the 1960s there was an absolute decrease in the numbers of both foreign-born and foreign-stock population. By 1970 no city census tract contained more than 8.3 percent foreign-born. Furthermore, despite an increase in the Hispanic population to almost one-third of the total population, one study has observed certain tendencies toward the weakening of traditional ethnic ties.[39] At the same time, income disparities widened; the number of families living on family incomes greater than $25,000 more than doubled, to 582 families; and there is now both an emergent residential suburban structure and a new middle class, marked by the near 40 percent increase between 1960 and 1970 in the proportion of the work force engaged in professional and technical occupations.

In many respects Pueblo's first half-generation of economic diversification has been accompanied by more acute conditions of economic instability and adversity. Since 1960 Pueblo's median family income has dropped further below state and national averages; since 1966 its per capita net effective buying income has dropped below nonmetropolitan Colorado state averages. Furthermore, despite a 33 percent decrease in the proportion of the population under age five and no change in the percentage of the population over age sixty-five, the county welfare caseload increased by almost 50 percent between 1960 and 1972—an increase that can be only partially explained by the softening of welfare criteria.[40]

All in all, this period of economic diversification and retrenchment has provided a rather mixed record for boosters and planners alike. Still, according to one reliable public opinion survey conducted just after Pueblo's "no growth" decade, more than 50 percent of eight hundred Pueblo households surveyed could identify only two attributes that best described their city—"growing" and "friendly."[41]

POLITICAL CHANGE IN CONTEMPORARY PUEBLO

The divided mandate, which had produced the "compromise" charter of 1954 and the notion of a professionally competent "caretaker government," survived a full half-generation until the critical elections of 1969 and 1971. The persistence of this mandate is apparent in the campaign platforms of council candidates, the types of candidates attracted to the post-1954 council, the initially high turnover rate of city managers, and the decisions and nondecisions of the city council.

The first order of business for the new city council was the inauguration of a long-awaited street paving program, fatefully delayed at the excavation stage by one of the worst snowstorms in Pueblo's history. In preparation for an era of expansion and prosperity, the city council approved a regional planning commission (1958), a planning and zoning commission (1961), and a new series of codes and ordinances intended to professionalize its bureaucracy. These policies were administered by a city manager (who served longer than any of his predecessors, from 1961 until 1967, when he left to become city manager of Colorado Springs) and the first permanent regional planning director. The latter helped shape the "progressive-cosmopolitan" campaigns for "orderly growth" during his long tenure, 1960–75.

Projects that challenged the original mandate could still divide the city council: the Union Avenue urban renewal project was defeated by a three-to-two council vote in 1961, despite the vigorous support of the local chamber of commerce—later criticized for this action by the United States Chamber of Commerce. The annexation of an Eastwood barrio in the southeast section of district four (map 6.2) was rejected in 1962 and finally approved after the Fountain Creek flood of 1965, along with the annexation of a Hyde Park barrio in the southwest section of district one (map 6.2). Finally, a deadlocked vote over the city's Model Cities application was broken by a special city council session, only to be rejected by the federal government in 1967, in part because of the city's "lack of unity."

In a curious mix, the divided mandate that created the "compromise" charter, the historical political tensions behind it, the socioeconomic correlates of Pueblo's "great change," an extremely underdeveloped institutional structure, and the promise of the New Frontier–Great Society (assisted by the successful efforts of local Democrats in 1964 to unseat the Republican congressional incumbent, Edgar J. Chenoweth, for the first time since 1948) all tended to mobilize a new constellation of community groups and coalitions while continuing to restrain the roles and activities of local government. The "compromise" charter served not only to define the framework of government but also to rearrange the political landscape that had developed around its adoption struggle. On the one hand, it provided a reasonable compromise in which most participating interests could claim a stake. On the other hand, the memories of its adoption struggle created a disquieting no-man's-land out of the original battle lines that would rarely be crossed. These two tendencies combined with the conservative inclinations of a new professional-managerial class to keep the roles of city government qua government on a straight and narrow path for some time to come.

The incredible range of long-delayed, noncontroversial citywide projects and the rather open membership rules of a community like Pueblo enabled many local groups to turn their attention and energies to a variety of new community development projects. However, the variety of noncontroversial programmatic needs combined with the memories of recent battles (particularly over urban renewal) and no small amount of "boosterism" to deflect public attention from more controversial issues.

The tangible results of this period are instructive. Since the founding of the state college, Pueblo's *cultural* landscape has been virtually transformed by the completion of several key facilities. A new regional library was approved by a majority of the city's voters in every precinct save one. The Impossible Players and the Pueblo Arts Council helped weld the city's "progressive-cosmopolitan" establishment, and the leaders of that establishment were able to secure county and federal funds for the new Sangre de Cristo Arts and Convention Center, for a variety of programs offered by the University of Southern Colorado, and even for a Pueblo Civic Symphony. Although Pueblo's *physical* landscape has not been transformed, its most hazardous features have been removed by the near completion of the city's street paving program, the modernization of the CF&I plant (assisted in the final stages by a 1971 voter-approved industrial revenue bond), the completion of the Arkansas River flood control plan, and the provision of basic services to the city's long-neglected barrio and urban fringe areas. In 1975 Pueblo voters approved a bond issue for the development of a downtown mall. Also in the mid-1970s, two locally owned banks (the economic pillars of a community like Pueblo, especially in a state with branch banking prohibitions) have "saved" the commercial life of two strategic neighborhoods: Minnequa, the "anchor" of the working-class community, and the downtown courthouse area.

Equally important are the changes in Pueblo's *institutional* landscape. Concurrent with other developments, the organizational structure of the Democratic party has been virtually reformed by a new generation of managerial leaders, and the percentage of registered Democrats has steadily increased since 1964 (see table 6.2). Also, the number of social clubs and social service institutions that first grew in response to the depression and the New Deal increased dramatically in the late 1960s and early 1970s. In more cases than not, the new social organizations of this period were products of Great Society programs, state hospital decentralization, state college extension efforts, and the emergence of the Chicano movement, which began, in Pueblo, with the founding of a local chapter of La Raza Unida in 1969. During the two peak years of institutional foundings (1970 and 1971), more social service organizations were established in Pueblo than in any ten-year period since the 1920s.[42]

Table 6.2. Party Affiliation as a Percentage of Pueblo's Registered Voters

Affiliation	1964	1968	1972	1976
Democratic	41.1	46.8	52.9	54.3
Republican	14.2	15.9	16.6	6.7
Unaffiliated	44.7	37.3	30.5	39.0

Throughout this half-generation, from 1961 into the late 1970s, certain basic features of Pueblo's order remained intact. Despite economic diversification, Pueblo still had a lagging economy susceptible to periods of economic instability, and Puebloans' standard of living continued to slip below national and state averages. Within the state's economic system, Pueblo was still regarded as a depressed area, one step ahead of the conditions of adversity that continued to plague the small towns and rural areas of southern Colorado. Within the state's political system, Pueblo was still regarded as a suspect community, and the local district attorney did not seem to suffer from lack of work.[43]

Equally important, Pueblo's local political system retained certain basic features. The city's 1954 charter remained in force throughout this period, as did the basic distribution of power between the city manager and council. Despite important changes in political leadership, the dominant pool of city-wide and regional leadership remained Anglo; and the predominant pattern of political action remained accommodative.

Not surprisingly, it was these very continuities that enabled the new leaders to bring about as many changes as they did. By pursuing noncontroversial projects, securing tangible results, identifying themselves as Puebloans first, and projecting a spirit of accommodation, the progressive cosmopolitan leadership of the 1960s was able to accomplish most of its objectives and, along the way, profoundly change the nature of the Pueblo community. The direction of that change can best be understood as a reconstituting of Pueblo's civil community along metropolitan and technological lines. To borrow from Norton Long, this has involved "the search for a potential metropolitan governing class, the institutions through which it can function and a set of ideal goals which it can embody and which will render its leadership legitimate in the eyes of the people."[44]

Between 1954 and the late 1970s, this reconstituting process was undertaken in four political stages. From 1954 to 1960, the groundwork for a metropolitan civil community was unintentionally laid through the adoption of a city manager form of government, the recognition of planning as a legitimate government function, and the hiring of a progressive-cosmopolitan planner to direct the city's new regional planning commission. The second stage, from 1961 to 1969, witnessed the emergence of a loose coalition of progressive-cosmopolitan leaders outside government, who worked (often under the tutelage of the new regional planner) to transform the city's cultural, physical, and institutional landscape along the lines previously described.

The third stage, from 1969 to 1971, was marked by two critical elections in which the new leadership succeeded in obtaining a council majority around a new consensus of public opinion and political interests. At the heart of the new consensus was the idea that local government should play a leading role both in widening the scope of community along metropolitan lines and in refining the meaning of community through a policy of "orderly growth." The fourth and culminating stage, lasting through much of the 1970s, witnessed the near completion of this agenda, first by expanding the roles and constituencies of city government and then by supplying an institutional basis for regional governance. The remainder of this chapter is devoted to these last two stages: the acquisition and use of governmental power by the new leadership.

The Critical Elections of 1969 and 1971. The sheer programmatic successes of the new coalition of groups that had developed throughout the 1960s forced a basic reassessment of the original mandate of 1954 under which the coalition had initially flourished. Each programmatic success seemed to justify the traditional laissez-faire terms of the compromise charter and its caretaker government. At the same time, the cumulative effect of the new coalition achievements was to increase the demands on local government for planning and supportive services while strengthening the practical experience, cooperative ties, and progressive expectations of a widening circle of community leaders.

The changes were bound to affect city government, despite the persistent orientation of a council majority toward the maintenance of caretaker government. In February 1967, two months before the divided council vote over Model Cities, the city council inadvertently hired a seasoned city manager who possessed an unusually successful, Missouri-bred combination of professional competence and political sagacity. By 1969 the newly hired city manager had demonstrated the ability to secure badly needed federal funds for capital improvements, introduce necessary administrative reforms, and build the requisite political bridges out from an otherwise caretaker administration. Elsewhere in local government, the more overtly cosmopolitan-oriented director of the regional planning commission continued to energize various elements of the community's more progressive leadership through the work of the Master Action Plan Committee (for downtown development), the Pueblo Arts Council (for the Sangre de Cristo Arts and Convention Center), and the Pueblo Symposium on the Seventies (attended by over three hundred local residents in March 1969).

In several respects the council election of 1969 proved a most opportune moment to challenge the original mandate of 1954. The progressive-cosmopolitan leadership was mobilized by the drive for county and federal funds for the Sangre de Cristo Center. One of the principal leaders of that drive declared her candidacy for one of the two at-large council positions (both uncontested by incumbents in 1969). Her husband had "tested the field," so to speak, receiving over ten thousand votes in his overwhelmingly successful bid for election to the influential water board in 1967. At the same time, the city's two recently designated urban renewal areas (in Eastwood and Hyde Park) were mobilizing around the need for capital improvements and the successful drive for federal water and sewer grants that had been orchestrated, in part, by the new city manager.

In the 1969 election voters approved a referendum to increase the limit on the city's bonded indebtedness for capital improvements from 3 percent to 10 percent of assessed valuation. They also elected a loose coalition of progressive council candidates, built around the at-large election of the candidate mentioned above. Other coalition victories included the at-large election of the owner of the city's Spanish-language radio station, who filled the seat vacated by the city's first Spanish-surnamed candidate, elected in 1965; the district one election of a lawyer who had been involved in the business community's search for a progressive slate; and the district three election of a Whiggish maverick over a longtime incumbent.

But these electoral changes were not the result of a unified electorate. Rather, they represented a newly divided mandate that was subsequently reinforced by a bitter contest in 1971 for the third at-large seat. This contest pitted a member of the progressive coalition (elected by a plurality of 34.4 percent of the votes cast) against the incumbent—a former police chief who was the new administration's most vociferous critic (receiving 31.1 percent of the votes cast). Idiosyncratic and ideological differences would subsequently divide the new council on many basic questions of administration: how strictly to adhere to the policy of "orderly growth" in matters of land use and zoning; how to strike a proper balance between the new roles of local government; and the requisite level of government expenditures. However, unlike local elections before or since, the opportunity for a basic reassessment, the clarity of the policy alternatives presented, and the intensity of the campaigns marked a turning point in Pueblo's political history. Voter turnout in the 1971 council election was 41 percent of eligible voters—higher

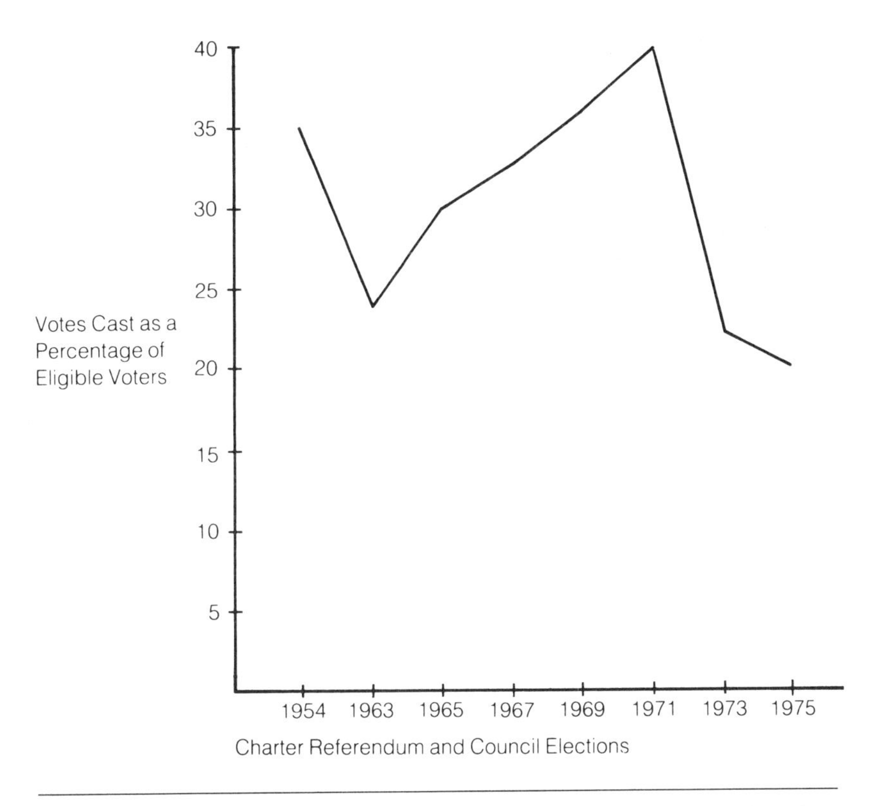

Fig. 6.1. Voter turnout in Pueblo council elections and the 1954 charter referendum (CHT).

than for other local elections during this period and higher than for the 1954 charter vote (see figure 6.1).

In 1954 the consensus that did exist centered on the notion of imbuing government with a representational base and a professional bureaucracy that would be better equipped than the commission form of government to provide traditional services to a rapidly growing population. Toward this end, all parties accepted the idea of a legislative council and an executive manager. The differences that did emerge were over the political questions of the proper criteria for legislative representation and separation of powers.

By 1969 Puebloans could look back on a full half-generation of unanticipated socioeconomic change and a period of vigorous community mobilization that had virtually transformed the terms of the original mandate of 1954. All parties seemed to agree that the time had come to reassess the terms of that mandate, and the general tenor of the 1969 and 1971 elections reflected this basic consensus. In those elections, one element in the community held that the terms of the original mandate should be restored and that the role of local government should continue to be restricted to the traditional caretaker functions set out in that mandate and its subsequent implementation. In the 1971 election, for example, much of the former police chief's council campaign centered on the claim that the new city manager had exceeded the terms of the original mandate. By contrast, a second element in the community held to the belief that its terms should be reconstituted in response to the great changes in Pueblo's socioeconomic order and that local government (and in human terms, the efforts of the new city manager and the regional planning director) should be invigorated by a new council leadership capable of consolidating those changes.

The most immediate effect of the elections of 1969 and 1971 was twofold: broadly, to shift the predominant element in city council and its divided mandate from the tendency toward noncentralization but not quite, to the tendency toward consolidation but not wholly; and specifically, to provide the new city manager with the strategic advantage of a new city council, containing none of the members who had appointed him.

New Directions and the Path of Least Resistance. In many respects the efforts of the 1970s to consolidate the political developments of the last half-generation can be traced to the critical elections of 1969 and 1971 and the newly divided mandate they established. In examining these ongoing efforts, several elements deserve special attention.

1. Roles of local government. Since 1969, the roles of local government in Pueblo have been broadened and strengthened locally not only in terms of its capacity to deliver traditional services but also in relation to those local nongovernment institutions that have traditionally performed the roles of "promoting economic growth" and "securing life's amenities." In 1971 Pueblo voters approved two capital-improvement bond issues (for storm and sanitary sewers and street improvements), rejected two other bond issues (for parks and a multipurpose arena), and approved an increase in the sales tax from 1 to 3 percent to finance capital improvements. In 1975 voters approved a bond issue for the development of a downtown mall. Equally important, city government has moved out of its restricted circle of activities and established two commissions that roughly parallel the regional planning commission: an industrial and economic development commission, which has emerged as a viable and in many respects dominant complement to the chamber of commerce in promoting economic growth; and a human re-

sources commission, which has begun to perform a meaningful coordinative role in the field of social services, even if it has been unable to significantly reduce the interagency conflicts in that field.

The composition of these commissions (fifteen members each) and the utilization of capital improvements for neighborhood development (first in Eastwood and Hyde Park) have brought together a considerable number of local government officials and citizens who might not normally come into direct contact. In contemporary Pueblo, unlike many other medium-sized cities, these contact points build on an existing sense of community. In this beleaguered city, governors and governed seem to share an appreciation of their special problems and prospects as citizens of a city of Pueblo's scale and location.

2. The scope of local government. The scope of local government and to a lesser extent of public attention has been increasingly widened along metropolitan lines, and it is now possible to discern the rudimentary framework of a metropolitan civil community. Puebloans have turned their Council of Governments (COG) to a rather uncommon use. Many of the political developments that have occurred in the city since 1969 are inextricably connected to the notion of the Pueblo County COG as a framework for political action. In terms both symbolic and actual, the purpose of the council has been "to strengthen local self government while combining total resources for meeting challenges of our area in an amiable and purposeful cooperation with state and federal agencies for the common good of all."[45] This purpose has been advanced by the council's recent acquisition of governmental powers, including the power to tax.

First, the city ordinance creating the Pueblo COG also incorporated the city's three commissions as standing commissions of the COG. Though the regional planning commission had functioned for more than a decade as a city commission, its natural tendency (and that of its director) had been inclined from the first toward metropolitan planning and development. Even during the brief existence of the city's economic development commission, the necessary match of county land and city workers in "promoting economic growth" was clear (recall map 6.1). The human resources commission was established from the first as a standing commission of the COG.

More important, there is an apparent willingness on the part of city and county officials to make their common council work, and work well, within its limited mandate. Breaking the conventional tradition of city-county parity elsewhere, the voting members of the council include all seven city councilmen, all three county commissioners, one member from each of the two school boards, and one member from the water board. The working nature of the COG is also apparent in council members' impatience to rush off to small working committees of the COG to discuss and resolve common problems through joint action, from the development of city-county purchasing agreements to a city-school parks and recreation program. It is also possible to distinguish increasing commonalities in the internal composition of each of the member units of government, especially since the mid-1970s adoption of a county manager plan.

These "incremental" yet functioning developments may not draw much public attention when compared with more dramatic cases of metropolitan federation and city-county consolidation. Yet for Pueblo these developments mark a most appropriate and natural course of action toward the gradual reconstituting of its civil community along metropolitan lines. By most standard measures of political economy, Puebloans do not yet face critical problems of inequities or inefficiencies that can be traced to the lack of more appropriate metropolitan devices, with the possible exception of the separate functioning of city and county school districts. In fact, the earlier annexations of Eastwood and Hyde Park barrio areas have corrected many of the most serious service inequities; and the immediate problems of uncontrolled suburbanization on the St. Charles mesa and the unregulated development of Pueblo West predate recent state land-use regulations. In historical perspective, there are also similarities between these responses and the recurring accommodative patterns found in the development of Pueblo's urban-industrial order. Only here it is possible to distinguish the simultaneous unfolding of two related spheres of government activity: one directed toward consolidating the economic and political changes in Pueblo's urban-industrial order, the other directed toward the commingling of centralizing and noncentralizing features to develop a potential framework for metropolitan political action.

One final note: the study of city politics as a field of political science qua science most typically involves the search for recurring patterns of political behavior and their explanations. Yet somewhat surprisingly, much of that search has recently turned toward the comparative investigation of different political issues while largely eschewing the historical (though nonetheless "comparative") search for recurrence in the political life of one or more communities at different times. In the study of national politics, the concept of political change constitutes a virtual field of political inquiry, yet the study of political change within local communities is stymied by a sort of temporal parochialism. If one attempts to explain the political differences between cities, is it not possible that our understanding of the variations in city politics can be deepened by the search for continuities and discontinuities within cities? Perhaps there is still some relevance to Aristotle's cautiously teleological instruction: "If, accordingly, we begin at the beginning, and consider things in the process of their growth, we shall best be able, in this as in other fields, to attain scientific conclusions by the methods we employ."[46]

7. Changing Expectations of Local Government in Light of the 1960s: The Cases of Champaign and Urbana

Rozann Rothman

The Setting

Champaign and Urbana, Illinois, are pristine examples of how political systems that "function in a given locality to provide it with the bundle of governmental services that can be manipulated locally to serve local needs in light of local values"[1] have responded to the pressures of the 1960s and 1970s as well as adapting them to their own purposes. The cities at first glance appear curiously isolated and remote from the challenges and opportunities of the federal system. If the citizens were queried concerning the need for and utility of government—federal, state, or local—a representative response might assert that government could and should be bypassed and that individual initiative and local spirit are all that either city requires. Yet in the 1960s the governments of both cities assumed new responsibilities, particularly with respect to securing civil rights for black citizens. Conflict over the rectification of racial injustice has created severe stresses in the federal system, but the experience of Champaign and Urbana revealed forces that led to reconciliation of national objectives and local traditions.

Accommodation is the result of a complex process that highlights adaptation. In the case of civil rights, Champaign and Urbana adapted national objectives to suit their purposes, even as national imperatives provided the catalyst for reshaping the structure and role of local government. The pattern is not atypical. In instance after instance—downtown redevelopment, zoning, environmental concerns, professionalization of staff—adaptation is the key factor in the process. Local values are embedded and strongly supported, but the problems of an urbanized present demand attention and remedies. Since solution of these problems depends on local implementation, adjustment to local values and concerns is necessary.

The product of this process is incremental change. The cumulative effects of such change eventually may produce radically different outcomes, but at the end of the postwar generation the politics of Champaign and Urbana could be described as transitional.

Neither Champaign nor Urbana is a microcosm of a larger universe; rather, politics in these civil communities presents a collection of contradictory and idiosyncratic responses to pressing contemporary problems. The contradictions arise from the pervasiveness of the individualistic, political subculture[2] that coexists with extreme dependence on state and federal governments for continued prosperity in the area. The idiosyncratic aspects of local political behavior are generated by the limited local awareness of the extent of local dependence on state and federal governments and the resulting neglect of the myriad relationships spawned by this dependence.

This combination of ambivalence and misperception can be attributed in part to the presence of the University of Illinois, which differentiates Champaign and Urbana forevermore from communities like Tolono or Villa Grove or Paxton, also situated in east-central Illinois. The university attracts residents to the cities, its major construction projects in the 1960s boosted the skilled trades, and its nonacademic employment needs provide opportunities for white-collar and unskilled labor. Throughout the postwar generation, unemployment was low in Champaign County, and more than half of the 60,000 or more wage and salaried employees worked for government. In 1970 the *Area Manpower Review* noted that the situation in Champaign and Urbana was atypical, "with problems unique to it and a few others."[3]

A local market of 34,000 students seemed to promise "permanent" prosperity for the retail and service sectors of the economy, and "good times" obscured the need for local efforts to attract new kinds of economic development or seek federal grants to ameliorate urban problems. Local business was dependent on university expansion to provide an ever expanding market, but most citizens failed to see the connection between university expansion and state or federal largesse.

The university does not participate in local politics, but university-affiliated persons provided the raw material for challenges to local habits and values. In the 1960s, faculty and students participated in protest demonstrations and joined the local political parties, infusing local politics with a new spirit of party competitiveness. Although the relationship between town and gown has overtones of antagonism, on the whole it is correct but limited. The most applicable generalization for the pattern of university participation is "neutral," and a little play with the word produces "neutralized."

Against the background of the Great Society programs, sporadic local black protest, and student demonstrations in opposition to the Vietnam War, local elites perceived the university primarily as a threat to local mores and values. When students and faculty entered politics en masse, they created their own organizations to advance their causes. In the one case where a local organization—the Champaign County Democratic party—was successfully infiltrated, the party was not "radicalized." Instead, an assimilative process developed within it; faculty and student activists challenged local preconceptions but eventually conformed to local political norms in order to enhance their effectiveness. The high point of faculty and student activism occurred during the late 1960s and early 1970s. But by 1973 it was clear that the respective civil communities had the means to contain or channel whatever "threat" they perceived from the technological and humanistic imperatives of the university people.

Objectively, the presence of the university meant that local government was confronted with the problem of providing services and amenities for an expanding population. Table 7.1 gives population figures and university enrollment from 1840 to 1970.

The sustained growth of the cities was not a function of local initiative, and local leadership lacked the resources to cope with population growth. In addition, students are a transient population, and until 1972 obstacles such as age and residence requirements hindered their participation in local elections, thus limiting their ability to influence local decision makers. In addition, the fragmented structure of local government—two cities, two park districts, and two school districts, as well as sanitary districts, obstructed concerted action to ameliorate the problems created by an expanding population. Action on these problems, of necessity, was piecemeal. The school and park districts had sufficient public support to pass the referenda needed for expansion. City government in the 1960s lacked the will to attack the problems; for example, zoning enforcement was minimal, and developers were in their element. Public services were neglected because no politician was in a position to impose unpopular assessments for amenities such as sidewalks.

During the 1960s, federal grants were available for urban projects, but Champaign and Urbana were prevented by pragmatic and ideological considerations from taking advantage of the opportunities. Although there were problems, "in the absence of any acute unemployment situation, visible pockets of substandard housing, or other crises, the municipalities were not motivated to reach out for Federal assistance. A general dislike of Federal intervention in any form with the subsequent threat to local autonomy and control which ensues, prompted local leaders to hold out as long as possible against participation in Federal programs."[4] In addition, federally financed developments, such as housing for the elderly, could not be taxed by local government, and local lenders wanted private capital for development so as not to lose potential sources of local revenue. By the 1970s the needs were

Table 7.1. Population Changes, Champaign-Urbana, 1840–1970

	Champaign County		Champaign		Urbana		
Year	Population	Percentage Increase	Population	Percentage Increase	Population	Percentage Increase	University Enrollment
1840	1,475	–	–	–	–	–	–
1850	2,649	80.0	–	–	210	–	–
1855	6,566	148.0	416	–	1,135	440.0	–
1860	14,629	123.0	1,727	315.0	1,370	21.0	–
1870	32,737	123.0	4,625	168.0	2,277	66.0	180
1880	40,863	25.0	5,103	10.0	2,942	29.0	434
1890	42,159	4.0	5,839	14.0	3,511	19.0	469
1900	47,622	12.0	9,098	39.0	5,728	63.0	2,234
1910	51,829	9.0	12,421	36.5	8,245	43.9	4,232
1920	56,959	10.0	15,873	27.8	10,244	24.2	7,839
1930	64,273	13.0	20,348	28.2	13,060	27.5	9,960
1940	70,578	10.0	23,302	14.5	14,064	7.7	11,676
1950	106,437[a]	51.0	39,563[a]	69.8	22,834[a]	62.4	19,521
1960	132,436	24.8	49,583	24.3	27,294	19.5	21,955
1970	163,281	23.3	56,532	14.0	32,800	20.2	34,018

Source: U.S. Bureau of the Census, *U.S. Census of Population,* 1950, 1970; Office of Information, University of Illinois, Urbana, Illinois.

[a]For 1950 and thereafter population data include students.

pressing, and new people promising changed policies won power in both cities. However, the Nixon and Ford administrations reduced the opportunities to obtain federal grants, and the cities did not have the personnel to compete in a more competitive game.

Given the limited participation of Champaign and Urbana in the grant programs, revenue sharing seemed to offer new possibilities for local initiatives. But by the time revenue sharing funds reached city coffers, pressing financial considerations minimized their impact. Although the funds strengthened the ties between the cities and the federal government, local perceptions of the relationship were shaped by established habits and understandings, and most citizens remained oblivious to the possibilities and significance of federal involvement. For these reasons, this chapter focuses on the subtleties of intergovernmental relationships in order to illustrate how these communities adapted state and national policies to their purposes, even as state and national procedures and objectives shaped local options and decisions.

Champaign and Urbana: Contrasts and Similarities

The cities, though they are adjacent and have similar populations, are very different political communities. They were founded at different times and for different reasons, and the politics of each has been influenced by its evolving location in time and space.[5] The founding of Urbana was circumstantial; if there was a reason for Urbana to be located on this site rather than some other, it has more to do with the whims of the original settlers who came to rest on top of its ridge as they moved westward than with rational or utopian designs for the future.

Champaign's founding was more rational but equally dependent on external decision rather than any intrinsic attraction of the particular site. In the 1850s the Illinois Central Railroad was laying the track that was to become "the Mainline of Mid-America." The track passed two miles west of Urbana, and the future site of Champaign was designated a division point on the line. The resulting commercial prospects attracted settlers, and the attraction continued through the years. From the beginning, Champaign's development was related to the linkage between the rural-land frontier and the urban-industrial frontier. It also coincided with the rise of the Republican party and its emergence as the political spokesman for local commercial interests.[6]

Although the cities have grown and changed, their origins generated different characters and political structures. Urbana was and continues to be the more cohesive community; it has a stronger and more rooted local elite. The city has been governed by the mayor-aldermen form of municipal government since the 1860s. The mayor serves on half time and is elected by partisan ballot for a four-year term. The city council is composed of fourteen aldermen elected for four years on party tickets, two from each of seven wards, with seven seats at stake every two years. The mayor is the executive officer of the city and presides over the city council but votes only in case of a tie.

This sketch of the mayor's formal authority does not convey its full potential. Urbana began to modernize its municipal administration in the latter half of the postwar generation. City personnel have come under civil service, and during the administration of Charles Zipprodt (1969–73) the full-time position of administrative officer was created. The administrative officer is responsible to the mayor; he compiles and analyzes information from the various departments and has an overview of the day-to-day operation of government that is invaluable for policymaking. This information is at the disposal of the mayor; the council does not have comparable staff, and some advantage thus accrues to the mayor in any conflict with the council.

Strong leadership of a different kind is a legacy from the recent past. Urbana's government has been classified as oligarchic, with periods of autocracy such as during the political life of H. I. Green, who was "boss" of Champaign County until the early 1950s.[7] The city council meetings were short, decisions were taken quickly, and most citizens were not involved or were touched only peripherally by the acts of government. Decisions reflected private undertakings rather than public affairs. If the public good was served by a decision that promoted private objectives, it was an incidental by-product of an individual effort to attain particular goals. Until the middle 1960s, municipal government provided minimum services, maintained a low profile, and served only limited purposes. There was little interest in improving the environment or altering the status quo. There was neither foresight nor authority to deal with the problems of an expanding population—for example, provision of adequate sewers, streets, and lights.

In 1959 the city council was solidly Republican; only one Democrat held a seat, and the Democratic party had the attributes of a permanent minority. However, in 1960 a group of "reform" Democrats, mostly associated with the university and imbued with national party ideals, began the formidable task of resurrecting a moribund party. One of their first objectives was to field a full slate of candidates for local elections, an objective that had seemed out of reach of the regular Democratic organization.[8] The insurgents were enthusiastic; they built their own networks of friends and neighbors, rang doorbells, and stressed local needs such as stop signs and better zoning. They were aided by the ward structure of Urbana; it is easier to work a ward intensively than to canvass even a small city, and gradually their efforts bore fruit.

Each election from 1963 to 1973 brought larger numbers of voters to the polls. In 1961 two Democrats were elected, and in 1963 three more were successful. While the number of Democrats remained constant in 1965, the first black Democrat won office. In 1967 the Democrats added a seat. After the elections in 1971 the council was evenly divided, and in 1973 the Democrats elected a mayor and a majority, with eight seats, on the city council.[9] The 1975 elections secured the Democratic grip, but as will be discussed below, majority status factionalized the party, and there is a question whether Democratic accommodation to the responsibilities of power blunted the reform Democratic objective of changing the contours and content of local politics.

In contrast, Champaign has a more heterogeneous population, more conflicts, more vocal interest groups, more calls for change, and less possibility for consensus than Urbana.[10] There has been more reliance on professional city administration as a substitute for the usual cement of community. Champaign has shown almost a faddish interest in experimenting with forms of government. The aldermanic form was used from incorporation until the state permitted the use of commission government. Commission government was adopted in 1921 and remained in effect until 1959, when the council-manager form of government was instituted. The council was elected on a nonpartisan, at-large ballot until 1972, when modified district representation was introduced. Under this plan, five council members are elected from districts, three are elected at large, and the ballot remains nonpartisan.

The mayor and councilmen are elected for staggered four-year terms. The council determines general policy, enacts the ordinances that govern the city, and is responsible for levying taxes and for appointing the city manager, city clerk, and treasurer. The city manager, within the limits set by the council, makes all administrative decisions, hires and fires all city employees except the city clerk and treasurer, and prepares the budget. When Warren Browning was city manager (1963–75), he established an easy working relationship with a majority of the city council and was, for a variety of purposes, the major decision maker. The relationship suffered when the composition of the city council was altered by the introduction of modified district representation, which produced a more activist council. When Browning resigned, the city council investigated candidates and selected

Eugene Miller as the new city manager. Miller proceeded to create a different and more accessible administration.

Partisan elections in Urbana and nonpartisan elections in Champaign call for different strategies for organizing and mobilizing the electorate. Aldermanic government in Urbana and a city manager system in Champaign provide different options for organizing administrative tasks and making policy decisions. Although both cities tend to adhere to the tenets of the individualistic political subculture that emphasize "the conception of the democratic order as a marketplace" and see government from a utilitarian perspective as meant "to handle those functions demanded by the people it is created to serve,"[11] the way they have organized to furnish that bundle of government services and activities has magnified and reinforced their distinctive characteristics. The tenets of the individualistic political subculture are manifested differently, and the complementary and contradictory manifestations can be viewed as variations on a cultural theme.

The recent efforts of "academics" to change the style and tone of local government came into conflict with this cultural predisposition. In their interest in ameliorating urban problems, the reformers wanted to seek federal grants to compensate for deficiencies in local resources. Some activists, particularly in Urbana, sought to transform local government into an energetic force to redress racial inequities, achieve a closer approximation to social justice, and safeguard and improve the environment. They sought to overcome the obstacles of government structure in order to mount a concerted attack on urban problems. All of these steps went against established community attitudes.

Thus the political controversies of the latter half of the postwar generation reflected the complex tensions that arise from the continual interjection of new people into an established community, as well as the conflict between allegiance to individualistic values and the new demands of an urbanized present. Individualistic beliefs shaped attitudes and the perception of options, while the needs of an urbanized present and future seemed to demand changes in both in the direction of more activist government. National objectives, such as integration, and the interests of autonomous governing bodies, such as school and park districts, further complicated this mixture of ambiguous perceptions and conflicting imperatives. These interactions and their consequences, especially the pressures toward accommodation, reflect the patterns of American federalism and suggest the continuing viability of the local community. The prerogatives of "local autonomy" may shift relative to shifts in the federal system, but "local autonomy" as a factor in the implementation of national and state policies can be neither discounted nor ignored.

Urbana and Federal Aid

The city of Urbana's involvement with federal grant programs in the 1960s was minimal. In some obvious ways, Urbana was unprepared to contemplate participation in the federal system. The League of Women Voters of Champaign County studied Urbana's financial structure and services in 1962 and concluded that there was no comprehensive overview of government activities or financial operations. City offices were in widely separated locations, city council committees functioned separately for the most part, and audit reports, which were prepared by several auditors, were not compiled and kept as a complete set of records in one office. In other words, it was "difficult to get any kind of complete, over-all picture of activities within the city."[12]

Charles Zipprodt, Republican mayor from 1969 to 1973, initiated the turn to professional administration in Urbana by hiring a part-time administrative assistant. The position soon became full time with expanded duties. Richard Franks was appointed by Mayor Zipprodt and continued in the office after the election of Hiram Paley, a Democrat, in 1973. In the Paley administration, the position was upgraded to administrative officer and became the central coordinating office with respect to the day-to-day operation of city government. The new emphasis on professional norms is illustrated by the retention of Franks, and professionalism has changed the style and increased the costs of local government. Formal recognition of the change came in 1975 when Urbana became an associate member of the International City Management Association.

However, acceptance of more professional administrative techniques occurred at the time when federal grant money for the cities was diminishing. In 1972 a small grant to finance the gathering of data for a neighborhood development program was received, but in 1973, as Urbana was preparing an application for a grant from the Department of Housing and Urban Development (HUD), the Nixon administration froze funds in preparation for the shift to revenue sharing and urban block grants. The Democrats, in opposition, advocated using federal grants to ameliorate urban problems, but it appeared that they came to power too late to effectively implement this strategy. Ironically, for Urbana, the shift in federal policy to revenue sharing and block grants seemed to promise an increase of federal money for urban projects. The promise was of course relative, based on the absence of federal grant money in the 1960s compared with the receipt of revenue sharing money and the acquisition of a Community Development Program in the 1970s.

The promise was not to be realized. The rising costs of city government and Urbana's limited tax base restricted the amount of revenue sharing money that could be allocated either to start urban redevelopment projects or to improve the conditions of minorities and the poor. For the first two years of revenue sharing, Urbana was in no financial position to allocate money to social service agencies.

The budget for fiscal year 1976 allocated $40,000 of revenue sharing money to social agencies in an operating budget of $3,246,207, and this generated a sharp debate. The allocation was not requested by the administration but was proposed by the Democrats and Independents on the city council. Republican aldermen contested the need to designate funds for social services and urged the traditional virtues of thrift, economy, and low taxes. The Democratic majority held firm, and the allocation was included. When the budget came up for final approval, the allocation was attacked by John Peterson, an Independent, who urged a larger appropriation. He was joined by three Republicans who were opposed to unnecessary spending and expressed their concern about a possible budget deficit.[13] Again, the Democratic majority held firm, and the $40,000 allocation remained in the budget. However, that such a small sum engendered such a heated debate suggests the strength of individualistic tenets in setting the priorities of local government.

The picture was brighter for improving housing conditions in the ghetto, primarily because Urbana received HUD money for community development ($133,000 in 1975 and $295,000 in 1976). However, the amounts allocated appear large only because Urbana had not previously received urban development money; they were small relative to the needs of the North End and the costs of staff and office. In addition, federal restrictions on how the money could be spent minimized the effect of the program. For example, there was interest in weatherizing older homes. To implement such a program required an intergovernmental effort; the Regional Planning Commission (RPC) and the County Office on Aging accepted applications, Community Development allocated $10,000 for materials, and Comprehensive Employment and Training Act (CETA) funds transmitted through the RPC were used to pay the workers. Supervisors were paid by the Office on Aging. The need for weatherstripping was widespread in the older areas of Urbana, but the project could be implemented only in the area designated for community development.[14] The number of homes to be weatherstripped was small, and their concentration in the designated area worked against widespread awareness of the federal contribution to a new initiative against urban blight. This example is representative of some of the constraints that prevent federal programs from making a visible impact either on the environment or on the attitudes and understanding of citizens.

The pattern of involvement obscures the contrast between citizens' perceptions of the significance of federal funds and the actual amount of federal funds that enter the community. Urbana was only peripherally involved in the grant programs of the 1960s, which reinforced citizens' perception of the nonsignificance of federal funds. However, the actual amount of federal funds that came into the community was in sharp contrast to this perception. In 1968 the federal government disbursed $66,764,975 in Urbana; in 1971 the sum was $57,136,236; and in 1972, $49,308,607 was distributed.[15] These totals include benefit payments to individuals, such as Social Security, railroad pensions, and military retirement benefits, as well as grants for research at the University of Illinois. Although these funds make an important contribution to the economic health of the community, they are not distributed in a way that impinges on the consciousness of citizens or officials.

City officials appeared unaware of the magnitude of these funds. When queried as to the federal funds received in Urbana, they estimated the amount at between $200,000 and $700,000 in any year—the amount actually received by the city government alone. The fragmented structure of federal allocations is the key here. For example, though the public schools receive money for the milk program from the Department of Agriculture, the schools are run by the school district, and city officials are at most peripherally aware of this allocation. The university receives grants from the National Science Foundation and the Department of Agriculture, but the university is autonomous, and few city officials could be expected to know of these allocations. Finally, a significant percentage of federal money goes to individuals who collect Social Security, military pensions, and railroad retirement benefits. Pension payments are accepted as routine, and the source of the funds and their contribution to the economy is easily overlooked.

Thus, in 1971 HUD allocated $133,503 to the park district for Open Space programs. The park district is autonomous, and city officials were unlikely to consider this a federal contribution to the city. In 1971 the Office of Economic Opportunity (OEO) allocated $144,162 for community action programs, but the money was divided between a variety of nongovernment agencies and did not loom large in city calculations.[16] In civil communities there would be sufficient integration of the elements composing the local government system to generate awareness of the total "package" of outside resources available. A political culture that emphasizes the centrality of private concerns and does not expect to find such an overwhelming government presence in its midst seems uniquely unsuited to grasp or understand the extent of the federal contribution to the viability of the community. Perception is selective, and cultural bias says government is unimportant except as a threat. If what needs to be accomplished is thought to be better accomplished by individual initiatives, the massive inflow of federal funds represents a threat to the local value system itself. The minimal visibility of federal allocations is reinforced by the small amounts earmarked for specifically urban problems. In 1972 the OEO allocated $17 for "concentrated community development" and $49,032 for community action programs.[17] The difficulty of initiating and conducting programs under conditions of financial uncertainty has been well documented, but more to the point for Urbana is the question, "What can be accomplished with such small and scattered allocations?" The projects are few, the focus is on amelioration at the fringes, and there is minimal impact on attitudes and behavior, since for the most part there is neither elite nor public awareness of the existence of these projects. No comprehensive picture of federal involvement is readily available; record keeping is a rather new dimension in Urbana and many other small cities and typically is spurred by federal or state insistence. However, habits change slowly, and as yet the results are skimpy. No local official has found it worthwhile to seek a comprehensive outline or understanding of federal involvement.

Local indifference to the cumulative effect of federal funds is one manifestation of the subtle interdependencies of the American system. Morton Grodzins described the system as a marble cake,[18] and the metaphor retains its validity despite various attempts to revamp federal relationships since the 1960s. Such efforts consistently have overlooked the discretion the existing system provides to local officials and the engrained cultural and political habits that support such discretion as well as the vested interests in local discretion. If Urbana is any example, the fears of conservatives and the hopes of liberals are equally misplaced. Federal financial contributions do not give rise to the situation described by the proverb "He who pays the piper calls the tune." The proverb is inappropriate when the right hand does not know what allocations it receives, let alone what the left hand is receiving or for what purposes.

A second manifestation of the subtlety of the relationship is that the political process generated by fragmentation of power on the national plane is copied on the local plane. For this reason national politics, even in a city that has not been consciously involved in federal programs, serves as the paradigm for the interaction of autonomous governing bodies in the local arena. Undertaking after undertaking in Champaign and Urbana seems to founder somewhere between plan and implementation, because no political actor either has the power to provide the ultimate push for successful project implementation or is willing to use whatever power he has accumulated. American presidents face similar problems in pushing their programs, but the problems of the mayor of Urbana are more acute. The mayor typically lacks charisma, local issues are not usually of the type that generate charismatic leadership, and the norms of individualistic culture, particularly the emphasis on a political marketplace, foster self-interest rather than a communal outlook. In Urbana the scattered and piecemeal allocation of federal funds, a fledgling professional administration, aldermen with districtwide rather than areawide constituencies, and Democratic leaders with few ties to the local business leadership suggest the need for coalitions to neutralize if not reconcile a collage of conflicting objectives and interests. The need resembles the pressures for bargaining and negotiation that define national politics, and in this way the paradigm of interaction on the national plane functions to shape the conduct of local politics.

Racial Integration in Urbana

The subtle interaction of federal relationships is also apparent in Urbana's response to the demands for black equality. Although conflict over demands for racial justice has highlighted some major weaknesses in the American federal system and occasioned severe stresses, in Urbana the opportunities and challenges of the 1960s produced an intermingling of national goals and local values that resulted in a complex process of adaptation and accommodation.

In 1948 Urbana was almost totally segregated, and residence, employment, and public schooling were determined by race.[19] In 1966 Urbana voluntarily became the first school district in the state of Illinois to implement a desegregation program. Circumstances were uniquely fortuitous; the school board made the decision while the superintendent was in Europe. The mechanics of integration were easily arranged; 80 percent of the children from Hayes School (since renamed the Martin Luther King, Jr., School), previously 99 percent black, were bused to elementary schools throughout the district, and the children from Orchard Downs, a university-operated housing project for married graduate students, foreign students, and visiting faculty, were bused to Hayes.[20] Although there was scattered local opposition, the addition of a few black children to classrooms throughout the district was unlikely to incite white parents, while transporting the children of transients obviously had little significance for permanent residents.

The implementation of this program without the immediate impetus of a court order can be attributed to the efforts of Democrats, liberals, the League of Women Voters, and civil rights groups. As noted above, the local Democratic party was transformed after 1960 by Democrats who professed allegiance to national party ideals. These Democrats soon began to win office on the school and park boards as well as the city council. Although the 1970s brought new racially connected problems in the schools to public attention and indicated that school desegregation was only a small step toward racial equality, the voluntary desegregation of the schools in 1966 suggests that the presence of sufficient numbers of activists with a commitment to federal goals can stimulate change in a local community.[21]

School desegregation failed to solve the problems of ensuring racial equality, and when the Democrats won the mayor's office and a majority of the city council in 1973, one of their priorities was the passage of a human rights ordinance. The city council began discussions on an ordinance forbidding discrimination in 1973, and at first it seemed that extending protection to homosexuals constituted the major stumbling block to legislation. The first ordinance making discrimination illegal was defeated by a seven-to-six vote in September 1973, and the Urbana Human Relations Commission (HRC), established in 1968, began rewriting it.[22] In October 1974 a new human rights ordinance, prohibiting discrimination on the basis of race, color, religion, sex, marital status, political affiliation, matriculation, sexual orientation, physical handicap, source of income, or place of residence or business, and applicable to employment, public accommodations, public services, and housing and commercial space was brought before the council. The ordinance was comprehensive and appeared to be ready for council action, but there were serious legal questions regarding constitutionality and application.

Although the chairman of the HRC criticized the decision, the council deferred action in order to discuss further the scope of the ordinance and amendments proposed by several Republicans. The ordinance was rewritten and returned to the council, and on 2 December the council again postponed action. This time the question was whether civil service regulations were in conflict with the ordinance. Further discussion occurred on 17 December, but no action was taken, and in January 1975, after an acrimonious debate that polarized the Democrats, the measure was returned to the HRC.[23]

The major obstacles to enactment were the inclusion of homosexuals and definition of the city's jurisdiction with respect to federal, state, and local agencies. The university, the Urbana park district, the Urbana school district, and Cunningham Township all sent letters to the mayor claiming that the city could not enforce the ordinance against them.[24] The HRC was undaunted; an ordinance again was brought to the council, and on 3 March the council approved the ordinance that declared the intent of the city "to secure an end to discrimination for any reason other than individual merit" but omitted housing discrimination because it was already prohibited by the Real Estate Licensing Ordinance, which had become effective in May 1968.[25]

However, the ordinance evaded the question of jurisdiction with respect to other government bodies. The Urbana school and park boards, the township, and the university continued to deny Urbana's jurisdiction over their employment practices, and the mayor vetoed the ordinance.[26] The matter rested until July, when the mayor announced that a rewritten human rights ordinance was again ready for council discussion. The new ordinance provided stronger sanctions, but rather than risking a lawsuit, it exempted state and federal agencies including the university, the largest employer in the city, from its provisions. Discussions continued for the next four months, and the prospect of increased intergovernmental conflict and other objections were again raised.[27]

In November the council in a four and a half hour special session debated amendments and by a seven-to-six vote excluded pregnant women from the protection of the ordinance. This exemption was a small victory for opponents of government regulation of business practices.[28] On 17 November the council finally approved the ordinance eight to five, with one amendment. State law forbids employers of twenty-five or more people from discriminating against pregnant women, and the council by voice vote withdrew the amendment that exempted them.[29]

Although opponents insisted that the ordinance was naive, impractical, dehumanizing, and likely to create friction between government units, it probably will have little effect on the lives of the citizens of Urbana. The ordinance may even be redundant, as opponents claimed, since federal and state statutes and regulations provide remedies for discrimination. Nevertheless, its passage is a significant measure of the slow percolation of national objectives into the nooks and crannies of the system.

It is especially significant that the long controversy over the ordinance, including a mayoral veto, attracted little public interest. The first ordinance, defeated in 1973, attracted public notice for its protection of homosexuals. In the long debate over the second ordinance, relations between the mayor and some Democrats became strained, some Republicans excoriated the city government's attempt to regulate individual practices, and other government bodies disputed the city's jurisdiction. But there were no public demonstrations, pro or con, nor was attendance at council sessions dramatically increased. Fifteen years earlier the passage of a human rights ordinance would have appeared visionary, perhaps even utopian; in 1975, despite delays and haggling over language and coverage, the dispute was not about the objective but about the means of achieving it. This greater tolerance of government intervention, including legal sanctions against discrimination, illustrates the slow transformation of attitudes in Urbana and suggests how national goals interact with and shape the objectives of local policy.

In this, too, federal activity played a major role. It was a United States

Supreme Court decision that enabled college students to claim rights of local residence in college towns, including voting rights, which strengthened the Democratic party in Urbana. Even in this case, however, the local factor made the major difference. Urbana's Democrats had begun their effort a decade earlier and were in a position to capitalize on the new voter residency requirements, while in the constellation of Champaign politics the change made less difference.

The new commitments increased the pressure on local administration and resources and generated new frustrations with government. The frustration was attributable in part to the activity generated by years of Democratic challenge and eventual victory, which increased the number of groups and individuals with a voice in the political process. It is just more difficult to make a decision, any decision, than it was fifteen years ago, largely because no "leader" has a strong enough base to act autonomously. It is hard to build cohesion on policy, and even more difficult to maintain cohesion. In this way the pattern of politics in Urbana has come to resemble more closely the pattern of national politics. The same tactics—dependence on persuasion, negotiations, and tact—were needed to produce results. The resemblance is an important indicator of the pervasiveness of federal relationships, for it highlights the deep-rooted attitudes, values, and needs on which such relationships are based.

In summary, Urbana is a "hard case" to use to describe the pervasiveness of federal relationships. There is still minimal awareness of the significance of federal actions for the viability of the community, and where there is awareness it typically is dominated by the perception of threat. Yet attitudes in Urbana have changed, and the catalyst has been population growth, spurred by university expansion. Democratic victory meant an expanded role for local government. The city undertook more commitments, ranging from stricter enforcement of the housing code and community redevelopment to a human rights ordinance, than were dreamed of fifteen years before. The commitments strengthened Urbana's ties to the federal government but had little effect on local understanding of the relationships spawned by interdependence.

Champaign Responds to External Pressures

Champaign exhibits a different pattern of response to the opportunities and challenges of the 1960s than does Urbana. Champaign's population is more heterogeneous, and the networks of friends and neighbors that played such a large role in Urbana politics have not developed. The distinctions between rich and poor are more acute, and real estate expansion has been more rapid. No clearly defined leadership core exists, and because neighborhoods lack community spirit and a sense of unity, joint action on problems is difficult.[30] Champaign opted for professional administration earlier than Urbana and has used council-manager government since 1959. Professional administration eased the way for the city to become directly involved with federal grant programs in the 1960s—it applied for and received an urban renewal grant. But in spite of—or perhaps because of—this experience, local elites seem more suspicious of federal assistance. The fear is endemic and can be attributed to the strength of individualistic tenets and to the greater difficulties facing "amateurs," such as the Democratic activists in Urbana, in building a political base in Champaign.

In specific cases, fears about federal control override what objectively could be described as self-interest. Two areas of Champaign were designated floodplain areas, and federal regulations specified that if a community with a designated floodplain area failed to join the Federal Flood Insurance Program by 1 July 1975, all forms of loans and grants, including mortgage and disaster loans from either federal agencies or banks and savings and loan institutions with Federal Deposit Insurance, would cease to be available.

Refusal to join the program had disastrous implications for construction activity, but two city council members voted no on a resolution authorizing Champaign's participation. Councilmen William Kuhne, a contractor, and William Bland, a union leader, who represented the working-class neighborhoods of North Champaign, defended their votes as a protest against unwarranted federal intervention in the affairs of local government. Two votes were sufficient to kill the resolution, because only six council members attended the session.[31] Defiance did not last long; within two weeks the council unanimously (six to zero) reversed the decision. Although several council members, including John Lee Johnson, a black activist, said they thought the proposal was in effect "legalized" blackmail, the council realized that the "city's federal Community Development application could be jeopardized by the city's refusal to join the flood insurance program."[32] Although the behavior can be dismissed as a purely rhetorical flourish in support of a lost cause, it indicates the strength of cultural preference and their potential to influence the political behavior of elites and citizens.

The deep-rooted aversion to federal assistance is illustrated by what is not done as well as by what is done. Champaign's downtown, securely established as the primary commercial district in the county in 1959, faced a severe challenge from suburban shopping centers by the end of the 1960s. Interest in downtown redevelopment, particularly a mall, was expressed as early as 1964, but discussions remained in preliminary stages until 1973, when a proposal for an outdoor brick mall, to cost approximately $710,000, was presented to the city council by businessmen. The proposal asked for city financing for one-sixth of the cost, while downtown businessmen took responsibility for the remainder.[33] Owing to financial problems and construction delays, the mall was not completed until eighteen months later, and the project probably will not reestablish the primacy of the downtown.

The meagerness of the effort to revitalize the downtown is one measure of the problem. In 1969 a $3,000,000 enclosed mall was proposed, but this proposal failed to attract support because of the expense. Neither local businessmen nor city officials suggested seeking federal funds. Redevelopment was perceived as assistance to downtown business, and city officials waited for those concerned to develop a plan. When the plan was finally presented, it was small-scale because private resources were simply inadequate for grand schemes, and thus the options were severely restricted. Limited objectives and the passivity of local elites and officials ruled out efforts to seek federal funds for the kind of large-scale redevelopment that might have secured the place of the downtown as a center of community life. What was not done illustrates the strength of the habits and attitudes of individualistic culture and sketches the limits of effective change in Champaign.

These examples of rejection or indifference to federal programs illustrate the difficulties of implementing change and obscure awareness of the extent of change during the 1960s. The trend toward an expanded role for local government, although reinforced by the shift to modified district representation, was not generated by dramatic events such as the shift from Republican to Democratic control in Urbana. Rather, the changes were intertwined in an incremental process that depended on shifts in administrative personnel and new conceptions of what was possible. With the exception of urban renewal, the objectives and policies of the federal government were peripheral to this process, but federal policy, interpreted and transmitted by the state of Illinois, became a factor in the allocation of state aid and thus had important consequences for the process.

The Case of Public Housing

An urban renewal program and its consequences for black employment illustrate the subtle interdependencies of the federal system, as do the steps taken to redress racial inequities. As in Urbana, remedial steps in racial matters were a matter of serious concern throughout the American system during the period under discussion here. Demands for rectification of racial inequities created severe stresses in Champaign. There has been conflict over school integration and affirmative action in employment, but typically the pattern in Champaign has been adaptation of outside imperatives to local objectives, and the resulting interplay leads to something resembling accommodation.

Champaign's history of urban redevelopment is long, convoluted, and continuing. Despite local ambivalence concerning further involvement with urban renewal, the shift to revenue sharing and block grants in the 1970s brought community development funds to Champaign. To understand the housing saga, however, it is necessary to begin with the late 1940s, when the need for remedial action on housing became apparent. Substandard housing had been in use before 1945, but patterns of residential segregation limited the impact on the general public until the influx of veterans after World War II placed apartments—any apartments—at a premium. The League of Women Voters gathered the first systematic data on housing conditions in 1948 and 1949 and wrote a report called "The Shack Study." Families lived in shacks with dirt floors; chicken coops were converted into housing; many houses lacked indoor plumbing or running water; rents were high, and residential areas were segregated.

At that time the League pushed for improved housing rather than integration, and application was made to the Public Housing Administration for construction of housing for low-income families. In 1950 units were built by the Champaign County Housing Authority with the stipulation that for each new construction a dilapidated unit was to be destroyed. However, lax enforcement resulted in limited destruction of inferior housing.

In 1957 the League updated "The Shack Study" and concluded that substandard housing in white areas had decreased but that conditions in the black community were substantially unchanged. The League's focus was still on improved housing. In the mayoral election of 1960, the problem of substandard housing was raised, and after the election of Mayor Emerson Dexter, a Citizens' Advisory Committee on Urban Renewal was formed. By 1962 data was being collected to prepare a "workable plan" to qualify for federal help, and Harland Bartholomew and Associates was hired to prepare a general neighborhood renewal plan.

As the preparations were being made, the issue that was to haunt urban renewal became explicit. Objections to segregated patterns of housing were raised in connection with the relocation of the families displaced by renewal. Not many black families could afford housing on the open market, and public housing in the renewal area was proposed. The director of the Urban League opposed the idea, arguing that it would perpetuate patterns of segregation.

The city evaded the racial question by affirming that choice ought to be limited only by the individual's means. Local activists tried to involve the federal government and wrote the regional office of the Public Housing Administration. They found that in 1963 federal officials may have been sympathetic toward integration in public housing, but they lacked legal power to pressure local housing authorities.[34] Urban renewal had city support, but the project moved slowly. The absence of public enthusiasm, the qualms of liberals about segregation, and questions about the effect of the project on neighborhood families reinforced ambivalence and contributed to the delays.

With the passage of the Civil Rights Act of 1964, the federal government received new powers to promote integration. In practical terms, however, the net effects were further delays. The city was required to provide additional documentation to support the location of public housing units in the renewal area. The documentation was at hand—costs outside the renewal area were estimated to exceed federal limits on costs per room, and the city needed the federal credits offered for public housing to meet its one-fourth share of renewal costs. However, the new emphasis on integration led to the proposal to locate sixty units in and sixty units outside the renewal area. By November 1966, when the city council approved the renewal plan,[35] it seemed that the last obstacles had been removed.

Civil rights activists continued to oppose the location of public housing in the renewal area. They were joined by two conservative city council members, elected in 1967, who were altogether opposed to urban renewal. Clearance began in January 1968, but the proposal to build sixty units of public housing in a white working-class neighborhood of north Champaign antagonized the neighborhood, and the residents organized to fight the program. Various rear guard actions fought against the construction of public housing between 1967 and 1973 did not succeed in blocking clearance work, but they further reduced public and official support for renewal and for public housing in particular.

In 1973 residents of the working-class neighborhood appealed to United States Congressman Edward Madigan for his help in fighting the project, and Madigan asked the Department of Housing and Urban Development (HUD) to prepare an audit. The audit revealed that the project was anomalous. It had been authorized years before under a housing program that had expired, and construction had not yet begun.[36] The Champaign County Housing Authority (CCHA) then voted to drop the project, to sell the site, and to seek a program for scattered-site housing. The shift to scattered-site housing was in accord with shifts in HUD policy that stressed racial integration.[37]

HUD had allocated $2,795,206 for the construction of public housing units in Champaign. As of 30 June 1973, the CCHA had spent $560,820 and had only a few scattered sites and two parcels of land that cost $185,000 to show for its activity. The perceptions and preferences of the community produced a mixture of opposition and apathy concerning public housing. Conservative opposition was to be expected, particularly in an area where the traditions of the individualistic culture are strong, but liberal opposition to the project increased as the drive for integration became the primary objective of civil rights activists. The opposition of families in the renewal area and in the working-class neighborhood of north Champaign provided fuel for both conservative and liberal opponents, and in the end no one supported the project. Federal money for the community willing to make the effort was intended to take the financial burden of housing improvement and rehabilitation off local tax resources, but in this case federal money did not provide sufficient motivation to overcome established preferences and perceptions.[38]

HUD officials were tolerant of the hesitations and delays surrounding the project. No move was made to prod the CCHA into quick action, to demand conformity, or to seriously attempt to cut off funds until Congressman Madigan intervened on behalf of opponents. It was neither federal red tape nor federal stringencies that killed the program; HUD carried the project for years, and when the unused funds were returned they were put in escrow for the development of a new program. Local delays and ambivalence and the changed climate of the late 1960s that transformed the project into an anomaly led to its demise. As noted above, efforts to ameliorate housing conditions are continuing; at present community development funds are being received. However, ambivalence of local elites and the public concerning federally financed initiatives that might promote change in community life-styles or attitudes is still evident and will continue to affect the implementation of programs.

Integration in Public Employment

Involvement in urban renewal left a mixed legacy; on the one hand, it reinforced perceptions of government ineptitude even as it strengthened fears about federal control. On the other hand, blacks were hired to administer the program, and when the program ended they took other positions in the administration. Thus in 1975 minorities were well represented at top administrative levels in Champaign and were represented above their proportion of the city's population in all but three departments.[39] The extent of the change in city policy is impressive; in 1948 employment opportunities for blacks were strictly segregated, and one policeman in Champaign was the only black working for the municipalities except in unskilled work.[40]

Changes in national objectives in the 1960s, tougher federal laws, and new state laws prohibiting discrimination in employment as well as local black demonstrations and two city ordinances contributed to the result. Although urban renewal programs served as the catalyst for employment of blacks in administrative positions, federal incentives or sanctions were not directly related to the shifts in employment policy. Threats of state sanctions regarding the transmission of federal money overcame resistance. For example, two of the three city departments that underutilize blacks are the fire and police departments. Their personnel policies are made by the Board of Fire and Police Commissioners, which operates independently of the city administration, in conformity with state law. Several activists on the city council made a determined effort to liberalize height and weight requirements in order to open up hiring, even threatening to use home rule[41] powers to bring the departments under stricter city control. The effort was dramatic but made little progress until the Illinois Law Enforcement Commission, the state agency dispensing grant money from the Federal Law Enforcement Assistance Administration, declared that a minimum height requirement may be discriminatory.[42] Within a week the Board of Fire and Police Commissioners reversed its decision, albeit grudgingly, so the city would be eligible for the grant.[43]

The exception is dramatic, but the primary pressure for open employment was local—the pressure of activists and changes in administrative personnel and attitudes. Champaign enacted an affirmative action ordinance in 1969, providing that contractors and vendors that did business with the city must supply a written commitment not to discriminate in employment. The ordinance seemed dictated by the times and national trends, but it was more a symbolic gesture than an instrumental measure.

Administrative difficulties, and controversy over the conduct of the community relations director, as well as over the director's position in the administrative structure, effectively vitiated enforcement of the ordinance. After the second community relations director was fired by the city manager in 1973, a newly elected black activist councilman began to lobby for a new affirmative action ordinance. The councilman was successful, and in 1974 a stronger affirmative action ordinance was enacted, which specified acts of discrimination and strengthened sanctions. It provided for greater accountability of the city manager, but the community relations director continued to be responsible to the city manager rather than to the city council.

The black community's perception of the city manager's commitment to affirmative action was not reassuring, and there were doubts concerning the effect of the new ordinance on policy. However, the city manager resigned in 1974, and hopes were concentrated on his replacement. Before the manager resigned, he hired a new community relations director. Then the new city manager as well as new administrative personnel eased the tensions that clustered around the implementation of the ordinance. The activists on the city council made their concerns evident, and the new city manager promised an open administration.

A more professional attitude in community relations created an atmosphere in which it was politically feasible to enforce the ordinance. Meetings were held early in 1975 to explain affirmative action requirements to vendors, and in July a vendor was terminated for noncompliance.[44] Although there continued to be local resistance to the ordinance at the generation's end and the administration continued to face obstacles in implementing it, the difference between 1973 and 1976 was significant. The former city manager appeared unwilling (at least to his critics) to carry out an affirmative action program; a new administration has demonstrated its commitment to the program and its determination to enforce the law.

Integrating the Public Schools

To complete the tale of change in Champaign, a brief sketch of school policy is needed. Schools in Champaign, as in Urbana, were totally segregated in 1948.[45] Champaign, like Urbana, integrated its schools voluntarily, that is, without the pressure of a federal court order. However, local resistance was stronger than in Urbana, and Champaign lacked a concentrated group of children who could be bused without creating a political backlash.

An Equal Education Opportunity Committee (EEOC) was created in 1967, and after deliberations it proposed that Washington School, in the black ghetto, become a model school, operated jointly by unit 4 and the College of Education at the University of Illinois. The proposal "finessed" the difficulty of gaining community support for busing white children to a black school. Only volunteers were to be bused to Washington, and the "carrot" offered was the promise of an innovative laboratory school with exceptional educational opportunities. The black students displaced from Washington were to be bused throughout the district so each school would have no more than 93 percent or less than 74 percent white students.[46]

The idea of a laboratory school with volunteer students was received by white citizens with reactions ranging from enthusiasm to relief. For proponents of integration, the creation of an integrated school system was the fulfillment of a moral imperative. For opponents, the proposal offered minimum involvement and, more important, minimum dislocation in neighborhood schools. Opposition to the EEOC proposal came from black families, who objected to the mandatory dispersion of their children, but opposition was spotty and poorly organized, and a majority of the black community accepted the plan. Integration was smoothly implemented in September 1968, and the racial ratios in the schools approximated the EEOC guidelines. Success was due in large part to the absence of coercion; individuals could choose for their children, and individualistic tenets were not violated.

However, integration did not solve the problem of racial balance. The racial composition of the schools became more salient after 1971, when the State Office of Education established guidelines that permitted a variation of 15 percent above or below the percentage of black population in the district. For Champaign, with a black school population of 15.2 percent, the maximum allowable black concentration in any school was 30.2 percent.[47] By the middle 1970s, population shifts and a sharp decline in school population increased the difficulty of local conformity with state guidelines. The board's decision to close three schools in the older neighborhoods of Champaign and reassign their students compounded the difficulties. Since failure to conform to state guidelines carried the threat of suspension of state aid, the school board was compelled to make the necessary adjustments. The result was increased parental opposition to board policy and dissipation of the belief that individual choice was the basic factor in creating racial balance. The absence of official coercion had helped smooth the path of desegregation in 1967, but by 1976 it was obvious that a conscious effort was needed to reach state-mandated objectives.

The increase in overt state pressure should not obscure the significance of local accommodation to national objectives. The primary pressure for integration was local, albeit legitimized by the national concern for racial equality. A solution that did not violate local values yet conformed to national expectations was devised and voluntarily implemented. Continuing state pressure may be needed to maintain this accommodation, but the crucial factor in change at the local level remains the complex interplay between national objectives and the way they are accepted and adapted locally.

Conclusion

The politics of Champaign and Urbana cannot be neatly summarized. From 1967 to 1975, local government undertook a series of initiatives that greatly expanded its responsibilities and had the potential to affect the lives of citizens more and more. These initiatives were related to an increase in political activism beginning in the early 1960s and were fueled by the excitements and disturbances of national politics. New expectations, new demands, new responsibilities, and new tasks were thrust upon the governments of the two cities. There has been opposition to the expanding role of local government, and rear guard actions have slowed and will continue to slow attempts to change. Progress comes slowly in Champaign County, and local activists must use some part of their energies to defend what has been won rather than to seek new victories. If these initiatives were to be evaluated, a number of specific endeavors to improve the quality of life could be applauded, the placid days of the past could be lamented, or the constraints on a new group of enlightened administrators and officials could be condemned. What such a summing up would accomplish is a graphic description of two city governments in transition.

The contradictory perceptions are generated by the contrast between individualistic tenets and the necessities of urban communities. On the one hand, local attitudes reject the necessity of interdependence, and the most common perception of government—especially the national government—is that it is a threat to the individual and to cherished liberties. For this reason, at first glance both cities seem curiously remote and isolated from the challenges and opportunities of the federal system. The cities, for the most part, ignored the possibility of using federal grants to revitalize downtown business districts, and when federal help was utilized, for example in Champaign's urban renewal program, the results seemed peculiarly inconsequential.

On the other hand, neither Urbana nor Champaign exists in a vacuum; they are integral parts of a complex system of government, situated in Champaign County in the state of Illinois in the United States of America. The decisions of larger units as well as the increase in relationships between units progressively shape and influence local decisions. For example, in the past fifteen years, county government has been jarred out of passivity into activism, and the new initiatives have generated an expanding chain of consequences for Champaign and Urbana. The county created a Regional Planning Commission (RPC) in the 1960s to provide professional knowledge to aid development. The RPC became the clearinghouse for federal grants, and its role was ever more important after the federal Bureau of the Budget promulgated circular A-95 as one means to bring order to the proliferation of grants and applications of the Great Society. Emphasis on planning and the resulting drive for active cooperation between local governments derives from the federal government's interest in coordination, but the objective cannot be realized unless local government shares the interest. The need to conform to federal standards has encouraged record keeping in the county and the cities, but habits change slowly, and the order is at times more apparent than real.

In addition, the RPC has the potential to coordinate development in the county, and this task has been strongly supported by HUD through budget contributions. Nevertheless, the efficacy of the RPC depends on local support, since approximately half its budget comes from Champaign, Urbana, and the county. Local support is at best ambivalent, not only because developers can exert pressures on local officials, but because each government demands preference for its concerns and threatens budget reductions if its demands are not met. The RPC must conform in some measure to local purposes, and such conformity leads to reinterpretation of national objectives, even as the national push for more order in local administration changes the structure of local government.[48]

New expectations about local government were created as the national government took a larger role in redressing the inequities of the past. The chain of consequences generated new demands on local government, and the assumption of new functions strengthened the connections between local government, the state, and the national government. Legal amelioration of racial injustice illustrates the complex interactions of the American federal system. Conflict over this problem has created severe stresses, yet the experience of Champaign and Urbana sketches the forces that push for accommodation. Champaign and Urbana were thoroughly segregated in 1948, and individualistic tenets that militate against government regulation were pervasive, but each city has endeavored to change by law the status of black citizens. Although much remains to be done to remedy the condition of blacks, the schools were integrated voluntarily, and each city has an open occupancy ordinance as well as ordinances prohibiting discrimination in employment.

The legal status of blacks was turned around without the impetus of direct national pressure or threat of sanctions. Changes in local attitudes were stimulated by changes in national policy, as reflected by the shift from pressure for improved housing to integration in the League of Women Voters. Local change was sparked by activists who came to Urbana and Champaign from other places and who carried national ideals with them. But it was the complex amalgamation of national goals and local values that produced the shifts in local policy. As government responsibilities expanded, political habits and cultural preferences functioned to soften the consequences. National imperatives were adapted to local perceptions, needs, and interests even as expanded responsibilities reshaped the role and structure of local government.

8. The Agricommercial Tradition on the Metropolitan Frontier: Decatur

Maren Allan Stein

> . . . and so, as surely as the corn rises straight and green each spring, Decatur rose in the midst of the fertile prairie. (Decatur Chamber of Commerce, "Decatur, Illinois")

Decatur sits in the center of Illinois, near the center of the nation. It is not immediately close to any large city, and the nearest medium-sized city is half an hour away by expressway. Statistical measures reveal Decatur as the most typical of United States heartland cities. It is prosperous, with a per capita income above state and national averages; homogeneous, with nearly 80 percent of the population born in Illinois; stable, with an annual rate of population growth or decline averaging less than 0.2 percent since 1940; and relatively self-sufficient in terms of business ownership and government revenue.

Decatur is one of the few cities on or off the prairie that so closely approximates the heartland ideal. There is a touch of irony in this source of Decatur's uniqueness. Unlike its sister cities of central Illinois, Decatur's political landscape is dominated by no single state institution or corporate enterprise. Unlike most cities of the prairie considered in this book, the 1960s and 1970s brought it no dramatic changes and very little difference in the way the city fathers (and a few mothers now) handle what they regard as the business of politics. In fact, there is a decided flatness to Decatur's political as well as physical landscape that has enabled the city to weather many of the storms of the post–World War II generation.

Geography has much to do with this. Decatur's river, the Sangamon, is not navigable; it is a river, as Edgar Lee Masters put it, "not distinguished for majestic scenery, nor for a battle, nor for a single historic event."[1] Isolated on the edge of the Grand Prairie, near no major city or navigable waterway, Decatur developed late and in closer relationship to the land than to its sister cities of the prairie. To this day Decatur is not "well connected" to the transportation or political system of the state and region of which it is a part.

At the same time, Decatur is hardly a backwater community like Cairo, Illinois, to the south, or Duluth, Minnesota, to the north.[2] In fact it is perhaps the quintessential case of a community that has managed to negotiate America's successive frontiers, albeit at its own pace and somewhat off the beaten path. The reason, we submit, has to do with Decatur's historical ability to weave the strands of agrarianism and commercialism into an "agricommercial" tradition that has proved remarkably adaptable to America's successive frontier opportunities. It is to understanding the makings of that tradition and its negotiation of the metropolitan-technological frontier that the remainder of this chapter is devoted.

Frontier Stages of the Agricommercial Tradition

The history of the Grand Prairie is most typically set out in agrarian terms. Agrarian it is, but in the commercial vein of the Middle States, not the backward subsistence farming of the upland South. As early as the 1950s, historians began to question the traditional notions of nineteenth-century prairie farmers and farm life as provincial and turned inward. In 1950 Henry Nash Smith challenged the nineteenth-century myth of the Mississippi valley as the "garden of the world."[3] Allan and Margaret Bogue wrote of the importance of money and commerce for the pioneer farmer and the prevalence of land speculation and scientific innovation on the prairie frontier.[4] Norman Pollack and others reinterpreted the midwestern populist response to industrial America as a matter of public control, not disdain for industry.[5]

Long before the valleys of California came to be dominated by large corporate farms, commercial farming was a way of life on the prairie. Based on a study of county biographical sketches of nineteenth-century Iowa and Illinois farmers, Bogue assessed the values and the reality of that way of life. As Bogue concluded: "It was good to have pioneered here, to have been an 'old settler,' and made virgin prairie 'productive' by stocking it with fine animals and raising bountiful crops. He had lived a good life who started with little and added to his acres so that in middle or old age he could start his sons on farms or rent to others."[6]

Missing from these histories is a theoretical framework capable of explaining the importance of the medium-sized city and its relation to agriculture and agrarianism on the prairie. Furthermore, just as historians of the Grand Prairie region have tended to overlook the role of its cities, historians of the urban West have bypassed those prairie cities that have grown to medium size in relation to their hinterland. Richard C. Wade has depicted the early towns of the Ohio River valley as "spearheads of the frontier."[7]

Harry N. Scheiber and others have focused on the nineteenth-century rivalries of Great Lakes cities, river cities, and prairie cities throughout much of the Old Northwest.[8] Arthur E. Bestor, Jr., has studied the transplanting of towns throughout the trans-Mississippi West as "patent-office models of the good society."[9] Yet none quite captures the development of priarie cities such as Decatur in relation to their surrounding farms and, now, suburbs.

One notable exception is Daniel J. Elazar's *Cities of the Prairie,* published in 1970.[10] In that study Elazar provides a theoretical framework that helps explain three important facets of central Illinois politics in general and Decatur's politics in particular: the linking of agrarian and commercial values; the interdependence of urban and rural economies; and the continuity of these relationships during the rural-land, urban-industrial, and metropolitan-technological stages of the American frontier experience. As to the linking of agrarianism and commercialism, Elazar suggests:

> In every form it has taken, American *Agrarianism* has had a strong *commercial* aspect, beginning with the American's desire to make a profit from the use of the land even while valuing closeness to it for moral reasons. Unlike feudal or peasant agrarianism, it has represented the effort to create a moral commonwealth of religiously-inspired freeholders actively engaged in commerce in its various manifestations. By the same token, the values of *Agrarianism* modify *commercial efficiency* at crucial points so that maximizing profits is not the only measure of efficiency in American life even as they are themselves tailored at some points to meet the demands of *Efficiency.* The politically defined limits of *Commerce* in America are set by the demands of *agrarian legitimacy.*[11]

In Decatur and Macon County at least, the "agricommercial" tradition remains alive and well, owing in no small part to the continued commitment of the city and the county to perpetuating its myths and its realities. Three such perpetuating factors, set out by Elazar, seem particularly appropriate to Decatur and to Macon County. Economically, commercial efficiency is still defined in terms of agriculture and agribusiness, which continue to dominate both the urban and the rural economies of the region. Socially, the maintenance of the agricommercial tradition remains cast in terms of a specific style of life—whether in urban, suburban, or rural surroundings—that places great value on "religiosity, individual self-reliance, and family solidarity," to use Elazar's terms. Politically, the public expression of the agricommercial ideal and the bias against "citification" comes as much from city as from county residents. Though city and county interests may differ, each has combined agrarianism and commercialism into "a single socioeconomic package and endowed it with high moral value."[12]

Lying adjacent to Illinois's Grand Prairie, Decatur was settled, founded, and incorporated later than many other Illinois cities, especially the river cities. Its first settlers arrived in the early 1820s. They saw only tough-rooted prairie grass and acres of swampy lowlands, though it was not long before the first was vanquished by the steel plow and the second by an almost universal system of tiling and ditching. Nonetheless, the pioneer stage of the land frontier lasted a full generation, since efforts to render the Sangamon River suitable for transportation were unsuccessful. Macon County was established in January 1928, and in June of that year the county commissioners court ordered that the town of Decatur be erected not as a "city upon a hill," but "after the form of Shelbyville," county seat of Shelby County to the south, from which Macon County had separated.[13]

Until the coming of the railroad in 1854, Decatur was a modest town, even by early-nineteenth-century standards. County settlements were sparse and patterned after the scattered homestead model of Pennsylvania and North Carolina. Agricultural produce and livestock were raised primarily for local consumption. Yet it was during this period that Decatur's position in relation to the American frontier experience was fashioned. Inadequate river transportation retarded population growth and agricultural production, yet it also discouraged excessive land speculation. The attendant isolation also encouraged local ingenuity, as in the case of breeding hogs for the overland trip to St. Louis markets, local self-reliance through the marketing of agricultural production for local use, and an agrarian-commercial orientation with the development of Decatur as a local agricultural service center. Interestingly, the delayed arrival of the railroad (in 1854) and an interstate highway connection (in 1974) would reinforce those characteristics at successive stages of Decatur's frontier experience.

In 1850 the population of Macon County was nearly 4,000; on the day the railroad arrived in Decatur, a local count revealed 1,500 residents of the town. Six years later, in 1860, the population of Decatur was only 4,000, while that of the county had increased dramatically to 13,738. The population of the city of Decatur would not reach 10,000 until the 1880s and would not surpass the combined population of other areas of the county until the 1910 census; yet the initial responses to the urban-industrial frontier were apparent. Within a decade of the coming of the railroad, Decatur had assembled the prototype of a diversified agri-industrial base: grain processing, farm-equipment inventions and manufacturing, an ironworks producing rails for the railroad, a brewery, a tile company, and a gunsmith's shop.

Political responses to growth and prosperity were swift and characteristic. In 1856 Decatur was incorporated as a city, and in 1860 county residents established township government, marked by the subdivision of the county into fourteen townships. The statewide expansion of railroad services in the 1870s and other factors brought an industrial boom to Decatur in the

1880s and 1890s, characterized by a flurry of local inventions, the expansion of the local agri-industrial base, and the introduction of the "motorwagon" industry. By 1900 Decatur's regional position on the urban-industrial frontier was secure, with no great sacrifice to either the agricommercial tradition or local ownership and control.

It was not until the twentieth century that Decatur attained an international position in the new world of "agribusiness." During the first quarter of the twentieth century, Decatur's reputation was tied almost exclusively to corn—corn flakes breakfast food, corn oil products (such as soap and salad oil), cornstarch, and corn feed for livestock. Then in 1922 Augustus Eugene Staley, Sr., owner of one of the largest corn processing companies in Decatur, adopted a little-known import from Manchuria (the soybean) and established the first soybean processing plant in the United States.[14] Decatur's reputation as "the soybean capital of the world" was complete when the Archer-Daniels-Midland Company (ADM) moved its divisions and international office from Minneapolis to Decatur.

Throughout the post–World War II period, Decatur has sought to negotiate the metropolitan-technological frontier without sacrificing agrarian and commercial ideals. The result is an expectedly mixed record. Since 1950, signs of suburbanization have begun to appear in townships such as Hickory Point (northwest of the city) and Mount Zion (to the southeast), raising concern among downtown merchants and county farmers alike. Yet according to one recent study, "while 6,453 acres were being converted from agricultural uses to other (mainly surburban) uses, 4,303 acres were being converted from other uses to agriculturally productive lands."[15] Decatur's economy has undergone similar changes.

Since the end of World War II, most of the area's new major employers have been corporate divisions and branch plants set up in Decatur or surrounding townships by international firms (Borg-Warner, 1948 and 1958; Pittsburgh Plate Glass, 1950; Caterpillar Tractor, 1954; and Firestone Tire and Rubber, 1963).[16] With the greater importance of absentee-owned plants, particularly in the automobile industry, Decatur's economy has been increasingly affected by swings in the national economy. Still, local firms (notably A. E. Staley) and locally transplanted firms (notably ADM) remain a major element of Decatur's economic base, as does the processing of agricultural produce and the manufacture of farm machinery. In short, agriculture and agribusiness are still major sources of wealth and regarded locally as uniquely reliable (given enough rain).

Though few Macon County residents farm for a living, agrarianism is still the preferred style of life. Residents continue to avoid the trappings of citification, and the county's new suburbs among the cornfields are an

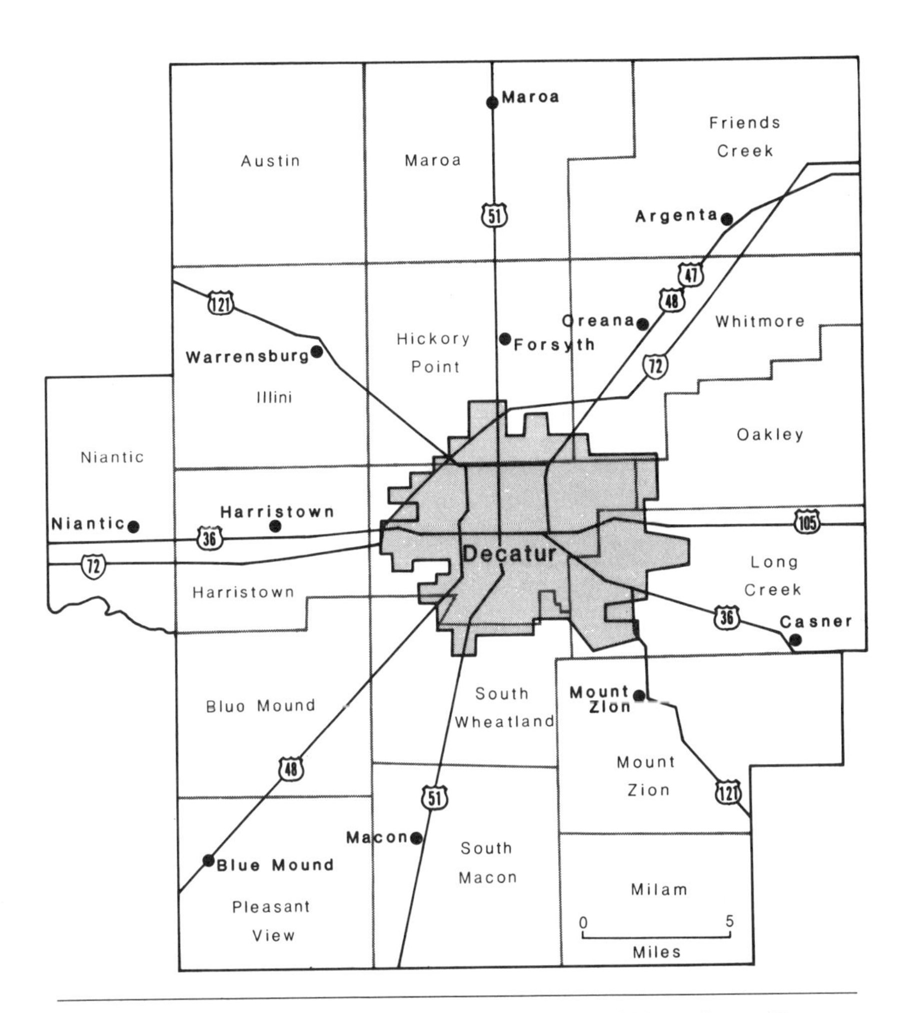

Map 8.1. Macon County. From O. T. Banton, *History of Macon County* (Decatur, Ill.: Macon County Historical Society, 1976). Courtesy of Macon County Historical Society.

expression of that traditional bias. Many Decaturites are one or two generations removed from a farm background, and having a few acres or a small farm in addition to a salaried job is not at all unusual today. Although small landholders became the minority a long time ago, many of the county's big farms are still worked by single families owing to the concentrated amount of time spent planting and harvesting in grain farming.

Politically, the values and interests of agricommercialism continue to inform Decatur's responses to the metropolitan-technological frontier. As one local official put it, the goal of the city is to keep the tax base low; the goal of the county is to preserve its agricultural base. This has fostered an increasingly accommodative response to federal and state funds and accompanying regulations, while the city retains an independent stance. Those goals also have fostered a reluctant commitment from local government in dealing with economic and, to a lesser extent, social needs traditionally viewed as beyond the scope of legitimate government activity. Finally, those goals have opened up new areas of conflict between city and county governments. The remainder of this chapter examines these three sets of political responses to the metropolitan-technological frontier.

Decatur in the Federal System

The number of intergovernmental relationships Decatur participates in has increased greatly since 1960. New federal and state regulations and entitlement programs account for a great many of those relationships; however, there is also more willingness to use the money. Even so, Decatur has seemed to prefer to remain as independent as possible, thereby avoiding some difficulties but also missing some opportunities.[17] There seems to be no sustained commitment to establish a political presence either in Springfield or in Washington. The local congressman is thought to be the agent, and what he does not do does not get done. A notable exception is the working relations established by the Decatur Housing Authority with the Washington and Chicago regional offices of the Department of Housing and Urban Development.

According to the city manager, who has served for eight years, the city has tried not to become over dependent on federal and state funds because they are viewed as unpredictable. This, and other hesitations, resulted in a period of relative neglect of capital improvements throughout the 1960s.[18] During the late 1960s, Decatur initiated planning in various project areas, supported in part by federal assistance; but it was not until the early 1970s that the city fully embarked upon a program of capital improvement.

Table 8.1. Intergovernmental Sources of Local Revenue, 1962–77

	Percentage of Local Revenue from State Aid		Percentage of Local Revenue from Federal Aid	
Year	Decatur	National[a]	Decatur	National
1977	29.9	34.9	7.2	9.5
1972	34.7	32.9	1.4	4.6
1967	22.9	33.0	0.2	3.6
1962	21.7	—	0.2	—

Source: U.S. Bureau of the Census, *County and City Data Book, 1962–1977*.
[a]National figures are for SMSAs of 100,000–200,000 population.

In many respects 1972 represented a fault line in Decatur's intergovernmental relations. The figures in table 8.1 serve as partial indicators of this. From 1972 to 1977 federal funds as a proportion of Decatur's total revenues increased from 1.4 to 7.2 percent, with a corresponding decline in state aid from 34.7 to 29.9 percent of total revenue. Behind those statistics, however, one finds greater willingness to utilize federal funds and an increased capacity to do so.

In 1972 Decatur received its first funds under federal revenue sharing, and the city council established a policy of earmarking half the money for surface water drainage improvements. In August 1972 the city began construction of a new water treatment plant at Rhea's Bridge, becoming the only city in the state to receive federal funding for that purpose. One month earlier, the city began operating the Decatur Public Transit System with the assistance of a $250,000 local bond issue, approved by a local referendum in November 1971 and $828,600 in state and federal grants. In November Decatur signed a contract with the federal government to begin redevelopment of the eleven-block Torrence Park Urban Renewal Project, which had been in the planning stage since 1969. In January 1973 the city began building a stormwater drainage system in its northeast quadrant. And throughout the early 1970s it was able to draw on needed Emergency Employment Act funds for some of these and other projects as one of twelve High Impact Demonstration Cities in the country.[19]

Although intergovernmental interaction is sought, political influence is not strenuously pursued. As a result, several basic items have remained on the agenda for years, in part owing to lack of success in Washington or Springfield. The Champaign-Springfield section of I-72, providing Decatur with an east-west interstate connection, was not completed until 1974, ten years after construction began.

Also among the unaccomplished agenda items is a north-south interstate linkup, known as the Midstate Expressway. Such a road would be part of a proposed Illinois highway system connecting all major cities in the state. The Midstate Expressway, linking Rockford and Decatur, was first proposed in 1963; however, Decatur has not been successful in the continuing Illinois struggle over which cities will gain access to the arteries. In the most recent round, Congress passed and the president signed a "special priority measure to fund the federal share of highway construction." However, the state's share was not forthcoming, on the grounds that it would force an increase in the gasoline tax.[20]

Another long-standing unsuccessful pursuit is the effort to increase the water supply. The land quality and the extensive area under cultivation in Illinois mean that lakes created to supply water eventually silt up. Such a fate is befalling Lake Decatur, and people in Decatur looking toward future industrial development have sought an additional reservoir since before the first study of the cities of the prairie.

The choice has been between dredging the present lake and creating a new one. Two sites that have been proposed for a new reservoir are one that would flood a historic nature reserve, Allerton Park, owned by the University of Illinois near Champaign-Urbana (Oakley) and another in the northern part of Macon County (Big Creek/Long Creek). Both sites have met opposition: the first from University of Illinois interests, the second from landowners. Without local consensus, area congressmen have not been able to lobby effectively in Washington, and local opposition has prevented use of available funds. Even when funding was obtained by Congressman William Springer in 1962, a local study by the United States Army Corps of Engineers precluded building the Oakley reservoir.[21]

Decatur's mixed record of intergovernmental dealings has not been limited to federal programs. During Governor Otto Kerner's administration, two state funding programs were begun with implications for local communities. One created a statewide system of mental health zone centers; the other provided for community college districts within the state. Decatur availed itself of the zone center option within a few years (1962–66), competing successfully for the Adolph Meyer (sixteen-county, east-central) Zone Center.[22]

Decatur was not as unified about the community college.[23] Although state enabling legislation was passed in 1965, Richland Community College did not open until 1972. Even then, controversy continued for another seven years over finding an alternative site to the bank building where Richland was first situated. The varieties of opposition to the college, and to a new site, ranged from a reluctance to being taxed for it to a latent sentiment against the inevitable liberalization of Richland's original vocational orientation.

The first alternative site, near the northwest city addition of Wilcox, aroused a county/city conflict and was defeated in two referenda, the second time, in 1978, by fewer than a hundred votes. Other sites were considered; two parties offered free land in the county, while others suggested using the mental health zone center if it closed. This last alternative brought the matter to the state level, and the governor decided to keep the zone center open. Finally, the option of leasing land in an industrial part northeast of the city was chosen and approved by the Illinois Community College Board. City interests, downtown merchants, and black leaders disapproved, but the lease extends only until 1987.

Decatur as a Reluctant Polity

Politics and government in Decatur have traditionally rested on the belief that "What's good for the chamber of commerce is good for the community" intersects with "What's good for the community is good for the chamber of commerce." It is in that area of intersection that the local political system operates. Traditionally this means that the public reason for any sought-after public action must be cast in terms of the good of the community, particularly its economic well-being. Furthermore, that rationale is expected of those who enter public life and is generally accepted by them.

One of the more important developments in Decatur over the past fifteen years has been the gradual broadening of that area of intersection within which legitimate public action occurs. Despite the prevalent belief that many matters should be attended to by individuals and groups in their private capacity, the line between private and public affairs has been crossed rather easily in recent years when it appeared that involvement in areas of former neglect would benefit the economic interests of the city. Businessmen now emphasize the need for good schools, for avoiding the appearance of poverty through urban renewal, and the like. One local businessman even noted that Decatur needs more cultural events to attract new businesses to the area.[24] It is in this way or not at all that the good of the deprived becomes associated with the good of the entitled.

There are several implications in all of this for the conduct of politics and the role of government in Decatur. Compared with many cities in other parts of the country, in Decatur politics is conducted in muted tones, making it difficult for the outsider to see the process, let alone appreciate it. In fact, there seems to be a strong sense of the need to maintain cordial relations.

More than that, "politics," in addition to having an unsavory taint, is seen as potentially disruptive. Conflict, where it exists, is hard to recognize because even the participants rarely define their actions in terms of competition over scarce resources. And since the resources are not as scarce as elsewhere, this is partially justified. In this way the myths and realities of the community good as a basis for public action support one another and, in turn, the agricommercial tradition on which they rest.

This set of attitudes has affected the role of political parties and interest groups in Decatur. The city government has been nonpartisan in fact as well as in name since 1959. Although school board elections can be acrimonious, as we shall see, general city elections are traditionally rather tame. In national and statewide elections, Decatur continues to vote Democratic except when the rest of Illinois votes Republican.

County politics is, however, a different matter, not simply because county elections remain partisan but because traditional attitudes have been more directly challenged by new political and social realities in the county than in the city. One such change was the 1970 Illinois state constitution, which required a shift in the membership of the county board of supervisors from township supervisors to members elected by districts, thereby somewhat eclipsing the role of the townships and introducing a new division in the old order. A second development is the effect of suburbanization on county politics, marked by the migration of Democratic city voters to county townships and villages. In 1976 a Democratic majority was elected to the Macon County Board of Supervisors, but in 1978 Republicans regained their majority on that board. In all likelihood, party contests will continue to dominate, and perhaps will invigorate, county politics for some time to come.

Interest-group politics in the city are generally conducted in subtle tones and around the center of the political continuum. Decaturites evince little or no commitment to class politics or fundamental changes in the distribution of power. Group identification on the basis of explicit ideological goals is also largely absent. One notable exception is the recent, albeit loosely organized, coalition among the Eagle Forum, Right-to-Life, CURB (a local group, Citizens United for Responsible Broadcasting), and various religious groups. However, as close as Decatur is to Phyllis Schlafly's home territory, the coalition's recent drive for a city ordinance banning the sale of pornographic literature did not meet with success.[25]

The foregoing is not meant to suggest that conflict is absent or that all needs are eventually met. The issue of where to locate the community college involved a hotly contested battle between city and county forces and raised a number of basic issues (such as community support for a broader than vocational education) that would normally remain quiescent. Still, though many groups were involved, debate was always couched in terms of what was best for the community college and, on the part of city forces, the downtown.

If the needs of any group go unmet, that group is certainly black citizens. The attempt to desegregate the schools is one illustration. Not untypically among American cities, the lag time between the United States Supreme Court's decision in *Brown v. Board of Education* and local efforts at racial desegregation was well over a decade. For Decatur, the issue of school busing was dramatic and divisive well into the 1970s. As recently as 1978, an election campaign resulted in the partial defeat of a desegregation plan.[26]

Decatur's formal response to the *Brown* decision began in the late 1960s, when a Commission on Community Integration developed a plan using busing to achieve school integration, proposing secondary-school busing in 1968 and elementary-school busing at the beginning of 1969. The latter ignited opposition.

Two organizations, United School Action (antiplan) and Keep Improving Decatur Schools (proplan), each with a candidate for the upcoming school board election, opposed each other in a series of meetings and confrontations. The antiplan candidate won. The opposition to the plan apparently came from both blue-collar workers and conservative professionals. Although a substantial core of voters supported the plan, they were simply not in the majority.[27] According to one 1975 public opinion survey, 33.4 percent of those surveyed ranked "racial difficulties" as the most pressing social problem in Decatur, with only 16 percent listing unemployment as the most serious problem.[28]

Vestiges of the agricommercial tradition are also apparent in the expected roles and forms of local government in Decatur. In many respects the city government of Decatur takes a "caretaker" role, attending to capital improvements where necessary and joining in economic development where appropriate. Per capita taxes from 1970 to 1975 averaged $98.42 in Decatur compared with a national mean of $265.02. Local per capita spending for improvements averaged $33.86 during that period compared with a national mean of $82.73.[29]

Decatur departs from caretaker governance, however, in the longstanding expectation of well-planned and soundly managed public policy. Decatur became one of the first cities in the nation to adopt a city plan in 1920, when a newly appointed City Planning Commission approved a plan developed by American Park Builders of Chicago. In fact, however, the term "commission" was a misnomer, for the commission was a committee of the Association of Commerce, which spearheaded the effort and sold the idea to the city council.[30] As early as 1939, the city council commissioned a city and regional plan, though the limits of caretaker government precluded city agencies' developing an internal planning capacity until the mid-1960s.

Decatur is atypical among blue-collar cities in its commitment to planning and management as legitimate core functions of government. Decatur voters approved a council-manager form of government in 1958, with a city council based entirely on at-large representation, and neither the manager orientation nor the citywide representation has ever been challenged significantly. Furthermore, there have only been three city managers since the plan went into effect in 1959, and their predominant style has been low-profile professionalism. As the current city manager put it, Decatur government is based on good management, responsible decisions by the electorate, and good planning.[31]

Since 1960 there has been a substantial increase in government functions and special constituencies in Decatur, as elsewhere, though there is no clear pattern for the institutional accommodation of these functions. There have been additions to the city council in the form of advisory boards and commissions, such as the Human Relations Commission, which hears complaints of discrimination; yet there also is a Department of Community Relations, established in 1968, that serves as staff to the commission and handles complaints outside the commission's jurisdiction. The city also has established a Department of Community Development, which now includes the planning division of the city. The county government shows similar additions.

The same names reappear on city advisory boards and commissions, and city officials complain that there is a limited pool of community residents who are willing to serve. The consequent ambivalence on the part of the electorate emerged in the Sangamon State University survey of 1975: 33 percent of those surveyed in Decatur expressed the view that local government officials do what the majority of citizens want, while 38 percent responded that local officials do what influential citizens want and 29 percent believed that local officials simply did what they themselves thought best for the community.[32]

The implication in all this for Decatur's "quality of life" is mixed. According to one well-known study by Ben-Chieh Liu, in terms of economic well-being, Decatur ranked seventh in a field of ninety-four comparable-sized cities. This finding is supported by the 1975 Sangamon State study, which found that 94 percent of Decatur respondents were very satisfied or somewhat satisfied with their standard of living. Understandably, however, Decatur scored low on Liu's political index, with government expenditures (and taxes) well below average. On the other hand, when asked, Decaturites offered a different view: according to the Sangamon State study, 67.9 percent of respondents reported that the quality of Decatur's public services (excluding health and education) was good or very good, and nearly 40 percent believed that local and state governments had improved the quality of life. (Views were somewhat more divided on whether the federal government improved or worsened the quality of life.)[33]

In both studies, Decatur scored lowest in the quality of health and educational services. In Liu's study, Decatur ranked sixty-seventh out of ninety-four cities in those service areas, partly because of low government expenditures and higher-than-average infant-mortality rates. Nearly 90 percent of respondents to the Sangamon State study reported that they had a specific doctor or clinic to visit when they needed medical assistance, and 70.5 percent were very satisfied with the medical care they received; however, a local newspaper reported that Decatur had only one prenatal clinic, and that one did not open until the summer of 1977.[34] Among all services included in the Sangamon State study, public education received the lowest rating in Decatur and other Illinois cities.

Conflict among the Cornfields

Disputes between centers of population in Macon County began as early as 1829, when the only two collections of cabins contended over which was to be the county seat. The compromise was to locate it in neither place.[35] This early incident signals a spirit of competition among settlements in the area that persists to this day.

Illinois's forms of local government supply abundant arenas for such competition. Thirty-two kinds of special districts, many of them intended to meet agricultural needs, are possible in addition to townships and municipalities.[36] Both the spirit and the forms make local independence a way of life that persists today in competition about population size and basketball teams and in resistance to entangling local agreements.

A further surviving sentiment is distrust of large centers of power. Proposals to centralize power or consolidate functions are equally suspect in Macon County, where residents clearly prefer a diversity of governments and a division of functions.

The importance of this for local responses to metropolitanization is clear. On one hand, city and village governments prefer to remain independent of each other in policy and administrative matters alike. Macon County governments are notable for their lack of formal or informal interjurisdictional arrangements. Mount Zion, a growing township southeast of Decatur, purchases water services from the city; villages buy planning services from the county. Informal arrangements do exist, but their main content is division of turf.

At the same time, much of today's political competition is cast in city/county terms. County interests pursue both the preservation of the agricultural lease and government independence, while the city is seen as land hungry and expensive. Conversely, city politicians see county politicians as being more oriented than they toward party politics and patronage. City leaders also tend to view the Regional Planning Commission as a county-based organization.

As in other regions, city/county conflict often centers on suburbanization and the issue of suburban shopping malls, though locational disputes can be further complicated by city interests outside the downtown and by antidevelopment forces in the county. Plans to "do something" about Decatur's downtown shopping and business area began in the early sixties with the hiring of a consultant to assess the situation. His recommendation that a street be closed to traffic for mall shopping was realized in 1970 with completion of the Landmark Mall. By that time, nine shopping malls were in operation outside the downtown but within the city. In 1972 the Decatur city council refused to annex an area in Hickory Point Township for a future shopping center that would have competed with downtown retail interests. However, this did not halt suburbanization. In 1978 Hickory Point Mall opened as the area's first regional mall, viewed locally as rampant metropolitanization. This development already has drawn some stores from downtown and will continue to take business and sales tax revenue away from the city.[37]

At the same time, efforts to maintain the downtown continue. A new civic center is near completion thanks to $10 million from state race track tax funds and $3 million from federal revenue sharing funds. Downtown interests sought unsuccessfully to retain Richland College downtown. Central Park has a new band shell, with 25 percent of the financing contributed by individual citizens, businesses, and civic groups.

Many government officials have come to recognize, however, that certain changes cannot be ignored. Population movement to county townships, both attracted by and carrying with it retail and industrial relocation, has placed more pressure on village and county officials for new schools and capital improvements. The most visible examples of the change in needs in the area since the mid-1960s are the new water and sewage systems being build in such villages as Harristown. A less visible example of change is that local governments and planning agencies are beginning a long-term annexation policy for Decatur in coordination with other incorporated areas. Least visible, but perhaps most important, is the growing need for and pursuit of regional planning through such devices as the Macon County Regional Planning Commission.

Conclusion

Local developments in Decatur during the second half of the post–World War II generation reflect the agricommercial nature of Decatur's past and present. Nowhere is this more apparent than in Decatur's economic base, which still relies on commercial uses of the land. One of the new plants successfully sought during Decatur's negotiation of the industrial frontier was a branch of Archer-Daniels-Midland, a manufacturer of grain products. In 1969 Decatur became the corporate headquarters of ADM. To make the bridging of the years complete, ADM sees itself as ready to begin producing gasohol from that same grain, and county villages are seeking HUD funds to build stills to meet some of their energy needs.

Settlement and land use have broadened from the city to include suburbanization and commercial development of the villages, but the concern for preserving farmland remains. A strong feeling of independence may preclude government mergers, but most public policy concerns are now implicitly set in a regional framework. In fact there are now some concerns that are cast in a central Illinois circle of medium-sized cities extending beyond the congressional district of which Decatur is a part and that transcend election day.

The city itself is faring well enough. The urban policies of the federal government are singularly appropriate for Decatur, even though they may not be appropriate for other cities on the new citybelt/cybernetic frontier.[38] Decatur still prefers to make improvements cautiously, a few steps at a time, which it can do with state and federal grants-in-aid. Equally important, necessary improvements are limited enough so that this has proved an effective strategy. At this point Decatur is somewhere between the problems of the Northeast and the promise of the Sun Belt.

Part of the promise lies in international trade. There is nothing, in fact, that better illustrates the contrasts in Decatur. Illinois has made an extensive effort to promote international trade, and Decatur has joined in that effort to the end that one-third of the jobs in Decatur in 1976 depended on it. Decatur's exports still include soybean and corn products, and "f.o.b. Decatur" has become an international marking. People who participate in trade missions to the People's Republic of China bring back word that there is nothing the Chinese need more than Illinois's varieties of hogs and soybeans.

In sum, Decatur remains one of the few cities, on or off the prairie, that has made those changes necessary to maintain its stability, benefiting from a combination of good fortune, good sense, and a measured response.

In every midwestern farm family of any size, there was a division among the children according to where they sought their fortunes. Some fled to the sophistication of Chicago; a smaller number went as far away as California or New York. Others stayed with what was called the "home place," usually referring to a farm, but more recently applicable to the place of one's origin and including a continuing, caring relationship with parents. The city of Decatur is the child of the prairie that never left home.

9. The Effect of External Factors on the Medium-Sized Civil Community: The Case of Joliet

Joseph Zikmund II and Daniel J. Elazar

Joliet: A City on the Prairie

The city of Joliet lies on the Des Plaines River, thirty-eight miles southwest of the Chicago Loop. In the network of nineteenth-century transportation it stood at the juncture between the man-made waterway or canal between Lake Michigan and the Mississippi River and the beltway railroad that connected all the rail lines entering Chicago. Unquestionably, the early development of the city was tied directly to the railroads, and in its early years some viewed it as a potential competitor to Chicago itself. Other factors also contributed to the area's initial economic development:

> Quarrying (limestone) comprised the area's first industry. . . . Named for the French adventurer Louis Jolliet who, with Father Marquette, explored the region in 1673, incorporation as a city . . . came in 1852. As with most communities of that era, business was geared to meet the needs of farmers with sawmills, grocers, implement dealers and gristmills. However, the completion of the Illinois and Michigan Canal in 1848 and the first connection by railroad with Chicago brought about the initial influx of industry. In addition to broadening the markets for plentiful limestone, Joliet's newfound transportation capabilities attracted the steel mills in 1870, an industry which still is a major factor in the Joliet economy. Soft coal mining, immediately south of the city, proved not only an industry unto itself, but an additional attraction in bringing about industrial expansion. The coal companies found strip mining . . . the most efficient method of unearthing this vital source of fuel.[1]

In this century the Joliet economy expanded with the arrival of the Illinois State Penitentiary (now employing more than one thousand persons), the Joliet Arsenal, and in 1950 Caterpiller Tractor Company (with more than three thousand employees). In the early 1960s Elazar classified the economic functions of the city in the following manner: first, a place for the manufacture of metals and heavy equipment, serving both the national and the world markets; second, the commercial center for its own immediate hinter-

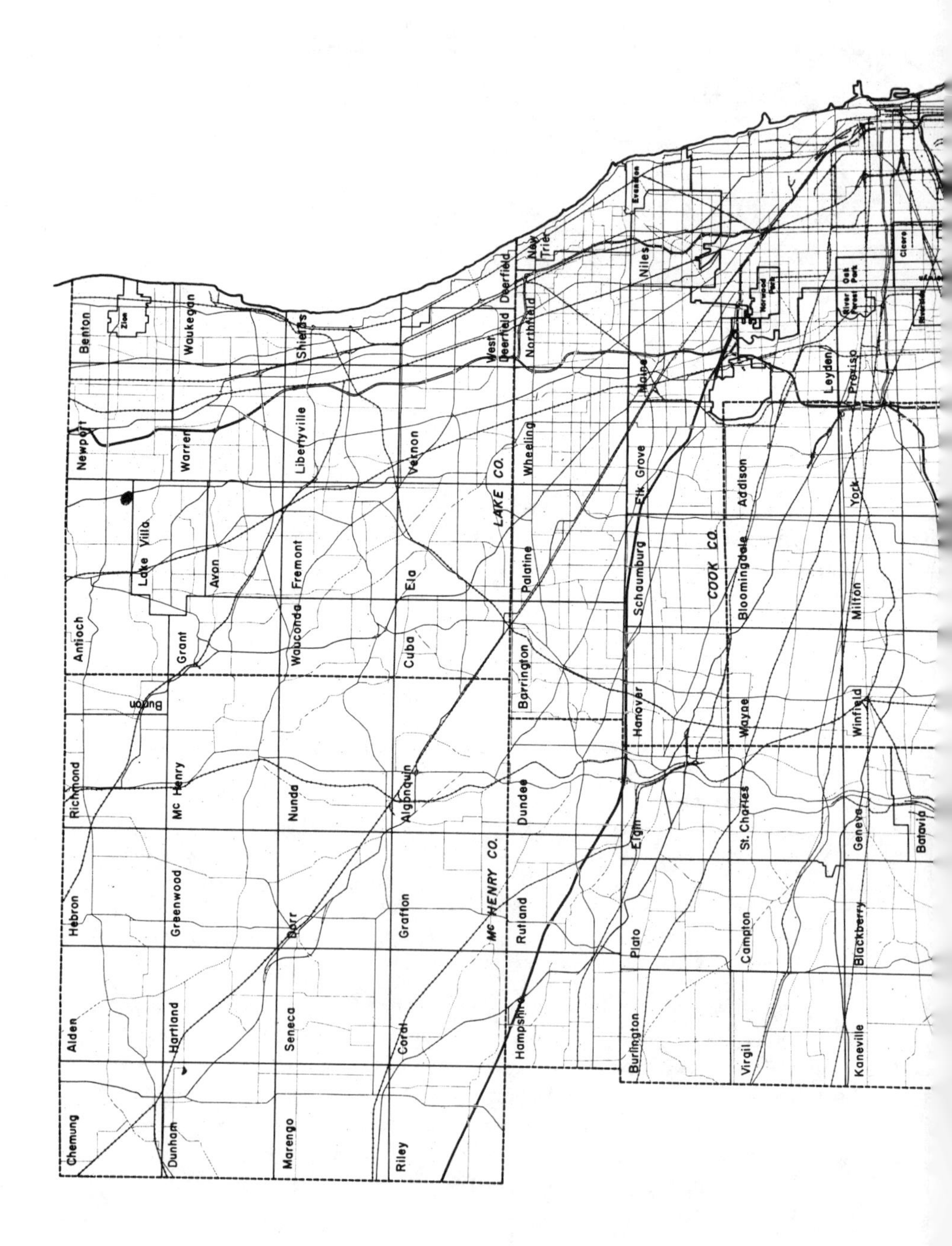
Benton
Zion
Waukegan
Shields
West Deerfield
Deerfield
New Trier
Northfield
Evanston
Niles
Norwood Park
Oak Park
Cicero
River Forest
Riverside
Maine
Leyden
Proviso
Newport
Warren
Libertyville
Vernon
Wheeling
LAKE CO.
Elk Grove
Addison
York
Lake Villa
Avon
Fremont
Ela
Palatine
Schaumburg
COOK CO.
Bloomingdale
Milton
Antioch
Grant
Wauconda
Cuba
Barrington
Hanover
Wayne
Winfield
Burton
Richmond
Mc Henry
Nunda
Algonquin
Dundee
Elgin
St. Charles
Geneva
Batavia
Hebron
Greenwood
Dorr
Grafton
Mc HENRY CO.
Rutland
Plato
Campton
Blackberry
Alden
Hartland
Seneca
Coral
Hampshire
Burlington
Virgil
Kaneville
Chemung
Dunham
Marengo
Riley

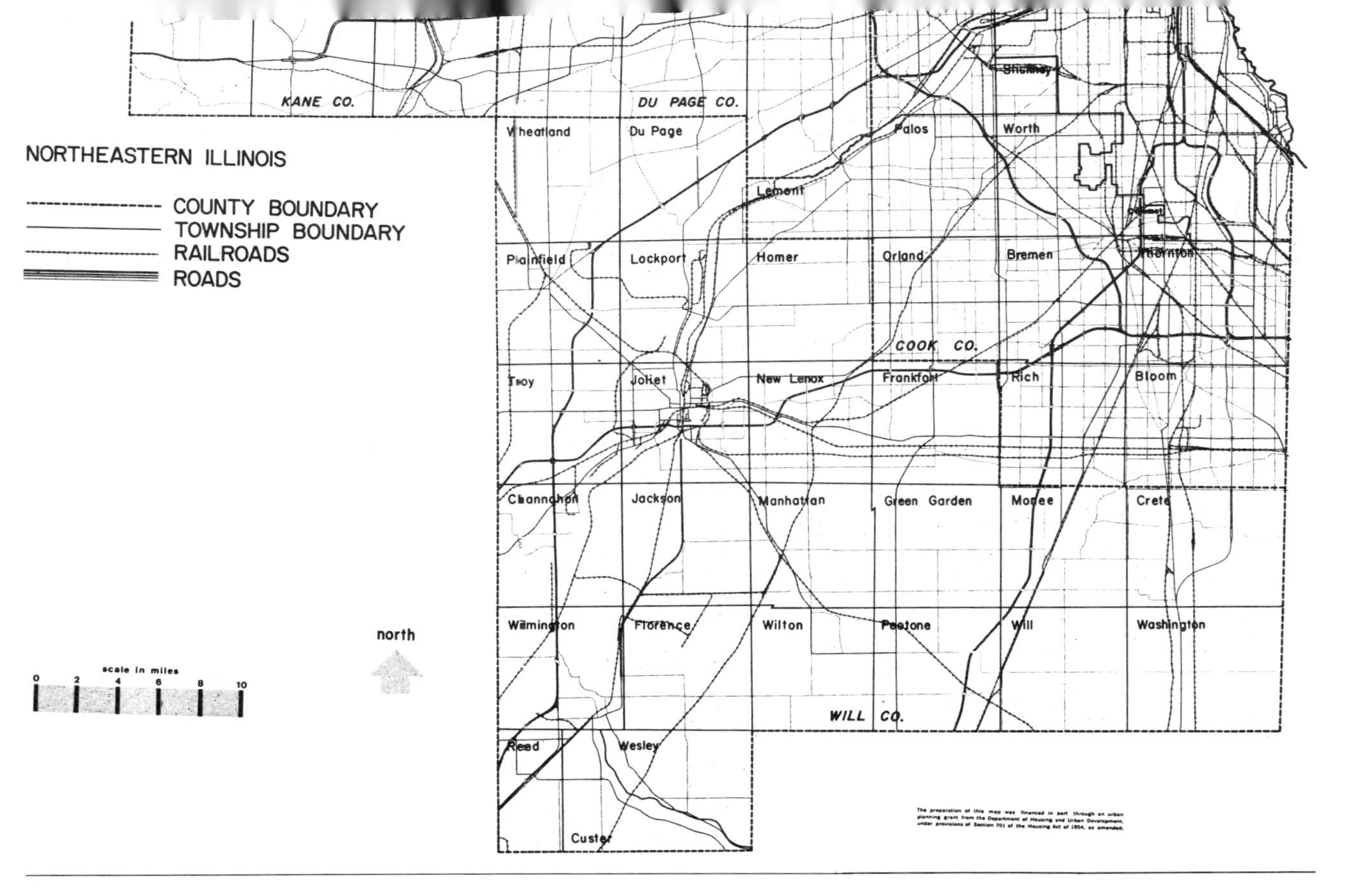

Map 9.1. Joliet in the northeastern Illinois region.

land (Will and Grundy counties); and third, the seat of government for Will County.[2]

The people who first came to Joliet saw it as a place of opportunity, as have successive waves of newcomers who continue to settle there. The result is a polyglot population created initially by Yankees who "entered the state through Chicago and spread out onto the prairie, rapidly engulfing the two northern tiers of counties, then thrusting south and southwestward."[3] Later came Jews from eastern Europe, the Irish, small groups of Scandinavians, Italians, Slovenians, Slovaks, Poles, Russians, Serbs, and Croatians. Typical ethnic neighborhoods were common. In 1960, 28.3 percent of the city's population still was identified by the Census Bureau as "foreign stock"; Italians, with 14.0 percent, were the largest single group in the area. Blacks at this time made up less than 4 percent.

Looking at Joliet city government and politics in the early sixties, Elazar focused on two topics: the geography of political cleavages and the workings of the new council-manager form of local government. For years political conflict in Joliet reflected its ethnic settlement patterns. The Des Plaines River runs through the city from the north to the southwest, dividing it into the middle-class northwest—settled by Yankee, English, Irish, and northern European peoples—and the poorer working-class east—dominated by eastern and southern European descendents and American blacks. Aided by a system of at-large elections for seats on the city council, the middle-class areas controlled city offices.

Joliet's experience with council-manager local government began during the late fifties as local business leaders sought to encourage reform to achieve "businesslike, efficient, economic, apolitical government." Elazar's description of the situation is short and to the point:

> after adopting the plan by referendum, the cosmopolitans almost immediately withdrew from the fray. The older politicians were returned to office by the locals and reduced the plan to a dead letter. The Mayor reasserted control, and the city manager was reduced to the level of an administrative assistant to him. After the one professional city manager who had been hired left in disgust, the mayor and the council appointed a local engineer to replace him, a man who knew how to function as a chief administrator within a political context and who did not try to be a city manager "by the book."[4]

However, not all of Joliet's problems with its city manager system in the early years were a product of local politics—at least in the most obvious sense; some were a result of the institutional structures that any incumbent manager had to cope with. The head of the police department was politically independent of both the council and the manager, and the city clerk and city treasurer were equal to the city manager in organizational position and independent of him. In 1967 the first major step was taken to strengthen the manager's authority when the appointment of the police chief was put directly in the manager's hands.[5] Police scandals apparently were a primary cause of the change.

Progress toward a strong, effective managerial office had begun in 1964 with the appointment of the city's third manager, a professional with previous experience in council-manager government. This trend slowed considerably in 1971 when the manager openly opposed the incumbent mayor in his bid for reelection. The electoral campaign quickly degenerated into a severe personality conflict between the two city officials. However, after the voters had returned the mayor to office, he made no attempt to change the system or the formal powers of the office of city manager. Needless to say, the errant city manager soon found employment elsewhere.[6] By the mid-1970s Joliet's council-manager government appeared to be secure and to be performing the routine functions of local administration effectively. The turnover in city managers has slowed considerably; the professional quality of managers has been uniformly high throughout the 1970s; and respect for and acceptance of the system itself seems unquestioned.

In the early 1960s Elazar saw the politics of Joliet in terms of polyarchy: "a continuing division of power among a number of groups in such a manner that no ongoing set of influentials can be said to 'control' decisions made locally but in which influential elements, groups and individuals (and the issues which particularly interest them) can be identified without great difficulty."[7] Today, group conflict and differing economic and social interests still give Joliet polyarchic political patterns.

Given the strength and diversity of the forces acting upon Joliet's urban system, to what degree does—or even might—the city adequately determine its own destiny? It is to these environmental factors that have influenced Joliet's development in the past fifteen years that we now turn.

Factors in the Urban System Environment Affecting Joliet since 1960

Four kinds of factors in the urban system environment can have an influence on a city like Joliet: the economic, the physical, the political, and the social. Examples of all four have affected Joliet's life and development over the past two decades. In the economic realm three are most obvious: the decision by the United States government to close the Joliet Armory, the construction of the Jefferson Square shopping mall outside downtown Joliet, and the placement of several new industrial and commercial facilities southwest of the city along the Des Plaines River. Physical and technological forces of considerable consequence have been the continued use of the river for commercial traffic and the junction of two major interstate highways on the outskirts of the city, again to the southwest. In addition, the continued aging of the city's housing stock has imposed increasing hardship on residents and has created innumerable problems for local officeholders. Probably the most important political factors have been the home rule portions of the new Illinois state constitution of 1970 and later pressures from state and federal officials to desegregate the city's public schools. Social pressures on Joliet during this time have included the general shifts in the population composition of the city, suburbanization around the city itself, and the spread of the Chicago metropolitan area out toward Joliet and its neighbors in Will County. These pressures provoked responses on the part of the city leadership that enabled the city to hold its own in the latter half of the postwar generation. We will now explore these themes in greater detail. In doing so, we will see once again how Joliet's existence as a separate political entity with its own jurisdiction and with various sets of boundaries—the city of Joliet, Joliet Township, and Will County—that can be used to separate it from other polities gave Joliet the opportunity to maintain significant control over these forces. Joliet's ability to take advantage of that opportunity was in turn dependent upon the degree to which it could function as a civil community.

Of the four kinds of environmental factors affecting Joliet, clearly the easiest to describe and analyze is the physical (spatial)/technological. At the same time these also provide the prerequisite geographic structure that influences all the other forces—both internal and external—acting upon the Joliet urban system. Transportation patterns, the arrival of new transportation technologies, and the physical condition of buildings owing to aging touch upon the place, shape, and flow of everything else.

Joliet was founded at the point where two transportation technologies—the Illinois and Michigan Canal and the railroads—came together. Oddly enough, today the canal dominates. In 1974 nearly twenty-eight million tons of cargo passed through Joliet by this route.[8] In the past the major industries that came to the city located on its banks. Today they continue to do so. The latest growth industry attracted to the area because of the canal is petrochemicals. Most of the attractive commercial sites along the water between Joliet and Chicago to the northeast are occupied. Thus new industry has gone in the other direction, along the Des Plaines River as it leaves Joliet headed south and west. Here industry competes for farmland with corn and hogs, not mushrooming suburban residences as to the northeast.

In the last quarter of the twentieth century the canal will be important to Joliet because it brings a transportation technology that, when combined with land suitable for industrial development, is especially appealing to modern growth industries.

Since the 1960s interstate highways also have made Joliet accessible to commerce and industry. The decisions regarding the placement—or more accurately the meeting—of two major interstate highways in the Joliet area were not made locally; they occurred outside Joliet's political environment. Yet their impact on development patterns in and around the city is tremendous. I-55 cuts across Illinois on the diagonal from Chicago to Springfield (the state capital) and St. Louis, then turns due south to Memphis and New Orleans. Beginning at McCormick Place at the south end of the Chicago Loop, I-55 leaves the city heading southwest and forms one of the five major expressway commuter links from the suburbs to the center city. It provides the transportation spine for one of the most rapidly suburbanizing areas on the Chicago metropolitan fringe. The highway approaches Joliet from the northeast, then bends around the northern and western sides of the city and meets I-80 to the southwest.

The second superhighway, I-80, is the westward extension of the Pennsylvania, Ohio, and Indiana tollways. It passes along the southern end of the Chicago SMSA, out through a diminishing strip of rural fringe, and under the southern edge of Joliet. From here it stretches across the prairies to Des Moines, Omaha, Cheyenne, Salt Lake City, and Portland, Oregon. It might seem that these two expressways reaching out to Joliet from the east and northeast would serve as encircling arms drawing Joliet into the center of the Chicago SMSA. This has not happened. In fact, a more appropriate analogy might be the crossed hairs in a rifle sight, which focus Joliet's development in precisely the opposite direction—to the southwest, away from Chicago. Thus, the combined impact of two distinctly different transportation technologies—water and highway—and of cheap abundant land has directed Joliet's growth not toward Chicago, but away from it.

The Joliet urbanized area is not moving closer to Chicago; it is running away pell-mell. This is fully in line with one of the continuing aims of Joliet as a civil community, namely to maintain its separate identity and particularly its separation from Chicago, the giant to the northeast. In this case Joliet's location enhances the civil community's capacity.

A final physical/technological factor affecting Joliet today is its aging housing stock. Joliet, like many older, freestanding industrial cities, is showing its age. In 1970 83 percent of its residential structures were over ten years old; more than 65 percent were at least twenty years old. Homes in Joliet look old and are old; neighborhoods are dingy and unattractive. Given a choice, most people would prefer to live elsewhere. Population patterns in and around the city—to be discussed in the next section—reflect the same social processes experienced by older cities across the nation, inner-city deterioration and middle-class suburbanization.

Three major social-demographic trends have influenced the growth and character of Joliet since 1960: the outward spread of the Chicago metropolitan complex, the suburbanization of the city of Joliet, and the changing pattern of residence within Joliet itself.

The city of Joliet is the county seat of Will County. When in 1949–50 the Bureau of the Census first introduced the concept of the standard metropolitan statistical area, all of Will County including the city of Joliet was excluded from the Chicago SMSA. Ten years later the entire county was added. What had changed? In part, the Census Bureau had modified its definitions. However, in that same period suburbanization had moved southward out of Cook County (Chicago) into Crete and Monee townships at the northeastern corner of Will County. Six other townships in Will County sharing a common boundary with Cook County also experienced significant growth (see table 9.1 and map 9.1). These eight townships accounted for a majority of the Will County population growth from 1950 to 1960 and included seven of the nine Will County townships that grew by more than 50 percent during that decade. Clearly, Will County's Chicago-fringe areas plus Joliet itself were the primary focus of population change in the county. As one might expect, this trend continued through the 1960s as well, with one important difference: population growth in Joliet Township (which contains the city of Joliet) virtually ceased. During the 1970s, Chicago's push to the southeast has continued. Spurred by the completion of I-55 (as noted) above), by the presence of Argonne National Laboratory, and by the availability of relatively inexpensive farmland, the Chicago urbanized area pushes on toward Joliet.

Around the city of Joliet itself there is another story, the suburbanization of the city. The urbanized area of Joliet includes the city, Joliet Township, and five other adjacent townships. Population figures for these seven civil units appear in table 9.2. From these data it is obvious that the Joliet region is growing, that Will County is growing, and that technical projections into the middle-range future suggest that this growth will continue. However, more important for our look at the city of Joliet itself is growth by annexation. In 1960 the city held 66,780 people, while the rest of Joliet Township contained 27,336, for a total of 94,116. Ten years later the city had 80,378 and the township only 15,623, a combined sum of 96,001. No, the

Table 9.1. Population Growth of Selected Townships in Will County, 1950–70

	1950–60		1960–70	
	Absolute	Percentage	Absolute	Percentage
Townships touching Cook County and facing Chicago[a]				
Dupage	3,670	348	15,312	324
Lockport	9,414	54	6,472	24
Homer	2,619	180	2,608	64
New Lenox	2,876	86	3,817	61
Frankfort	2,473	75	3,849	67
Green Garden	36	6	113	17
Monee	3,394	195	2,109	41
Crete	5,357	84	3,533	30
Total	29,839	84[b]	37,813	58[b]
Average	3,730		4,727	
Joliet Township	17,420	23	1,855	2
All other townships[c]	10,022	45[b]	16,510	51[b]
Average	668		1,101	

Source: Suburban Factbook 1973 (Chicago: Northeastern Illinois Planning Commission, 1973), p. 12.
[a]Townships ordered geographically from northwest to southeast.
[b]Total percentage is the percentage increase for all these townships together.
[c]This category includes fifteen townships, only two of which in 1950–60 had increases of more than 50 percent: Troy with 152 percent and Wesley with 111 percent. Troy lies immediately west of Joliet and experienced some suburbanization from Joliet during this period. In 1960–70 only three of these townships increased by more than 50 percent: Plainfield with 66, Wheatland with 75, and again Troy with 269.

people were not flocking to the city from the surrounding countryside. Rather, the city had annexed several heavily populated areas in the township.

One way to illustrate the effect of these annexations on the city is to look at the population changes occurring only in that portion of the city's area that existed ten years earlier (table 9.3). Both the city and the township experienced most of their growth during the 1950s. However, during the 1960s that part of the city within the 1960 boundaries actually lost population despite the official total city gain of 13,598 people, all of whom came from Joliet Township through annexations. Once again, all of Joliet Township—the city and the outlying areas—had little real population gain from 1960 to 1970. In this the Joliet region seems to reflect very closely the pattern of other old but markedly larger SMSAs such as Chicago and Detroit.

Table 9.2. Population Patterns for Joliet and Surrounding Townships

Total Population	Will County	City of Joliet	Joliet Township[a]	Lockport Township (north)	Plainfield and Troy Townships (west)	Homer and New Lenox Townships (east)
1950	134,336	51,601	25,095	17,468	4,815	4,484
1960	191,617	66,780	27,336	26,882	9,334	10,310
1970	247,825	80,378	15,623[b]	33,354	22,596	16,735

Sources: Suburban Factbook 1973 (Chicago: Northeastern Illinois Planning Commission, 1973), pp. 4, 12, 53; *Joliet Regional Fact Book* (Joliet: Joliet Region Chamber of Commerce, 1974), 3:4.
[a]Joliet Township here means that portion of the township not part of the city of Joliet.
[b]The apparent loss of population in the township is due to a number of annexations by the city of Joliet during the sixties.

What is particularly important, however, is that the city of Joliet did annex additional territory and population, especially those areas crucial to its ability to continue to control its economic base (see below) and to allow it room for suburban-style population growth within the city limits. In this way the civil community used its governmental powers to come to grips with the changing sociodemographic environment.

The third sociodemographic influence affecting Joliet over the past twenty years has been the rapid increase in black and Spanish-speaking minorities within the city. As indicated before, Joliet had been a polyglot community almost from the beginning. During the 1950s and early 1960s Italians made up the largest identifiable ethnic group in the city; they remained so in 1970, but not by much. In 1950 blacks were a mere 4 percent of Joliet's population; by 1960 they had increased to almost 7 percent; and at the time of the 1970 census their numbers had reached just under 12 percent. Spanish-speaking people, who were present in statistically insignificant numbers before the mid-1960s, constituted some 4 percent of Joliet's population in 1970. Together blacks and Hispanics represented 15.8 percent of the city's population that year.

Even more important is the geographic spread of blacks through the city and into the rest of Joliet Township. In 1960 blacks were concentrated in a narrow band running north to south through the center of the city, but lying always on the east side of the Des Plaines River (the major white middle-class areas are across the river to the northwest). In addition, blacks made up a large portion of the population to the south of the city of Joliet in Joliet Township (36.4 percent). At the same time, within the city itself

Table 9.3. Effect of Annexations on City and Township Populations, 1960–70

	1960	1970
Population of total city area	66,780	80,738
Population for total area ten years earlier	(–)51,601	(–)66,780
Official population change for decade	15,179	13,598
Population in areas annexed over previous decade	(–)10,390	(–)13,840
Real population change within city's area ten years earlier	4,789	–242
Real population growth rate for previous decade (percentage)	9.3[a]	–0.4[a]

Source: Suburban Factbook 1973 (Chicago: Northeastern Illinois Planning Commission, 1973); *Joliet Regional Fact Book* (Joliet: Joliet Region Chamber of Commerce, 1974).
[a]Growth rate calculated by dividing row 5 by row 2.

blacks accounted for no more than 38.5 percent of any one census tract area. Ten years later the pattern of black residents looked virtually the same. The one significant change was in the proportion of blacks per tract. The four tracts with the largest black concentrations in 1960 had relatively small boundary changes from 1960 to 1970. Thus for our purposes we can assume that they had virtually the same areas in both years. The tract at the northeast corner of the township jumped from 36 to 73 percent black; the north central-city tract went from 22 to 33 percent; the south central-city tract leaped from 25 to 60 percent. However, the tract to the south of the city experienced a slight decline in black residents, from 36 to 31 percent. This last downward change probably was a result of white suburbanization out into the township in this direction.

What is most important about other demographic patterns in Joliet is the absence of significant change during the 1960s. Table 9.4 presents selected—but by no means atypical—data about the city itself and about the somewhat larger Joliet urbanized area. We see that between 1960 and 1970 the proportion of foreign stock in the city declined, the average age of the population increased owing both to a decline in those under eighteen and to a slight increase in the number of those sixty-five and over, and the educational level of the adults over twenty-five years of age improved. Despite this change in potential skill level, 33 percent of the employed workers still had jobs in manufacturing establishments (compared with 33.2 percent in 1960). While manufacturing has held constant, white-collar jobs—in whatever

Table 9.4. Population Characteristics of Joliet, 1960–70

Characteristics	City of Joliet 1960	City of Joliet 1970	Joliet Urbanized Area 1960	Joliet Urbanized Area 1970
Percentage foreign stock	28.3	23.1	21.0	19.3
Age				
Percentage twenty-five years old or more	33.0	22.6	—[a]	37.3
Percentage sixty-five or more	10.1	11.2	8.6	8.1
Adult education				
Percentage of those twenty-five or more with four years of high school	42.1	49.7	38.6	50.7
Employment				
Percentage of workers in manufacturing	33.2	33.0	36.9	35.9
Percentage of workers holding white-collar jobs[b]	45.7	40.4	40.5	42.6

Source: Suburban Factbook 1973 (Chicago: Northeastern Illinois Planning Commission, 1973); *Joliet Regional Fact Book* (Joliet: Joliet Region Chamber of Commerce, 1974).

[a]Data not available.

[b]Managerial, professional, sales, and clerical.

kind of industry—among Joliet city residents dropped by 5.3 percentage points. Comparing data for the city versus the urbanized area produces few surprises. In 1960 the city had higher levels of education and white-collar employment, but this was reversed by 1970. Only the higher proportion of manufacturing workers living outside the city in 1960 and 1970 might be considered contrary to our expectations. This, however, reflects a pattern common to medium-sized cities in Illinois and its region, whereby many blue-collar workers, originally from rural areas, settle on the city's fringes so as to maintain at least a semirural style of life.

To summarize the sociodemographic changes affecting Joliet in the past decade, one is impressed with how typical Joliet's patterns were of other cities in the East and the Midwest. The black population increased in the center of the city and became ghettoized in the older, less well kept residential areas. White-collar whites moved outward to the edges of the city and into the surrounding fringe (suburban) areas. The city's population aged; the suburban population became slightly younger. All in all, the neighborhoods remained remarkably stable, as did the population characteristics for the city and the broader urbanized areas.

The principal economic forces in the environment of Joliet's urban system are economic base and commercial sales. Joliet is so typical of other cities, whatever their size, that it can serve as a model for illustrating the system effect of external corporate (economic base) decisions on the capacity of all cities to cope with modern times.

The economic base of Joliet—as we noted above—is manufacturing. Despite the fact that Joliet is known to much of the world as the location of Stateville, the Illinois Penitentiary, the prison is more of a millstone around the city's neck than a boost to the local economy. (Who wants to live/locate next to a lot of criminals?) In any case the prison has not been the source of most local employment. Up to 1970 that role was carried by the Joliet Ammunition Plant, operated by the United States government; then a decision was made in Washington to phase out the installation. As a result the plant's contribution to the local economic base dropped from 3,000 employees in 1971 to 420 in 1977, a loss of almost 2,600 jobs. Once again the civil community rose to the challenge, in this case through one of its government arms. Since 1971 the Joliet Region Chamber of Commerce has actively sought to bring new industry to the area. It has been relatively successful; more than forty new establishments have come, bringing jobs for more than 3,600 persons to the region. Yet the net gain for the past six or seven years is only about 1,000. The loss of 2,600 jobs through one economic decision means it has required twenty to thirty positive location decisions and much promotional hard work for the Joliet area to break even.

The second major economic factor in the Joliet system environment has been commercial competition for the downtown shopping area from fringe malls. Before 1970 downtown Joliet was the major regional shopping center to the southwest of Chicago. Then in 1974 a new suburban-type mall opened west of the downtown—though still within the city limits. Its effect on the original city center was significant but not catastrophic. Before the Jefferson Square Mall, the downtown had 33 percent of regional sales; a year after the mall opened (1975) the center-city shopping area had dropped to 29.5 percent of regional sales. These patterns have continued. By the end of the postwar generation, however, Jefferson Square was on its way to becoming a secondary threat to downtown boosters. The Homart Corporation, a private real estate firm from outside the area, was constructing the Louis Joliet Mall on the northwestern fringe of the city—out of the built-up area but recently annexed to the city proper. It was planned to be several times larger than the Jefferson Square Mall. The last two major department stores in the downtown area—Sears and Penneys—were closing out their inner-city facilities and moving to Louis Joliet. If Jefferson Square did not kill downtown Joliet, Louis Joliet is likely to do so.

In this case the city's ability to annex the sites of these shopping centers has ensured its tax base and general control over regional retail sales even though downtown Joliet is significantly downgraded. Thus the civil community, which cannot control the nationwide trend to shopping malls, is able to remain on top of such developments by properly utilizing its governmental powers.

Besides the obvious external government decisions affecting Joliet that have already been discussed—the positioning of the interstate highways and the closing of the Joliet Ammunition Plant, several political-governmental factors have influenced the operation of the Joliet urban system. Of these, we will mention just three: Illinois's adoption of a new state constitution in 1970, the great increase in the size and scope of federal and state funding of local government and certain public nongovernment activities, and the pressures from federal and state agencies leading to the desegregation of the Joliet public schools.

One consequence of the 1970 Illinois state constitution and the enabling legislation that followed was to induce the city of Joliet to modify somewhat its system of representation on the city council through a charter change that modified the constitutional reform introduced near the end of the postwar generation. Previously the council had consisted of six members, elected three at a time to staggered four-year terms, all chosen at large. The result was that the area to the west of the Des Plaines River totally dominated the city's electoral politics. This pattern not only underrepresented the east side of the city geographically, but also underrepresented the working-class and especially minority residents living on that side of the river. In the early 1970s the electoral system was changed to provide for five geographically defined council districts plus three council seats at large. Two of the districts are east of the Des Plaines River and three are to the west, one in the newly settled far western fringe of the city.

The change itself rounds out the generation's constitutional activity in Joliet in an appropriate way. The generation began with a strong pull on the part of the middle-class cosmopolitans for a charter change that would eliminate old-style, localistically rooted organization politics and bring in "businesslike" government. The charter change itself was only the beginning of a struggle to achieve its intended purposes that continued throughout most of the generation, since in the second municipal election after the referendum the old political forces resumed control over the city government. Only in the 1970s was the intent of the constitutional change substantially realized, at which point it became apparent that it would have deleterious consequences for the real access and representation of the blue-collar and minority populations of the city. In the spirit of the end-of-generation tendency to tie up loose ends, the circle of constitutional reform was completed by the introduction of district elections.

The result of this modification has been to change the names and faces on the council—only two of the 1978 incumbents were on the council before 1970. It has given representation to the eastern part of the city. It has brought one black onto the council. It is hard to say that this change has significantly altered the ultimate distribution of power within the city. Five of the present eight council members either predate the change or are newly elected west side residents. Geographically, at least, the effect of the 1970 constitution appears to be more a change in form than a fundamental redistribution of power in city government. At the same time, especially in a city like Joliet, access and representation are important for localistic reasons even more than for cosmopolitan ones. Those avenues had been preserved for the east side during the 1950s and 1960s because the old politicians were in control of the at-large council. Now they were restored, and for the first time extended to blacks, through district elections.

It is relatively easy to illustrate the effect of intergovernmental transfers of money on the Joliet system. In 1967 less than 1 percent of city revenues came from other planes of government. The early 1970s found Joliet experiencing severe budget deficits. In 1977 the city received $3,268,000 from federal and state sources and was operating with a fiscal surplus. The reversal in Joliet's municipal finances cannot be attributed solely to the flow of money from the national and state governments, but unquestionably these dollars have helped considerably.

Of course the city of Joliet was but one civil entity in the civil community and, for that matter, the one least eligible for federal funds before the introduction of general revenue sharing. The local school districts, Will County, and the various special districts had been receiving substantial state and federal support even earlier, but they too were the beneficiaries of great increases in that support once the Great Society and New Federalism programs began to reach them.

A third example of external political forces affecting the Joliet urban system was the pressure from federal and state sources that led to the adoption of a voluntary school desegregation plan for the Joliet public schools in 1976. As an informational pamphlet published by the board of education notes, Joliet was not forced to desegregate by court order.[9] At the same time, the very real threat of a suit did encourage the school district to develop a voluntary plan in order to avoid what appeared to many to be inevitable. Voluntary school desegregation in Joliet has primarily meant busing black students to provide better educational opportunities for minority students and the integration of teachers at all schools. Although the plan has generated some controversy, conflict has been kept within reasonable bounds and meaningful progress has been achieved.[10] Here Joliet as a civil community took the lead in warding off external pressures through local initiative.

Observations and Conclusions

The first observation one can make at this point is that over the past two decades the Joliet civil community has spent much time and effort responding to outside pressures. Political systems often are thought of as steering a course of government activity much as a ship steers across the seas from port to port. At the same time, evidence from the Joliet experience since 1960 suggests that much, if not most, of the urban system's time and effort recently has been spent simply keeping the ship afloat in the wind and waves of external pressures. Those who would see the civil community—at least as reflected by Joliet—as a self-determining entity overwhelmingly responsible for its own destiny simply overlook the realities of the American situation.

In fact, Joliet's most persistent goal has been to be able to continue to make measured responses to environmental forces so as to preserve its own civil and political integrity, economic base, and public services—that is, meaningful survival. That goal has been attained. Thus it certainly would be inappropriate to see Joliet in the context of an oversimplified stimulus-response model.

What differentiates Joliet from such a model is the range of response options that have been open to the city and the particular response choices it has made. Joliet's freedom, so to speak, has been its capacity to respond to outside pressures with some measure of creative choice. The continuing influence of external forces has dominated its collective attention, but the city has retained the opportunity to decide among several alternative responses. It has not been reduced, in other words, merely to a knee-jerk, no-choice reaction.

How has the Joliet civil community retained this internal flexibility in coping with external pressures? Three internal factors seem important: the maturation of the city manager form of government; the development of an urban planning capability; and much aggressive, dogged hard work on the part of public nongovernment institutions maintained by the private sector.

The transformation of Joliet's city manager form of government was described earlier. Since Elazar looked at Joliet at the beginning of the 1960s, planning has become a major component in the city's decision process. The size of the local planning staff has expanded, and its competence has been upgraded—principally with federal funds acquired through the state government. More important, its role in city government is now central. It is the planners who appear to have anticipated environmental changes, analyzed their potential effect on the system, and recommended constructive, alternative responses. While the planners' proposals have not always been accepted by the community, their track record, so to speak, seems relatively good. Equally important, their advice to the city generally has been effective. Certainly the planners do not run the city. However, they are making very genuine contributions to Joliet's effort to cope effectively with pressures and problems imposed from without.

Finally, Joliet's continued capacity to function as a relatively self-determining unit of local government results from a strong, and again effective, effort by public nongovernment bodies maintained by the private sector—especially the Joliet Region Chamber of Commerce. Whether hustling for employers after the closing of the Joliet Ammunition Plant or planning and implementing the Downtown Joliet renewal project, local citizens working through private organizations have improved the capacity of the Joliet urban system to respond positively to outside forces. This reflects the essence of the civil community concept.

The Joliet experience, then, suggests three distinct conclusions about the functioning of the medium-sized civil community generally and about the forces of growth versus nongrowth in civil communities of this scale. First, the capacity of such places to program their future and to move in planned, controlled steps toward some ideal community goal is quite limited, if not totally lacking. As emphasized in *Cities of the Prairie,* the output of the urban system simply cannot be adequately understood by looking only at the forces operating within the civil community itself. Second, the larger environment continually imposes strains on the civil community that at best require ongoing attention and can at times threaten its capacity to function at all. This is not because civil communities represent the lowest level in some putative American government hierarchy. Indeed, no such hierarchy exists. For their purposes, cities, counties, townships, and school and special districts are not only formally autonomous cells within the matrix of the American polity, but also primarily governments fully responsible for the fulfillment of certain public tasks. As such they command the attention, loyalty, and interest of wide segments of the public, at least for those purposes.[11] Still, each civil community is only a small part of the much wider and more complex American social, economic, and political system within which it must constantly readjust its location.

What is impressive about the Joliet civil community in the second half of the postwar generation is its capacity to control its responses to environmental forces and to significantly influence, if not perfectly program, its future. Obviously, catastrophic forces from the environment can overwhelm the civil community and destroy or cancel out its operations. But under more normal conditions the medium-sized civil community that tries can develop a constructive and purposeful relationship with the world around it and, at the same time, achieve meaningful self-governance.

Notes

Introduction

1. Glenn V. Fugitt and Calvin Beale, "Recent Trends in City Population Growth and Distribution," in *Small Cities in Transition: The Dynamics of Growth and Decline,* ed. Herrington Bryce (Cambridge, Mass.: Ballinger, 1977), pp. 13–37.
2. Herrington Bryce, "Characteristics of Growing and Declining Cities," in *Small Cities in Transition,* ed. Bryce, pp. 29–47.
3. Lincoln Steffens, *The Autobiography of Lincoln Steffens* (New York: Harcourt, Brace and World, 1931); Ida Tarbell, *All in the Day's Work* (New York: Macmillan, 1939).
4. Robert S. Lynd and Helen M. Lynd, *Middletown: A Study in American Culture* (New York: Harcourt, Brace and World, 1956).
5. Charles E. Merriam, Spencer D. Parrott, and Albert Lepawsky, *The Government of the Metropolitan Regions of Change* (Chicago: University of Chicago Press, 1933); Harold F. Gosnell, *Machine Politics: Chicago Model* (Chicago: University of Chicago Press, 1937).
6. C. Wright Mills, *The Power Elite* (New York: Oxford University Press, 1956); I. L. Horowitz, ed., *Power, Politics and People: The Collected Essays of C. Wright Mills* (New York: Ballantine Books, 1963); Floyd Hunter, *Community Power Structure: A Study of Decision Makers* (Garden City, N.Y.: Anchor Press, 1963); Robert Dahl, *Who Governs?* (New Haven: Yale University Press, 1962).
7. Edward C. Banfield and Morton Grodzins, *Government and Housing in Metropolitan Areas* (New York: McGraw-Hill, 1958); Morton Grodzins, *The American System: A New View of Government in the United States* (Chicago: Rand McNally, 1966); Alan A. Altshuler, *The City Planning Process: A Political Process* (Ithaca: Cornell University Press, 1965); idem, *Community Control* (New York: Pegasus Books, 1970); Douglas St. Angelo, "The 'Broker Role' of Local Political Parties and Federal Administration," *Research Reports in Social Science* 8 (August 1965): 14–25; idem, "Formal and Routine Control of National Programs," *Southwestern Social Science Quarterly* 45, 4 (March 1966): 416–27.
8. These themes are delineated in full in Daniel J. Elazar, *Cities of the Prairie: The Metropolitan Frontier and American Politics* (New York: Basic Books, 1970), appendix B, pp. 454–60.
9. The original research design is presented in full in Elazar, *Cities of the Prairie,* appendix A, pp. 433–53.

10. Daniel J. Elazar, *The Politics of Belleville: A Profile of the Civil Community* (Philadelphia: Temple University Press, 1971), pp. 3–4.
11. Daniel J. Elazar, "Constitutional Change in a Long-Depressed Civil Community: A Case Study of Duluth, Minnesota," *Journal of the Minnesota Academy of Sciences* 33, 1 (January 1965): 49–66.
12. Benjamin R. Schuster, "The Relationship between Economic and Political Power in Three Midwestern Cities" (doctoral dissertation, Temple University Department of Political Science, 1978).
13. Rozann Rothman, *The Great Society at the Grassroots: Local Adaptation to Federal Initiatives of the 1960s in Champaign and Urbana, Illinois* (Washington, D.C.: Center for the Study of Federalism, 1984).
14. In 1980 a study appeared of nine of the Illinois cities of the prairie: Daniel Milo Johnson and Rebecca Monroe Veach, eds., *The Middle-Size Cities of Illinois: Their People, Politics and Quality of Life* (Springfield, Ill.: Sangamon State University, 1980). This volume is built around a quality-of-life survey conducted in those cities in 1976 and 1978. It consists of chapters on each city or set of cities treated in a particular metropolitan area, written by different authors. One, the chapter on Champaign-Urbana by Rozann Rothman, was based on our resurvey. This book is a useful, if somewhat brief, summary of the general political situation in those cities in the mid-1970s (at the end of our resurvey period), plus the results of a survey of citizens' satisfaction with their communities.
15. John Kincaid, "Political Success and Policy Failure: The Persistence of Machine Politics in Jersey City" (doctoral dissertation, Temple University Department of Political Science, 1981).
16. Stephen L. Schechter, "Ten Cities in Search of Themselves," the unpublished outline of his book, *The Political Development of Metropolitan Civil Communities* (Philadelphia: Center for the Study of Federalism, 1976); idem, "The Founding of American Local Communities: A Study of Covenantal and Other Forms of Association," *Publius* 10, 4 (Fall 1980): 165–85.

1. The Civil Community in the Federal System

1. Ferdinand Toennies, *Community and Society* [*Gemeinschaft und Gesellschaft*], trans. and ed. Charles P. Loomis (New York: Harper and Row, 1963).
2. The communications network model follows that of Karl W. Deutsch in *The Nerves of Government: Models of Political Communication and Control* (New York: Free Press of Glencoe, 1963). It was applied by H. Paul Friesma to the Quad Cities metropolitan area, one of those included in this study, in *Metropolitan Political Structure: Intergovernmental Relations and Political Integration in the Quad Cities* (Iowa City: University of Iowa Press, 1971).
3. Herrington J. Bryce, ed., *Small Cities in Transition: The Dynamics of Growth and Decline* (Cambridge, Mass.: Ballinger, 1977).
4. Daniel J. Elazar, *Cities of the Prairie: The Metropolitan Frontier and American Politics* (New York: Basic Books, 1970).

5. See, for example, Daniel J. Elazar, *The American Partnership: Intergovernmental Co-operation in the Nineteenth Century United States* (Chicago: University of Chicago Press, 1962), and Morton Grodzins, *The American System: A New View of Government in the United States,* ed. Daniel J. Elazar (Chicago: Rand McNally, 1966).
6. John Shannon and John Ross, "Cities: Their Increasing Dependence on State and Federal Aid," in Bryce, *Small Cities in Transition,* p. 189.
7. Shannon and Ross, "Cities," pp. 199–201.
8. Shannon and Ross, "Cities," pp. 202–4.
9. Jane A. Altes and Robert E. Mendelson, "East St. Louis: A Persevering Community," in *The Middle-Size Cities of Illinois: Their People, Politics and Quality of Life,* ed. Daniel Milo Johnson and Rebecca Monroe Veach (Springfield, Ill.: Sangamon State University, 1980), p. 108.
10. See Hal Nelson, "Rockford: A Blending of Cultures," in *Middle-Size Cities,* ed. Johnson and Veach, pp. 148–49.
11. See Nathan-Adams index in Bryce, *Small Cities in Transition,* p. 207.
12. See, for example, Roscoe C. Martin, *Metropolis in Transition: Local Adaptation to Change* (Washington, D.C.: Housing and Home Finance Agency, 1965).
13. Daniel J. Elazar, " 'Fragmentation' and Local Organizational Response to Federal-City Programs," *Urban Affairs Quarterly* 2, 4 (June 1967): 30–46.
14. Nelson, "Rockford," p. 161.
15. James Krohe, Jr., and Cullom Davis, "Springfield: An Evolving Capital," in *Middle-Size Cities,* ed. Johnson and Veach, p. 212.
16. See "Quality of Life Survey Findings," in *Middle-Size Cities,* ed. Johnson and Veach, pp. 224–34.

2. Closing the Metropolitan Frontier

1. The thesis advanced here is presented in greater detail in Daniel J. Elazar, *Cities of the Prairie: The Metropolitan Frontier and American Politics* (New York: Basic Books, 1970), and idem, *The Metropolitan Frontier: A Perspective on Urbanization in America* (New York: General Learning Press, 1973).
2. Samuel Lubell, *The Future of American Politics* (New York: Harper and Row, 1965).
3. This was forecast in Daniel J. Elazar, *Some Social Problems of the Northeastern Illinois Metropolitan Area* (Urbana: University of Illinois Institute of Government and Public Affairs, 1960).
4. Rothman, *Great Society.*
5. See chap. 9.
6. See John M. Sumansky, "Peoria: The Growth and Development of a River Town," in *Middle-Size Cities,* ed. Johnson and Veach, pp. 123–42.
7. See Hal Nelson, "Rockford: A Blending of Cultures," in *Middle-Size Cities,* ed. Johnson and Veach, pp. 143–64; William Ward, "Rock Island-Moline: The Quad Cities," in *Middle-Size Cities,* ed. Johnson and Veach. See also the field notes of Daniel J. Elazar.
8. Hal Nelson, "Rockford," p. 155.

9. See Schuster, "Three Midwestern Cities," and the field notes of Daniel J. Elazar.
10. See chap. 6 and the field notes of Daniel J. Elazar.
11. See the field notes of Benjamin R. Schuster.
12. See chap. 6.
13. See, for example, Elazar, *Cities of the Prairie,* appendix A, pp. 443–53.
14. Rozann Rothman, *The Great Society at the Grassroots: Local Adaptation to Federal Initiatives of the 1960s in Champaign and Urbana, Illinois* (Washington, D.C.: University Press of America and Center for the Study of Federalism, 1984).
15. John M. Sumansky, "Peoria: The Growth and Development of a River City," in *The Middle-Size Cities of Illinois: Their People, Politics and Quality of Life,* ed. Daniel Milo Johnson and Rebecca Monroe Veach (Springfield, Ill.: Sangamon State University, 1980), pp. 123–42.
16. Field notes, Daniel J. Elazar and Benjamin R. Schuster. These and subsequently noted field notes are housed in the archives of the Center for the Study of Federalism, Philadelphia.
17. See U.S. Bureau of the Census, *City and County Data Book, 1977* (Washington, D.C.: U.S. Government Printing Office, 1978).
18. Jane A. Altes and Robert E. Mendelson, "East St. Louis: A Persevering Community," in *Middle-Size Cities,* ed. Johnson and Veach, pp. 89–122.
19. Jane Altes, *East St. Louis: The End of a Decade* (Edwardsville: Southern Illinois University Press, 1970); Robert E. Mendelson and David C. Ranney, *Central City—a Neighborhood Analysis* (Edwardsville: Southern Illinois University, Public Administration and Metropolitan Affairs Program, 1967).
20. Altes and Mendelson, "East St. Louis," p. 118.
21. Leon Cheres, "In Defense of a Lady," *Alestle* (Southern Illinois University at Edwardsville), 27 October 1977.
22. Civic Design Study, *Rocky Mountain and Great Plains Area* (Colorado Springs: Colorado College, 1962).
23. See chap. 6.
24. See chap. 9.
25. Benjamin R. Schuster, "The Relationship between Economic and Political Power in Three Midwestern Cities" (doctoral dissertation, Temple University Department of Political Science, 1978).
26. H. Paul Friesma, *Metropolitan Political Structure: Intergovernmental Relations and Political Integration in the Quad Cities* (Iowa City: University of Iowa Press, 1971).
27. Ann Elder, "Decatur: A City at the Crossroads," in *Middle-Size Cities,* ed. Johnson and Veach, p. 69. See also *Decatur Herald and Review* 11, 18 May 1984.
28. See chap. 8.
29. See Daniel J. Elazar, "The 1980s: Entering the Citybelt-Cybernetic Frontier," *Publius* 10, 1 (Winter 1980): 13–27; idem, "The Meaning of the 1970s," *Society* 17, 2 (January 1980): 7–11; Ralph I. Weidner, "A Fourth Stage in Our National Development?" in *Small Cities in Transition: The Dynamics of Growth and Decline,* ed. Herrington Bryce (Cambridge, Mass.: Ballinger, 1977); Werner Z. Hirsch, "The Coming Age of the Polynucleated Metropolis," in *Small Cities,* ed. Bryce, pp. 267–81; Bryan J. L. Berry, "The Transformation of the Nation's Urban

System: Small City Growth as a Zero-Sum Game," in *Small Cities,* ed. Bryce, pp. 283–98.

30. Elazar, *Cities of the Prairie,* chap. 3.
31. See, for example, Civic Design Study, *Rocky Mountain.*

3. Political Culture and Local Politics

1. Alex Inkeles and D. J. Levinson, "National Character," in *The Handbook of Social Psychology,* ed. G. Lindzey and E. Aronson, 2d ed., vol. 4 (Chicago: Aldine, 1964).
2. See for example, Gabriel A. Almond, "Comparative Political Systems," *Journal of Politics* 18 (August 1956): 391–409; Lucien Pye, "Political Culture," in *International Encyclopedia of the Social Sciences* (New York: Macmillan and Free Press, 1968), 12:218–25; Lucien Pye, "Culture and Political Science: Problems in the Evaluation of the Concept of Political Culture," *Social Science Quarterly* 53 (September 1972): 285–96; Lucien Pye and Sidney Verba, eds., *Political Culture and Political Development* (Princeton: Princeton University Press, 1965); Gabriel Almond and Sidney Verba, *The Civic Culture* (Boston: Little Brown, 1963).
3. Daniel J. Elazar, *Cities of the Prairie: The Metropolitan Frontier and American Politics* (New York: Basic Books, 1970), chap. 4 and appendix C.
4. Elazar, *Cities of the Prairie,* pp. 258–65.
5. See, for example, Daniel J. Elazar and Murray Friedman, *Moving Up* (New York: American Jewish Committee, 1976); Elazar, *Cities of the Prairie,* chap. 4.
6. Elazar, *Cities of the Prairie,* "Postscript," p. 424.
7. Hal Nelson, "Rockford: A Blending of Cultures," in *The Middle-Size Cities of Illinois: Their People, Politics and Quality of Life,* ed. Daniel Milo Johnson and Rebecca Monroe Veach (Springfield, Ill.: Sangamon State University, 1980), p. 157.
8. Cullom Davis and James Krohe, Jr., "Springfield: An Evolving Capital," in *Middle-Size Cities,* ed. Johnson and Veach, p. 210.
9. William Ward, "Rock Island-Moline: The Quad Cities," in *Middle-Size Cities,* ed. Johnson and Veach, pp. 183–84.
10. Ward, "Rock Island-Moline," pp. 184–85.
11. Jane A. Altes and Robert E. Mendelson, "East St. Louis: A Persevering Community," in *Middle-Size Cities,* ed. Johnson and Veach, p. 108.
12. See chap. 6.
13. Altes and Mendelson, "East St. Louis."
14. John M. Sumansky, "Peoria: The Growth and Development of a River City," in *Middle-Size Cities,* ed. Johnson and Veach, p. 125.
15. Ward, "Rock Island-Moline," p. 182.
16. See Harold M. Rose, "Black Residential Clusters in the Suburban Ring," in *Small Cities in Transition: The Dynamics of Growth and Decline,* ed. Herrington Bryce (Cambridge, Mass.: Ballinger, 1977), p. 85.
17. See, for instance, Daniel J. Elazar and Joseph Zikmund II, eds., *The Ecology*

of American Political Culture (New York: Thomas Y. Crowell, 1975). The current state of the art in the application of this typology is presented in John Kincaid, ed. *Political Culture, Public Policy and the American States* (Philadelphia: ISHI Publications, 1982).

18. Esley I. Hamilton, "A Portrait of East St. Louis, Illinois: 1969–1975" (research paper, University of Wisconsin, Madison, 1975).
19. Rozann Rothman, *The Great Society at the Grass Roots* (Washington, D.C.: University Press of America and Center for the Study of Federalism, 1984).
20. See Kincaid, *Political Culture.*
21. Elazar, *Cities of the Prairie,* p. 309.
22. Gary Michael Sandrow, "Political Subcultures and the Progressive Era: An Exploration" (senior honors thesis, Political Science Honors Program, Temple University, 1967).
23. An exception was the vote for George Wallace in the 1968 general elections, which revealed an almost perfect correlation with the map of American political subcultures. See Daniel J. Elazar, *American Federalism: A View from the States,* 2d ed. (New York: Thomas Y. Crowell, 1972), p. 138.

4. Continuing the Generational Rhythm

1. For an elaboration of the generational thesis, see Daniel J. Elazar, "The Generational Rhythm of American Politics," *American Politics Quarterly* 6 (January 1978): 55–94, and idem, *The Politics of Belleville: A Profile of the Civil Community* (Philadelphia: Temple University Press, 1971).
2. See, for example, Deil Wright, *Understanding Intergovernmental Relations,* 2d ed. (North Scituate, Mass.: Duxbury Press, 1982), and Daniel J. Elazar, "The Evolving Federal System," in *The Power to Govern,* ed. Robert M. Pious, Proceedings of the Academy of Political Science, vol. 34, no. 2 (New York: Academy of Political Science, 1981), pp. 5–20.
3. See Vincent Ostrom, *The American Experiment in Constitutional Choice* (Bloomington: Indiana University Department of Political Science, 1976).
4. Charles M. Haar, *Between the Idea and the Reality: A Study in the Origin, Fate and Legacy of the Model Cities Program* (Boston: Little Brown, 1975).
5. Ivo Duchacek, *Power Maps: Comparative Politics of the Constitutions* (Santa Barbara, Calif.: Clio Press, 1973).
6. Aristotle, *The Politics of Aristotle,* ed. Ernest Barker (New York: Oxford University Press, 1962).
7. See Daniel J. Elazar, *Cities of the Prairie: The Metropolitan Frontier and American Politics* (New York: Basic Books, 1970), part 3.
8. See, for example, Daniel J. Elazar and Douglas St. Angelo, " 'Cosmopolitans' and 'Locals' in Contemporary Community Politics," *Journal of the Minnesota Academy of Sciences* 31, 2 (May 1964): 171–77.
9. Daniel J. Elazar, *Community and Polity: The Organizational Dynamics of American Jewry* (Philadelphia: Jewish Publication Society of America, 1976), pp. 260–61.

10. Rozann Rothman, *The Great Society at the Grassroots: Local Adaptation to Federal Initiatives of the 1960s in Champaign and Urbana, Illinois* (Washington, D.C.: University Press of America and Center for the Study of Federalism, 1984).
11. C. Hal Nelson, "Rockford: A Blending of Cultures," in *The Middle-Size Cities of Illinois: Their People, Politics and Quality of Life,* ed. Daniel Milo Johnson and Rebecca Monroe Veach (Springfield, Ill.: Sangamon State University, 1980), pp. 155–56.
12. See Herrington Bryce, Gloria J. Cousar, and Stephanie Fain, "Planning the Need of Small Cities," in *Small Cities in Transition: The Dynamics of Growth and Decline,* ed. Herrington Bryce (Cambridge, Mass.: Ballinger, 1977), p. 315.
13. See chap. 6 for further discussion.
14. For a full discussion of these roles, see Daniel J. Elazar, "Local Government in Intergovernmental Perspective," in *Illinois Local Government,* ed. Lois Pelekoudas (Urbana, Ill.: Institute of Government and Public Affairs, 1960). For parallel experience in other countries, see Mark Kesselman and Donald Rosenthal, *Local Power and Comparative Politics* (Beverly Hills, Calif.: Sage Publications, 1973).
15. Rozann Rothman, *Great Society at the Grassroots.*
16. Jane A. Altes and Robert Mendelson, "East St. Louis: A Persevering Community," in *Middle-Size Cities,* ed. Johnson and Veach, p. 101.
17. The history of Rockford politics during this period is recorded in the field notes of Benjamin R. Schuster and in Nelson, "Rockford."
18. See the field notes of Stephen L. Schechter. See also Cullom Davis and James Krohe, Jr., "Springfield: An Evolving Capital," in *Middle-Size Cities,* ed. Johnson and Veach, p. 208.
19. William Ward, "Rock Island–Moline: The Quad Cities," in *Middle-Size Cities,* ed. Johnson and Veach, pp. 177–78.
20. John M. Sumansky, "Peoria: The Growth and Development of a River City," in *Middle-Size Cities,* ed. Johnson and Veach, pp. 133–34.
21. See chaps. 7 and 8.
22. On the issue of mandating in general, see Catherine Lovell, "Mandating: Operational Domination," *Publius* 11, 2 (Spring 1981): 59–78.

5. Federalism versus Managerialism

1. Two excellent analyses of this shift from very different perspectives can be found in Samuel Beer, "The Modernization of American Federalism," and Robert Pranger, "The Decline of the American National Government," both of which appear in *The Federal Polity,* ed. Daniel J. Elazar (New Brunswick: Transaction Books, 1979). The volume is also available as *Publius,* vol. 3, no. 2 (Fall 1973).
2. For an elaboration of what follows, see Daniel J. Elazar, "Harmonizing Government Organization with the Political Tradition," *Publius* 8, 2 (Spring 1978): 49–58.

3. See, for example, Daniel J. Elazar, " 'Fragmentation' and Local Organizational Response to Federal-City Programs," *Urban Affairs Quarterly* 2, 4 (June 1967): 30–46.
4. See a special forum, "Is Federalism Compatible with Prefectorial Administration?" *Publius* 11, 2 (Spring 1981): 3–22, for a full discussion of the subject.
5. See chap. 7.
6. John M. Sumansky, "Peoria: The Growth and Development of a River Town," in *The Middle-Size Cities of Illinois: Their People, Politics and Quality of Life,* ed. Daniel Milo Johnson and Rebecca Monroe Veach (Springfield, Ill.: Sangamon State University, 1980), p. 130.
7. Cullom Davis and James Krohe, Jr., "Springfield: An Evolving Capital," in *Middle-Size Cities,* ed. Johnson and Veach, p. 204.
8. C. Hal Nelson, "Rockford: A Blending of Cultures," in *Middle-Size Cities,* ed. Johnson and Veach, p. 163.
9. William Ward, "Rock Island–Moline: The Quad Cities," in *Middle-Size Cities,* ed. Johnson and Veach, p. 175.
10. Rozann Rothman, "Champaign-Urbana: The Politics of Transition," in *Middle-Size Cities,* ed. Johnson and Veach, pp. 55–56.
11. H. Paul Friesama, *Metropolitan Political Structure: Intergovernmental Relations and Political Integration in the Quad Cities* (Iowa City: University of Iowa Press, 1971).
12. William Ward, "Rock Island–Moline: The Quad Cities," in *Middle-Size Cities,* ed. Johnson and Veach, p. 186.
13. See chap. 8.
14. See, for example, Daniel J. Elazar and Douglas St. Angelo, " 'Cosmopolitans' and 'Locals' in Contemporary Community Politics," *Journal of the Minnesota Academy of Sciences* 31, 2 (May 1964): 171–77.
15. My first encounter with this phenomenon was in the study of the initial defeat of the city-county consolidation proposal in Nashville-Davidson County, Tennessee, in 1958. See Daniel J. Elazar, *A Case Study in the Failure of Metropolitan Integration: Nashville and Davidson County, Tennessee* (Chicago: National Opinion Research Center, 1961).
16. See, for example, Daniel J. Elazar, "Political Culture and the Contemporary Reform Movements," in *Cities of the Prairie: The Metropolitan Frontier and American Politics,* chap. 7 (New York: Basic Books, 1970), pp. 305–14.
17. John Dewey offers useful guidance on what is public in *The Public and Its Problems* (Chicago: Swallow Press, 1954).
18. See, for example, Norton Long, "The Three Citizenships," in "Serving the Public in a Metropolitan Society," *Publius* 6, 2 (Spring 1976): 13–32.
19. For an elaboration of the concept of civil community, see Daniel J. Elazar, *Building Cities in America* (Washington, D.C.: University Press of America and the Center for the Study of Federalism, 1985).
20. See Jean Gottman, *Megalopolis: The Urbanized Northeastern Seaboard in the U.S.* (Cambridge: MIT Press, 1964).
21. I forecast many of these trends in "Megalopolis and the New Sectionalism," *Public Interest* 2 (Spring 1968): 62–85.

6. Pueblo

1. Francis Parkman, *The Oregon Trail: Sketches of Rocky Mt.-Prairie Life* (New York: Doubleday, 1945; originally published 1849), p. 260.
2. As quoted by Paul Horgan, *Lamy of Santa Fe* (New York: Farrar, Straus, and Giroux, 1975), p. 298.
3. Neal R. Peirce, *The Mountain States of America* (New York: W. W. Norton, 1972), p. 46.
4. The acceptance of these reputational images is so widespread throughout the state that most can be found, in no uncertain terms, in a Colorado state document, *The Colorado Front Range Corridor,* prepared by the State Planning Office (September 1969) and later suppressed by the governor's office following a considerable furor in both Denver and Pueblo. The particularly bold language of this report was taken from a more prudent, locally prepared special report, cited in note 5 below. For a history of this issue, see "Statement by Allan Blomquist," 10 March 1970, then director of the Pueblo Regional Planning Commission and of the South Front Range Team, which prepared the 1968 special report.
5. *The South Front Range in 2020*, A Special Report to Governor John A. Love, prepared by the South Front Range Team, December 1968.
6. Daniel J. Elazar, *Cities of the Prairie: The Metropolitan Frontier and American Politics* (New York: Basic Books, 1970), pp. 348-49.
7. See Daniel J. Elazar, "Constitutional Change in a Long-Depressed Civil Community: A Case Study of Duluth, Minnesota," *Journal of the Minnesota Academy of Sciences* 33, 1 (January 1965): 49-66.
8. See Herman R. Lantz, *A Community in Search of Itself: A Case History of Cairo, Illinois* (Carbondale: Southern Illinois University Press, 1972).
9. Pueblo is the northern apex of a historical triangle, with other points at San Antonio and San Diego, that still contains highly stratified Spanish-speaking communities composed of Spanish-speaking persons whose ancestors were never part of Mexico proper and who object to any "Mexican" designation; Mexican-Americans, both foreign- and native-born, of Mexican ancestry; and Mexican citizens, legally or illegally residing in the area. (According to one conservative estimate of the Pueblo Office of the United States Department of Immigration and Naturalization, 2,000 or more illegal aliens resided in the Pueblo area in the mid-1970s. See *Pueblo Star-Journal,* 18 May 1975.)

   The matter is further complicated by the fact that the Arkansas River (which served as the United States-Mexican territorial border between 1821 and 1836 and the northern border of the disputed Texas claim between 1836 and 1848) divides Pueblo into northern and southern sections. The contemporary southern section, including the former towns of South Pueblo and Bessemer, was originally part of the Nolan Spanish land grant. See Herbert O. Brayer, *William Blackmore: The Spanish-Mexican Land Grants of New Mexico and Colorado, 1863-1878* (Denver: Bradford, Robinson, 1949).
10. For a discussion of ethnicity and residential stability in Pueblo, see Bernard

L. Bloom, *Changing Patterns of Psychiatric Care* (New York: Behavioral Publications, 1975), pp. 69–76, 181–83.

11. Leo Grebler, Joan W. Moore, and Ralph C. Guzman, *The Mexican-American People: The Nation's Second Largest Minority* (New York: Free Press, 1970), p. 275.

12. For a classic series of accounts of life in a New Mexican village near Las Vegas, which was one source of this temporary and permanent migration, see Olen Leonard and C. P. Loomis, *Culture of a Contemporary Rural Community, El Cerrito, New Mexico* (Washington, D.C.: Department of Agriculture, 1941), based on 1939 surveys; Charles P. Loomis, "Wartime Migration from the Rural Spanish-Speaking Villages of New Mexico," *Rural Sociology* 7 (December 1942): 384–95; and Charles P. Loomis, "El Cerrito, New Mexico: A Changing Village," *New Mexico Historical Review* 33 (January 1958): 53–75, based on 1956 resurveys.

13. The statistics in this paragraph are drawn from the *Pueblo Design Quarterly*, no. 2 (June 1973), pp. 4, 7, published by the Pueblo Regional Planning Commission, Pueblo, Colorado.

14. *Pueblo Chieftain*, 22, 30 January 1943; *Rocky Mountain News*, 16 November 1949; and *Denver Post*, 6–8 March 1950.

15. Bloom, *Psychiatric Care*, p. 94.

16. Justice Hays, dissenting opinion, *City of Pueblo et al. v. Flanders*, 225 P. 2d 838 (1950).

17. Peirce, *Mountain States*, p. 46.

18. *South Front Range in 2020*, p. 8.

19. Fred M. Betz, *Let's All Be Politicians* (Lamar, Colo.: published by the author, 1960), p. 21.

20. A history of this issue can be found in *City of Pueblo v. Grand Carniolian Slovenian Catholic Union of the United States of America*, 358 P. 2d 13 (1960).

21. For background information on the events leading up to the 1954 charter, see Gordon Alexander Shomaker, "The Government of Pueblo, Colorado 1908–1952" (M.A. thesis, University of Colorado, 1953); and Ralph C. Taylor, "Pueblo Has Been Looking for Good Government, Hundred Years," *Pueblo Chieftain*, 21 February 1954.

22. William H. Whyte, Jr., *The Organization Man* (Garden City, N.Y.: Doubleday, 1957), p. 9.

23. John H. Kessel, "Governmental Structure and Political Environment: A Statistical Note about American Cities," *American Political Science Review* 56 (September 1962): 615–20. However, even the most elementary measures reveal that these tendencies are particularly significant among those medium-sized cities composed almost entirely of native-born residents, having locally owned service and trade economies, and situated in states with one-party dominant or weak party systems. On the general question of bureaucracy and city size for this period, see Robert R. Alford, "The Bureaucratization of Urban Government," reprinted in *Social Change and Urban Politics*, ed. Daniel N. Gordon (Englewood, N.J.: Prentice-Hall, 1973), pp. 263–78.

24. Oliver P. Williams and Charles R. Adrian, *Four Cities* (Philadelphia: University of Pennsylvania Press, 1963), pp. 23-26.
25. Elazar, *Cities of the Prairie,* p. 352.
26. Williams and Adrian, *Four Cities,* p. 24.
27. For a detailed account of this episode, see Herbert C. Brayer, *William Blackmore: Early Financing of the Denver and Rio Grande Railway and Ancillary Land Companies,* 1871-1878, vol. 2 (Denver: Bradford, Robinson, 1949).
28. David Lavender, *The Rockies* (New York: Harper and Row, 1975), p. 356.
29. Elazar, *Cities of the Prairie,* p. 350.
30. Williams and Adrian, *Four Cities,* pp. 24-26.
31. Lavender, *Rockies,* pp. 299-300.
32. Ben-Chieh Liu, *Quality of Life Indicators in U.S. Metropolitan Areas, 1970,* (Kansas City, Mo.: Midwest Research Institute, 1975). Of ninety-five standard metropolitan statistical areas with fewer than 200,000 inhabitants, Pueblo ranked ninth in voter turnout in presidential elections (1968-72) and fourth in the level of violent crime per 100,000 inhabitants. According to Liu's indicators, Pueblo also joins three of the top ten "politically outstanding" cities of this size range that possess a significantly lower rating than expected in terms of socioeconomic factors. The other three cities are La Crosse, Wisconsin, Ogden, Utah, and Sioux Falls, North Dakota. See p. 181.
33. Pueblo West is a "new town" with a 1976 population of no more than 2,500. Early in 1977, seven years after the first land sales, McCulloch Properties, Incorporated pleaded guilty to nineteen counts of criminal fraud that largely centered on the developer's failure to provide basic services (water, sewer, roads) guaranteed in original land sales.
34. See Samuel H. Beer, "The Dynamics of Modernization," in *Patterns of Government,* ed. Samuel H. Beer and Adam B. Ulam, 3d ed. (New York: Random House, 1973), pp. 73-74.
35. Cf. Martin Diamond, "The Ends of Federalism," in *The Federal Polity,* a special issue of *Publius: The Journal of Federalism,* ed. Daniel J. Elazar (Fall 1973), p. 130.
36. Letter to the city of Pueblo from the National Short Ballot Organization, reprinted in the *Pueblo Chieftain,* 24 August 1911.
37. District court rulings and judgement were disapproved by the Colorado Supreme Court in *People of the State of Colorado v. Joseph E. Spinuzzi,* 369 P. 2d 427 (1962).
38. By 1976 the proportion of the work force engaged by the two largest employers (CF&I and the state hospital) had dropped to an estimated 15 percent; and though the third largest employer is still the army depot, massive cutbacks have reduced the depot's share of the work force to approximately 2 percent. Based on 1976 estimates of the Colorado Department of Employment, the distribution of employment by sector is as follows: government, 24.2 percent (army depot, down to approximately 8.5 percent of that amount owing to depot cutbacks); wholesale and retail trade, 20.3 percent; manufacturing, 19.0 percent (CF&I, down to approximately 68 percent of that amount owing to auto-

mation and sectoral diversification); services, 18.9 percent (state hospital, down to approximately 17.5 percent of that amount owing to professionalization of hospital staff and to major expansion elsewhere in the service sector); transportation, communications, and public utilities, 6.5 percent; contract construction, 5.1 percent; finance, insurance, real estate, 3.6 percent; and agriculture, 2.4 percent. More important than the increased balance among the four principal sectors are the qualitative changes within each sector toward increased professional, technical, and managerial occupations and the decreasing reliance on the city's traditional major employers within each sector. Still, according to estimates of the University of Colorado Business Research Division for 1977, manufacturing sales accounted for almost 50 percent of the total retail sales receipts for Pueblo county.

39. Bloom, *Psychiatric Care,* pp. 197-201.
40. Statistics in this and the previous two paragraphs are drawn from the *Pueblo Design Quarterly* and the *1970 Census of Population and Housing* (Washington, D.C.: U.S. Department of Commerce, Bureau of the Census, 1972).
41. *Community Attitude Survey* prepared for the Pueblo Regional Planning Commission by Research Services, Inc., of Denver (July 1971).
42. Data are drawn from Pueblo Human Resources Commission, *Inventory of Human Resources* (Pueblo, Colorado, 1972).
43. In the mid-1970s, the Pueblo county district attorney exhibited a much-publicized zealousness to root out public corruption—a crusade that has produced an extraordinary number of criminal cases filed by indictment, two concurrently impaneled grand juries, running battles with one district court judge, and a recall petition drive by the Coalition against Grand Jury Abuse.
44. Norton E. Long, "Self-Government and the Metropolis," in *The Polity,* ed. Charles Press (Chicago: Rand McNally, 1962), p. 175.
45. "Preamble," in *By-Laws of Pueblo Area Council of Governments.*
46. Aristotle, *Politics,* section 1252a.

7. Champaign and Urbana

1. Daniel J. Elazar, *Cities of the Prairie: The Metropolitan Frontier and American Politics* (New York: Basic Books, 1970), p. 5.
2. Elazar, *Cities of the Prairie,* pp. 259-60: "The individualistic political subculture emphasizes the conception of the democratic society as a marketplace. In its view, government is instituted for strictly utilitarian reasons, to handle those functions demanded by the people it is created to serve. . . . Since the individualistic culture emphasizes the centrality of private concerns, it places a premium on limiting community intervention—whether governmental or nongovernmental—into private activities to the minimum necessary to keep the marketplace in working order."
3. Illinois State Employment Service, *Area Manpower Review* (February 1970), p. 1.
4. Marilyn Flynn and A. Alexander, "Preliminary Report on the Indigenous

Social Change Process in Champaign County, Illinois" (unpublished manuscript, Department of Social Work, University of Illinois, 1968), pp. 7-8.

5. Elazar, *Cities of the Prairie,* pp. 7-10.
6. Elazar, *Cities of the Prairie,* p. 8.
7. Elazar, *Cities of the Prairie,* pp. 208-9.
8. Lois Pelekoudas, "Minority Party Activity in a Central Illinois Political Community: Champaign-Urbana, 1956-62" (unpublished manuscript).
9. *Champaign-Urbana News Gazette,* 3 April 1963, 7 April 1965, 2 April 1967, 2 April 1969, 2 April 1971, 4 April 1973, 2 April 1975.
10. Flynn and Alexander, "Champaign County, Illinois," pp. 12-13.
11. Elazar, *Cities of the Prairie,* p. 260.
12. Champaign County League of Women Voters, *Urbana Government: Financial Structure and Service Departments* (Champaign, Ill.: League of Women Voters, 1965), p. 1.
13. *Champaign-Urbana News Gazette,* 12 May 1975, 1 July 1975.
14. *Champaign-Urbana News Gazette,* 2 August 1976.
15. *Federal Information Exchange Systems,* City Program Summary as of 30 July 1968, pp. 180-86; *Federal Information Exchange Systems,* City Summaries-Agency Operations, fiscal year 1971, pp. 38-39, and FY 1972, pp. 40-41.
16. *Federal Information,* FY 1971, p. 38; *Federal Information,* FY 1972, p. 40.
17. *Federal Information,* FY 1971, p. 39; *Federal Information,* FY 1972, p. 41.
18. Morton Grodzins, "Centralization and Decentralization in the American Federal System," in *A Nation of States,* ed. Robert Goldwin (Chicago: Rand McNally, 1963).
19. League of Women Voters of Champaign County, *Report on the Status of the Negro in Champaign County, 1968* (Champaign, Ill.: League of Women Voters, 1968), p. 4.
20. League of Women Voters of Champaign County, *Report on the Status of the Negro, 1968,* p. 4.
21. For an extended discussion, see Rozann Rothman, *The Great Society at the Grass Roots* (Lanham, MD: University Press of America, 1984), chap. 6.
22. *Champaign-Urbana News Gazette,* 13 December 1973.
23. *Daily Illini,* 18 December 1974; *Champaign-Urbana News Gazette,* 21 January 1975.
24. *Champaign-Urbana News Gazette,* 30 January 1975; see also *Daily Illini,* 31 January 1975.
25. *Champaign-Urbana News Gazette,* 4 March 1975.
26. *Champaign-Urbana News Gazette,* 18 March 1975.
27. *Champaign-Urbana News Gazette,* 3 July 1975, 12 August 1975, 23 October 1975.
28. *Champaign-Urbana News Gazette,* 11 November 1975.
29. *Champaign-Urbana News Gazette,* 18 November 1975.
30. Flynn and Alexander, "Champaign County, Illinois," pp. 13-14.
31. *Champaign-Urbana News Gazette,* 19 February 1975.
32. *Champaign-Urbana News Gazette,* 5 March 1975.
33. *Champaign-Urbana News Gazette,* 23 May 1973. See also Elaine Johnson, "A Study of the Decision Making Process in Champaign, Illinois: The Downtown Pedestrian Mall" (unpublished manuscript).

34. Letter to Jean Burkholder, 9 April 1963. See also C. Patton, "Urban Renewal and Negro Involvement: A Case Study of Negro Politics in Champaign, Illinois" (unpublished manuscript in files of Champaign County League of Women Voters, 1968).
35. Patton, "Urban Renewal and Negro Involvement," p. 55.
36. *Champaign-Urbana News Gazette,* 5 April 1973, 6 July 1973, 12 September 1973.
37. *Champaign-Urbana News Gazette,* 2, 4 October 1973.
38. I am indebted to Heywood Saunders for his suggestions on housing policy.
39. Michael Preston, "Minority Employment in the Public Service: Focus on Illinois" (unpublished manuscript available through University of Illinois, 1975).
40. League of Women Voters of Champaign County, *Report on the Status of the Negro in Champaign County, 1948* (Champaign, Ill.: League of Women Voters, 1948), pp. 53–54.
41. The Illinois constitution of 1970 provided home rule options for municipalities.
42. *Champaign-Urbana News Gazette,* 25 July 1974.
43. *Champaign-Urbana News Gazette,* 30 July 1974.
44. *Champaign-Urbana News Gazette,* 11 June 1975, 2 July 1975.
45. League of Women Voters of Champaign County, *Report on the Status of the Negro, 1948.*
46. *Champaign-Urbana Courier,* 4, 17 September 1968.
47. *Champaign-Urbana Courier,* 1 January 1972.
48. For an extended discussion, see Rothman, *Great Society at the Grass Roots,* chap. 3.

8. Decatur

1. Edgar Lee Masters, *Sangamon* (New York: Farrar and Rinehart, 1942), p. 342.
2. See, for instance, Herman R. Lantz, *A Community in Search of Itself: A Case History of Cairo, Illinois* (Carbondale: Southern Illinois University Press, 1972); and Daniel J. Elazar, "Constitutional Change in a Long-Depressed Civil Community: A Case Study of Duluth, Minnesota," *Journal of the Minnesota Academy of Sciences* 33, 1 (January 1965): 49–66.
3. Henry Nash Smith, *Virgin Lands: The American West as Symbol and Myth* (Cambridge: Harvard University Press, 1950).
4. Allen G. Bogue and Margaret B. Bogue, " 'Profits' and the Frontier Land Speculator," *Journal of Economic History* 17 (March 1957): 1–24.
5. Norman Pollack, *The Populist Response to Industrial America* (New York: W. W. Norton, 1962).
6. Allen G. Bogue, *From Prairie to Corn Belt: Farming on the Illinois and Iowa Prairies in the Nineteenth Century* (Chicago: University of Chicago Press, 1963), p. 287.
7. Richard C. Wade, *The Urban Frontier: The Rise of Western Cities, 1790–1930* (Cambridge: Harvard University Press, 1959), p. 1.
8. Harry N. Scheiber, "Urban Rivalry and Internal Improvements, 1820–1860," *Ohio History* 71, 3 (October 1962): 227–39; Francis P. Weisenburger, "The Urbanization of the Middle West: Town and Village in the Frontier Period,"

Indiana Magazine of History 61 (1945): 19–30; and Bayrd Still, "Patterns of Mid-Nineteenth Century Urbanization in the Middle West," *Mississippi Valley Historical Review* 28 (1941): 187–206.

9. Arthur E. Bestor, Jr., "Patent-Office Models of the Good Society: Some Relationships between Social Reform and Westward Expansion," *American Historical Review* 58, 3 (April 1953): 505–26.
10. Daniel J. Elazar, *Cities of the Prairie: The Metropolitan Frontier and American Politics* (New York: Basic Books, 1970).
11. Daniel J. Elazar, *American Federalism: A View from the States,* 2d ed. (New York: Thomas Y. Crowell, 1972), pp. 92–93.
12. Elazar, *Cities of the Prairie,* p. 137.
13. John W. Smith, *History of Macon County, Illinois, from Its Organization to 1876* (Springfield, Ill.: Rokker's Printing House, 1876), p. 23.
14. O. T. Banton, *History of Macon County, 1976* (Decatur, Ill.: Macon County Historical Society, 1976), p. 224.
15. Macon County Regional Planning Commission, *Agricultural Base Study/1977: Comprehensive Plan Update,* report no. MCRPC 77-6 (Decatur, Ill., 1977), p. 11.
16. Banton, *History of Macon County,* p. 232 and passim.
17. Decatur's status as a home rule city, possible since the 1970 Illinois constitution, probably has reinforced this stance because there is less need to make requests of the state legislature.
18. Interview with city manager Leslie Allen, 15 July 1978.
19. City of Decatur, *Report to Citizens,* 1973.
20. Coverage of the present road controversy was presented in *Decatur Review* articles during 1978 and 1979, particularly "Inflation Stymies Freeway System," 30 July 1978.
21. Interviews with Hobart Riley, director, Macon County Regional Planning Commission, 12 July 1978, and Ralph and Ellen Allan, local environmentalists, 15 July 1978. Material filed at the University of Illinois library used in Elazar, *Cities of the Prairie* contains *Decatur Review* articles published in 1960–62 dealing with this question.
22. Banton, *History of Macon County,* p. 308.
23. The Richland Community College case is based on numerous articles in the *Decatur Review* and on local interviews, particularly with Larry Klugman, a faculty member, and Don Baird, a college board member, the week of 12 July 1978.
24. Interview with Bob Kowa, owner of a Decatur printing firm, 13 July 1978.
25. " 'Decent People's Revolt Possible,' Anti-Pornography Leader Believes," *Decatur Review,* 21 July 1978.
26. A 22–28 April 1978 *Decatur Review* series revisited the civil rights scene in 1968–69. The articles, by Bob Sampson, appeared in his "Off the Beat" column.
27. Interview with city councilman William Oliver, 20 July 1978; city manager Leslie Allen, 12 July 1978; and the director of the Decatur Housing Authority, 14 July 1978.
28. Daniel Milo Johnson, Don C. Shin, and Robert V. Hillman, "The Quality

of Life in Three Illinois Middle-Size Cities" (Springfield, Ill.: Center for the Study of Middle-Size Cities, 1976).

29. "Study: Decatur Finances Good," *Decatur Review,* 21 March 1979.
30. "The City Practical," the Decatur plan made for the City Plan Commission by Myron West (Decatur, 1920).
31. Interview with Leslie Allen, 15 July 1978.
32. Johnson, Shin, and Hillman, "Quality of Life."
33. References in this and the following paragraph are to Ben-Chieh Liu, *Quality of Life Indicators in the U.S. Metropolitan Areas, 1970* (Kansas City, Mo.: Midwest Research Institute, 1975), and Johnson, Shin, and Hillman, "Quality of Life."
34. "Prenatal Clinic Care for Some Poor Women May Be in Jeopardy," *Decatur Review,* 24 April 1978.
35. Banton, *History of Macon County,* p. 36.
36. Stephanie Cole, "Illinois Home Rule in Historical Perspective," in *Home Rule in Illinois,* ed. Stephanie Cole and Sam Gove (Urbana: Ill.: Institute of Government and Public Affairs, 1973), p. 12.
37. *Decatur Review* articles published in 1978 and 1979 deal at length with this development.
38. Daniel J. Elazar, "Urban Partnership on the Citybelt–Cybernetic Frontier," "The State of American Federalism," *Publius* 10, 1 (Winter 1980).

9. Joliet

1. Richard N. Vaughan, *Joliet Was, Joliet Is, Joliet Will Be: The Joliet Region Brochure* (Joliet, Ill.: Chester Galuska, 1976), p. 3.
2. Daniel J. Elazar, *Cities of the Prairie: The Metropolitan Frontier and American Politics* (New York: Basic Books, 1970), p. 74.
3. Elazar, *Cities of the Prairie,* p. 162.
4. Elazar, *Cities of the Prairie,* p. 311.
5. Joliet *Herald News,* 8 November 1967.
6. Joliet *Herald News,* 12 March 1971.
7. Elazar, *Cities of the Prairie,* p. 211.
8. Vaughan, *Joliet Was,* p. 21.
9. *Desegregation: Questions and Answers* (Joliet, Ill.: Joliet Public School District, n.d.).
10. Chicago *Tribune,* 22 August 1976, 29 January 1978.
11. For a fuller description of this model, see Daniel J. Elazar, "Harmonizing Government Organization with Political Tradition," *Publius* 8, 2 (Spring 1978): 49.

Bibliography

Publications by Daniel J. Elazar
Resulting from the Original Study

BOOKS AND MONOGRAPHS

Cities of the Prairie: The Metropolitan Frontier and American Politics. New York: Basic Books, 1970.

The Politics of Belleville: A Profile of the Civil Community. Philadelphia: Temple University Press, 1971.

The Metropolitan Frontier: A Perspective on Urbanization in America. New York: General Learning Press, 1973.

Building Cities in America. Washington, D.C.: University Press of America and Center for the Study of Federalism, 1985.

ARTICLES

"Churches as Molders of American Politics." *American Behavioral Scientist* 4 (May 1961): 15–18.

" 'Cosmopolitans' and 'Locals' in Contemporary Community Politics." (With Douglas St. Angelo.) *Journal of the Minnesota Academy of Sciences* 31, 2 (May 1964): 171–77.

"Constitutional Change in a Long-Depressed Civil Community: A Case Study of Duluth, Minnesota." *Journal of the Minnesota Academy of Sciences* 33, 1 (January 1965): 49–66.

"Are We a Nation of Cities?" *Public Interest* (Summer 1966), pp. 42–58.

" 'Fragmentation' and Local Organizational Response to Federal-City Programs." *Urban Affairs Quarterly* 2, 4 (June 1967): 30–46.

"Local Government in Intergovernmental Perspective." In *Illinois Local Government.* Urbana: University of Illinois, 1961. Revised edition appears in *Cooperation and Conflict: Readings in American Federalism,* ed. Daniel J. Elazar. Itasca, Ill.: F. E. Peacock, 1969.

"Community Self-Government and the Crises of American Politics." *Ethics* 81, 2 (January 1971): 91–106.

"Smaller Cities in Metropolitan Society: The New American 'Towns.' " Working Paper of the Center for the Study of Federalism. A slightly different version appeared as "Suburbanization: Reviving the Town on the Metropolitan Frontier." *Publius* 5, 1 (Winter 1975): 53–80.

Books and Dissertations
Resulting From the Second Study

Kincaid, John. "Political Success and Policy Failure: the Persistence of Machine Politics." Temple University, 1981.

Rothman, Rozann. *The Great Society of the Grass Roots: Local Adaptation to Federal Initiatives of the 1960's—Champaign-Urbana.* Lanham, MD: University Press of America, 1984.

Schuster, Benjamin. "The Relationship Between Economic and Political Power in Three Midwestern Communities." Temple University, 1978.

General References

Alonso, William. "The Economics of Urban Size." *Papers of the Regional Science Association* 26 (1971): 67–83.

Alonso, William, and Fajans, M. *Cost of Living and Income by Urban Size.* Working Paper no. 128. Berkeley: University of California, Center for Planning and Development, 1970.

Altes, Jane. *East St. Louis: The End of a Decade.* Edwardsville: Southern Illinois University, Regional and Urban Development Studies and Services, 1970.

———. *Population and Housing in Metro-East 1950–1960–1970.* Edwardsville: Southern Illinois University, Center for Urban and Environmental Research and Services, 1973.

Auld, D., and Cook, G. "Suburban-Central City Exploitation Thesis: One City's Tale." *National Tax Journal* 23 (1970): 117–39.

Ault, David. *A Study of the Need for and Spatial Distribution of Hospital Beds in the St. Louis SMSA.* Edwardsville: Southern Illinois University, Center for Urban and Environmental Research and Services, 1974.

Babcock, R. *The Zoning Game.* Madison: University of Wisconsin Press, 1969.

Bahl, Roy. *Metropolitan Population and Municipal Government Expenditure in Central Cities.* Lexington: University of Kentucky Press, 1969.

Bahl, Roy; Firestine, R.; and Phares, D. "Industrial Diversity in Urban Areas: Alternative Measures and Intermetropolitan Comparisons." *Economic Geography* 47 (1971): 414–25.

Bahr, R. C.; Meiners, M. R.; and Makayama, F. "New Consumer Price Indices by Size of City." *Monthly Labor Review* 3 (August 1972): 3–8.

Ballance, C. *History of Peoria.* Peoria: Bradley University, 1970. Originally published 1870.

Barry, Thomas. "Springfield, Illinois: How to Get over Being a State Capital." *Look,* 10 March 1970, pp. 66–67.

Bean, F. D.; Poston, D. L.; and Winsborough, H. "Size, Functional Specialization, and the Classification of Cities." *Social Science Quarterly* 53 (1972): 20–32.

Bernard, Jessie. *Marriage and Family among Negroes.* Englewood Cliffs, N.J.: Prentice-Hall, 1966.

Berry, B., and Garrison, W. "The Functional Basis of the Central Place Hierarchy." *Economic Geography* 34 (1958): 145–54.
Bi-State Metropolitan Planning Commission. *1995 Forecasts.* Rock Island, Ill., 1973.
Borukhov, E. "Optimal Service Areas for Provision and Financing of Local Public Goods." *Public Finance* 27 (1972): 267–81.
Bradford, D.; Malt, R.; and Oates, W. "The Rising Cost of Local Public Services: Some Evidence and Reflections." *National Tax Journal* 22 (1969): 185–202.
Bray, Jim. "City Elections in East St. Louis." *Illinois Issues* 5, 4 (April 1979): 16–17.
Brazer, Harvey E. *City Expenditures in the United States.* New York: National Bureau of Economic Research, 1969.
Bryce, Herrington J., ed. *Small Cities in Transition: The Dynamics of Growth and Decline.* Cambridge, Mass.: Ballinger, 1977.
Burgess, Charles E. "Mason Requests Help for His City's Image." *St. Louis Globe-Democrat,* 17 July 1975.
Center for the Study of Middle-Size Cities. *The Quality of Life in Three Middle-Size Cities.* Springfield, Ill.: Sangamon State University, Center for the Study of Middle-Size Cities, 1976.
Chamberlain, Neil W. *Contemporary Economic Issues.* Homewood, Ill.: Richard D. Irwin, 1969.
Chears, Leo. "In Defense of a Lady." *Alestle,* 27 October 1977.
Chinitz, B., and Vernon, R. "Changing Forces in Industrial Location." *Harvard Business Review* 38 (1960): 126–36.
Clark, C. "The Economic Functions of a City in Relation to Its Size." *Econometrics* 13 (1945): 97–113.
Cohen, Benjamin. "Trends in Negro Employment within Large Metropolitan Areas." *Public Policy* 22 (Fall 1974): 614–15.
Creamer, Daniel B. *Is Industry Decentralizing?* Philadelphia: University of Pennsylvania Press, 1935.
———. *Changing Location of Manufacturing Employment.* New York: National Industrial Conference Board, 1963.
Creamer, Daniel B., et al. *Migration and Economic Opportunity.* Philadelphia: University of Pennsylvania Press, 1935.
Crowley, R. W. "Reflections and Further Evidence on Population Size and Industrial Diversification." *Urban Studies* 10 (1973): 91–94.
Curry, George E. "The City That Lifted Itself from Mud to Mudslinging." *St. Louis Post-Dispatch,* 25 October 1977.
Curry, George E., and Malone, Roy. "East St. Louis: Optimism amid Blocks of Decay." *St. Louis Post-Dispatch,* 23 October 1977.
Curtis, Henry. "Public Decision-Making in the Annexation of Unincorporated Areas of Richwoods Township to Peoria, Illinois." M. A. thesis, University of Illinois, 1970.
Davis, Elliot, Jr. "One Big Family?" *Crusader Weekly Newspaper* (East St. Louis, Ill.); reprinted in *St. Louis Post-Dispatch,* 15 September 1978.
Dillman, Donald, and Dobash, Russell P. "Preferences for Community Living and Their Implications for Population Redistribution." In *Washington Agricultural Experiment Station Bulletin,* 764. Pullman: Washington State University, 1976.

Drake, St. Clair, and Cayton, Horace R. *Black Metropolis.* New York: Harcourt-Brace, 1945.

Duncan, Otis, et al. *Metropolis and Region.* Baltimore: Johns Hopkins Press, 1960.

Duncan, Otis, and Spengle, J., eds. *Demographic Analysis: Selected Readings.* Glencoe, Ill.: Free Press, 1956.

Elgin, Duane, et al. *City Size and the Quality of Life.* Washington, D.C.: National Science Foundation, 1974.

Franklin, Donald E. "Ironic Twist in East St. Louis Government Change." *St. Louis Post-Dispatch,* 4 April 1974.

Friesma, H. Paul. *Metropolitan Political Structure: Intergovernmental Relations and Political Integration in the Quad Cities.* Iowa City: University of Iowa Press, 1971.

Fuchs, V. R. *Differentials in Hourly Earnings by Region and Size, 1959.* Washington, D.C.: National Bureau of Economic Research, 1967.

Fuguitt, Glen V., and Zuches, James J. "Residential Preferences and Population Distribution." *Demography* 12 (August 1975): 491–504.

Gabler, L. R. "Population Size as a Determinant of City Expenditures and Employment: Some Further Evidence." *Land Economics* 47 (1971): 130–38.

Ganz, Alexander, and O'Brien, Thomas. "The City: Sandbox, Reservation or Dynamo?" *Public Policy* 21 (Winter 1973): 107–24.

Goldberg, Kalman. "Quality of Life in Peoria." Unpublished report, Urban Affairs Institute, 1975.

Gorham, William, and Glazer, Nathan, eds. *The Urban Predicament.* Washington, D.C.: Urban Institute, 1976.

Hadden, Jeffrey, and Borgatta, Edgar F. *American Cities: Their Social Characteristics.* Chicago: Rand McNally, 1965.

Hamilton, Esley. "A Portrait of East St. Louis: 1969–1975." Master's research paper, University of Wisconsin, Madison, 1975.

Harrison, Shelley. *The Springfield Survey: A Study of Social Conditions in an American City.* New York, 1918.

Hawkings, Brett W. *Politics and Urban Policies.* Indianapolis: Bobbs-Merrill, 1971.

Hirsch, Werner Z. "Cost Functions of an Urban Government Service: Refuse Collection." *Review of Economics and Statistics* 47 (1965): 87–92.

———. "Expenditure Implications of Metropolitan Growth and Consolidation." *Review of Economics and Statistics* 41 (1959): 232–41.

———. "The Supply of Urban Public Services." In *Issues in Urban Economics,* ed. H. Perloff and L. Wings, pp. 81–140. Baltimore: Johns Hopkins Press, 1968.

———. *Urban Life and Form.* St. Louis: Institute for Urban and Regional Studies, 1963.

Hoch, Irving. "Income and City Size." *Urban Studies* 9 (1972): 299–328.

———. "Urban Scale and Environmental Quality." In *Population, Resources and the Environment,* ed. R. Redker, pp. 231–86. U.S. Commission on Population Growth and the American Future Reports, vol. 3. Washington, D.C.: U.S. Government Printing Office, 1972.

Hoover, E. *An Introduction to Regional Economics.* New York: Knopf, 1971.

Illinois Capital Development Board. *The East St. Louis Area: An Overview of State Capital Projects and Policies.* Springfield: Illinois Capital Development Board, 1977.

International City Management Association. *Municipal Yearbook.* Washington, D.C.: International City Management Association, published annually.

Johnson, Daniel Milo, and Veach, Rebecca Monroe, eds. *The Middle-Size Cities of Illinois: Their People, Politics and Quality of Life.* Springfield, Ill.: Sangamon State University, 1980.

Judd, Dennis, and Mendelson, Robert. *The Politics of Urban Planning: The East St. Louis Experience.* Urbana: University of Illinois Press, 1973.

Keyes, Fenton. "The Correlation of Social Phenomena with Community Size." *Social Forces* 36, 4 (May 1958): 311.

Kingcade, Carolyn. "East St. Louis Canvass Cuts '80, 86 Names from Voter Roll." *Metro-East Journal,* 1 November 1978.

Landon, Pat. "Profile: The Peoria Park District." In *History of Peoria,* p. 44. Peoria, Ill.: Peoria Area Jaycees, 1975.

Lasswell, Thomas Ely. "Social Class and Size of Community." *American Journal of Sociology* 64, 5 (March 1959): 505–8.

League of Women Voters of Champaign County. *Report on the Status of the Negro in Champaign County, 1948.* Champaign, Ill.: League of Women Voters of Champaign County, 1948.

———. *Report on the Status of the Negro in Champaign County, 1968.* Champaign, Ill.: League of Women Voters of Champaign County, 1968.

———. *This Is Champaign County.* Champaign, Ill.: League of Women Voters of Champaign County, 1972.

———. *Urbana Government: Financial Structure and Service Departments.* Champaign, Ill.: League of Women Voters of Champaign County, 1965.

Levy, Frank; Meltoner, Arnold J.; and Wildavsky, Aaron. *Urban Outcomes: Streets, Schools and Illinois.* Berkeley: University of California Press, 1974.

Lichtenberg, R. *One-Tenth of a Nation.* Cambridge: Harvard University Press, 1960.

Lindall, Ruth, and Berner, William. *Financing Public Library Expansion: Case Studies of the Three Defeated Bond Issues.* Urbana: Library Research Center, University of Illinois, 1968.

Liu, Ben-Chieh. *Quality of Life Indicators in the U.S. Metropolitan Area, 1970.* Kansas City, Mo.: Midwest Research Institute, 1975.

Luna, Mel. "Era of Irish Politics Fading in East St. Louis." *St. Louis Globe-Democrat,* 27 November 1973.

McCarthy, Gerald. "Quality of Life in Peoria." Transcript of television documentary produced by Urban Affairs Institute, Bradley University, 1975.

McKenzie, Roderick C. *The Metropolitan Community.* New York: McGraw-Hill, 1933.

Malone, Roy, and Curry, George E. "East St. Louis Payroll Up, Population Is Down." *St. Louis Post-Dispatch,* 24 October 1977.

Martin, John B. "The Town That Reformed." *Saturday Evening Post,* 1 October 1955.

Mazek, Warren, and Laird, William E. "City Size Preferences and Population Distribution: The Analytical Context." *Quarterly Review of Economics and Business* 14 (Spring 1974): 113–22.

Mazie, Sarah M., and Rawlings, Stephen. "Public Attitude toward Population Distribution Issues." In *Population Distribution and Policy,* ed. S. M. Mazie, p.

605. U.S. Commission on Population Growth and the American Future Reports, vol. 5. Washington, D.C.: U.S. Government Printing Office, 1973.

Mendelson, Robert E., and Ranney, David C. *Central City—a Neighborhood Analysis.* Edwardsville: Southern Illinois University, Public Administration and Metropolitan Affairs Program, 1967.

Mera, K. "On the Urban Agglomeration and Economic Efficiency." *Economic Development and Cultural Change* 21 (1972): 309–24.

Mills, E. "Economic Aspects of City Sizes." In *Population Distribution and Policy,* ed. S. M. Mazie, pp. 383–94. U.S. Commission on Population Growth and the American Future Reports, vol. 5. Washington, D.C.: U.S. Government Printing Office, 1972.

———. *Studies in the Structure of Urban Economy.* Baltimore: Johns Hopkins Press, 1972.

———. *Urban Economics.* Glenview, Ill.: Scott, Foresman, 1972.

———. "Welfare Aspects of National Policy toward City Size." *Urban Studies* 9 (1972): 117–24.

Moline Chamber of Commerce. *Moline, Illinois, Presents the Metropolitan Quad Cities.* Moline: D.R. Light, 1969.

Monpenny, Phillip, and Steiner, Gilbert. "Merger? The Illinois Consolidation Case." In *Cases in State and Local Government,* ed. Richard T. Frost, pp. 267–79. Englewood Cliffs, N.J.: Prentice-Hall, 1961.

Morrow, Elise. "The Cities of America—Peoria." *Saturday Evening Post,* 12 February 1949.

Muller, Thomas. *Growing and Declining Urban Areas: A Fiscal Comparison.* Washington, D.C.: Urban Institute, 1975.

———. *Intergovernmental and Intrametropolitan Cost Differentials.* Washington, D.C.: Urban Institute, 1977.

Muller, Thomas, and Christensen, C. *State-Mandated Evaluation: A Preliminary Assessment.* Washington, D.C.: Urban Institute, 1976.

Muller, Thomas, and Dawson, Grace. *The Economic Effect of Annexation.* Washington, D.C.: Urban Institute, 1976.

Muller, Thomas; Neils, Kevin; Tilney, John; and Dawson, Grace. *The Economic Impact of I-295 on the Richmond Central Business District.* Washington, D.C.: Urban Institute, 1977.

Muller, Thomas, and Peterson, George. "Public Service Costs." Draft, Urban Institute, 1976.

Nathan, Richard P., and Adams, Charles. "Understanding Central City Hardship." *Political Science Quarterly* 91, 1 (Spring 1976): 47–62.

National League of Cities. "State of the Cities: 1975—a New Urban Crisis?" Washington, D.C.: National League of Cities, 1976.

Neenan, W. "Suburban-Central City Exploitation Thesis: A Comment." *National Tax Journal* 25 (1972): 595–97.

Neutze, G. M. *Economic Policy and the Size of Cities.* Clifton, N.J.: Augustus M. Kelly, 1965.

O'Gara, Mary, and Ward, William, eds. *Quad-Cities Resources, Problems, and Prospects.* Rock Island, Ill.: Augustana Center for the Study of Urban Affairs and Changing Society, 1975.

Ogburn, William F., and Duncan, Otia D. "City Size as a Sociological Variable." In *Contributions to Urban Sociology,* ed. Ernest W. Burgess and Donald Bogue, pp. 129–47. Chicago: University of Chicago Press, 1964.

Paraskevopoulos, C. "Population Size and the Extent of Industrial Diversification: An Alternative View." *Urban Studies* 12 (1975): 105–7.

Park, Robert E., et al. *The City.* Chicago: University of Chicago Press, 1925.

Pensoneau, Taylor. "Panel Holds Little Hope for East St. Louis." *St. Louis Post-Dispatch,* 2 September 1977.

Perloff, Harvey S., and Wingo, Lowdon, Jr. *Issues in Urban Economics.* Baltimore: Johns Hopkins Press, 1968.

Pettigrew, Thomas F. "Attitudes on Race and Housing: A Social Psychological View." In *Segregation in Residential Areas,* p. 43. Washington, D.C.: National Academy of Sciences, 1973.

Pickaske, David R. "Reports and Comment—Peoria." *Atlantic,* 4 November 1974.

Plague, Sheldon J., and Handler, Joel F. "The Politics of Planning for Urban Redevelopment: Strategies in the Manipulation of Public Law." *Wisconsin Law Review* 3 (Summer 1976): 720–27.

Puryear, D. "A Programming Model of Central Place Theory." *Journal of Regional Science* 15 (1975): 307–16.

Ramsey, D. "Suburban-Central City Exploitation Thesis." *National Tax Journal* 25 (1972): 599–604.

Ranney, David C.; Mendelson, Robert E.; Cannon, Jamie; and Bortnick, Bernard. *Rush City Analysis and Proposals.* Edwardsville: Southern Illinois University, Public Administration and Metropolitan Affairs Program, 1967.

Reissman, Leonard. *The Urban Process.* New York: Free Press, 1964.

Rice, James. *Peoria: City and County Illinois.* Chicago: S. J. Clarke, 1912.

Richardson, Harry W. *The Economics of Urban Size.* Lexington, Mass.: Saxon House/Lexington Books, 1973.

Richmond, Mabel E., ed. *Centennial History of Decatur and Macon County.* Decatur, Ill.: Decatur Review, 1930.

Riew, J. "Economics of Scale in High School Operation." *Review of Economics and Statistics* 48 (1966): 280–87.

Ryffel, Robert E. "The Machine Runs Amuk." *St. Louis Globe-Democrat,* 19 February 1976.

Schettler, Clarence. "Relations of City-Size to Economic Services." *American Sociological Review* 8 (1953): 60–62.

Schnore, Leo F., and Varley, D. W. "Some Concomitants of Metropolitan Size." *American Sociological Review* 20 (1955): 408–14.

Shabecoff, Philip S. "Seeing Ourselves . . . as Others See Us." *Peoria Star Journal,* 12 May 1971. Originally published in *New York Times,* 8 May 1971.

Shapiro, Harvey. "Economics of Scale and Local Government Finance." *Land Economics* 39 (1963): 175–86.

Solberg, Winston. *The University of Illinois, 1867–1894: An Intellectual and Cultural History.* Urbana: University of Illinois Press, 1968.

Spohn, Larry. "Convicted Officials Hired for Project." *Metro-East Journal,* 2 November 1978.

Stafford, H. A., Jr. "The Functional Bases of Small Towns." *Economic Geography* 39 (1963): 165–75.

Strahler, Steve. "Jail Referendum: Both Sides Speak." *Peoria Star Journal,* 29 April 1979.

Sundquist, James. "Where Shall They Live?" *Public Interest* 18 (1970): 88–100.

Sviekauskas, L. "The Productivity of Cities." *Quarterly Journal of Economics* 89 (1975): 393–413.

Taeuber, Irene B. "The Changing Distribution of the Population of the United States in the Twentieth Century." In *Population Distribution and Policy,* ed. S. M. Mazie, pp. 31–109. U.S. Commission on Population Growth and the American Future, Reports, vol. 5. Washington, D.C.: U.S. Government Printing Office, 1972.

Taylor, J. "A Note on the Definition of Industrial Diversification." *Journal of Economic Studies* 2 (1967): 105–13.

Taylor, Marjorie. "Peoria Barkeeps Are Never Tried with Impunity." *Louisville* (Kentucky) *Courier Journal,* 29 July 1940.

Thompson, W. *A Preface to Urban Economics.* Baltimore: Johns Hopkins Press, 1965.

Tiebout, C. "Economies of Scale and Metropolitan Governments." *Review of Economics and Statistics* 42 (1960): 431–38.

———. "A Pure Theory of Local Expenditures." *Journal of Political Economy* 64 (1956): 416–24.

Tolley, G. "The Welfare Economics of City Bigness." *Journal of Urban Economics* 1 (1974): 324–45.

Ullman, E. L., and Dacey, M. F. "The Minimum Requirements Approach to the Urban Economic Base." *Papers of the Regional Science Association* 6 (1960): 175–94.

United States Bureau of the Census. *County and City Data Book, 1977.* Washington, D.C.: Government Printing Office, 1977.

———. *County and City Data Book, 1983.* Washington, D.C.: Government Printing Office, 1983.

———. *1972 Census of Governments.* Vol. 5. *Local Government in Metropolitan Areas.* Washington, D.C.: Government Printing Office, 1975.

United States Office of Management and Budget. *Budget of the United States, FY 1977.* Washington, D.C.: Government Printing Office, 1977.

Vanneman, Reeve D., and Pettigrew, Thomas A. "Race and Relative Deprivation in the Urban United States." *Race* 13, 4 (1972): 461–86.

Vaughan, Roger J. "The Urban Impacts of Federal Policies. In *Economic Development,* vol. 2. Washington, D.C.: Rand Corporation, 1978.

Walzer, N. "Economies of Scale and Metropolitan Governments." *Review of Economics and Statistics* 54 (1972): 280–87.

Weber, Adna T. *The Growth of Cities in the Nineteenth Century.* New York: Macmillan, 1899.

Weisman, Joel D. "East St. Louis: A City in Flight." *Washington Post,* 1 April 1975.

Wickstrom, George W. *The Town Crier.* Rock Island, Ill.: Augustana Book Concern, 1948.

Woodbury, Coleman, ed. *The Future of Cities and Urban Redevelopment.* Chicago: University of Chicago Press, 1953.

Index